ENVIRONMENTAL POLICY CHANGE IN EMERGING MARKET DEMOCRACIES

Central and Eastern Europe and Latin America Compared

Studies in Comparative Political Economy and Public Policy

Editors: MICHAEL HOWLETT, DAVID LAYCOCK (Simon Fraser University), and STEPHEN MCBRIDE (McMaster University)

Studies in Comparative Political Economy and Public Policy is designed to showcase innovative approaches to political economy and public policy from a comparative perspective. While originating in Canada, the series will provide attractive offerings to a wide international audience, featuring studies with local, subnational, cross-national, and international empirical bases and theoretical frameworks.

Editorial Advisory Board

For a list of books published in the series, see page 251.

Environmental Policy Change in Emerging Market Democracies

Central and Eastern Europe and Latin America Compared

JALE TOSUN

UNIVERSITY OF TORONTO PRESS
Toronto Buffalo London

© University of Toronto Press 2013
Toronto Buffalo London
www.utppublishing.com
Printed in Canada

ISBN 978-1-4426-4409-0

Printed on acid-free, 100% post-consumer recycled paper with vegetable-based inks.

Library and Archives Canada Cataloguing in Publication

Tosun, Jale, author
Environmental policy change in emerging market
democracies: Central and Eastern Europe and Latin America
compared / Jale Tosun.

(Studies in comparative political economy and public policy)
Includes bibliographical references and index.
ISBN 978-1-4426-4409-0 (bound)

1. Environmental policy – Europe, Central.   2. Environmental policy –
Europe, Eastern.   3. Environmental policy – Latin America.   I. Title.
II. Series: Studies in comparative political economy and public policy

GE170.T68 2013   363.7   C2013-903343-2

University of Toronto Press acknowledges the financial assistance to its
publishing program of the Canada Council for the Arts and the Ontario
Arts Council.

University of Toronto Press acknowledges the financial support of the
Government of Canada through the Canada Book Fund for its publishing
activities.

Contents

Illustrations

Tables

Figures

Preface

This book is the result of a lengthy research project that I was able to conduct at the Department of Politics and Public Administration of the University of Konstanz, Germany. It builds on and extends my doctoral thesis, which I completed in December 2009 under the supervision of Christoph Knill. This book would not have been possible without his continuous professional and personal support. In addition, this study benefited greatly from many thoughtful remarks of Katharina Holzinger, who co-supervised my doctoral thesis. I made many significant changes to the original thesis during a research stay at the Edward J. Bloustein School of Planning and Public Policy of Rutgers University, from March until June 2010. I want to thank Radha Jagannathan, Michael Greenberg, and Joseph Seneca for their interest in my research and for providing me with fresh ideas about how to approach the topic.

I acknowledge friends and colleagues who read the chapters or commented on presentations of parts of the manuscript: Tim Balint, Michael Bechtel, Julian Bernauer, David Blair, Ken Coats, Michael Dobbins, Stephan Heichel, Carin Holroyd, Christina Kannenberg, Nerina Muzurović, Janine Reinhard, Raphaela Schlicht, Sophie Schmitt, Thomas Sommerer, and Eva Vögtle. I would further like to express my gratitude to the Environmental Law Center of the International Union for Conservation of Nature at Bonn, Germany, and the following colleagues and students who provided me with research assistance: Zekie Aliosman, Ingrid-Heidi Boszoki, Elina Brutschin, Alexander Dietrich, Adelina Dobreva, Dominic Fritz, Héctor Manuel Garcia Lozada, Ann-Kathrin Heß, Eva Hübner, Szilvia Kéfer, Ivo Krizic, Romina Laumann, Audriuas Paura, and Brit Tammiste. I thank Christina Kannenberg for proofreading as well as Tim Roll and Dorothea Winter for supporting me in the preparation of the final manuscript. I am alone responsible for any remaining errors or omissions.

In addition, I record my gratitude to the editors of the series, Michael Howlett, David Laycock, and Stephen McBride as well as editor Daniel Quinlan of the University of Toronto Press for an efficient and delightful collaboration. I thank two anonymous reviewers for their thought-provoking comments and suggestions, which helped me to clarify my arguments and to strengthen the book's analytical and empirical merits. Finally, I gratefully acknowledge the financial support of the German Research Foundation for my research stay at Rutgers University and the realization of the publication project.

This book is dedicated to my mother Zekiye Tosun and my husband Marc Debus, who have been constant sources of encouragement.

Jale Tosun
Mannheim, December 2012

Abbreviations

AIC	Akaike Information Criterion
BIC	Bayesian Information Criterion
BOD	Biological oxygen demand
CEE	Central and Eastern Europe(an)
CO_2	Carbon dioxide
DOTS	Direction of trade statistics
EPA	Environmental Protection Agency
EU	European Union
FAO	Food and Agriculture Organization of the United Nations
FDI	Foreign direct investment
GATT	General Agreement on Tariffs and Trade
GDP	Gross domestic product
GM	Genetically modified
GMO	Genetically modified organism
IMF	International Monetary Fund
INECE	International Network for Environmental Compliance and Enforcement
INGO	International non-governmental organization
IUCN	International Union for Conservation of Nature
LA	Latin America(n)
Mercosur	Southern Common Market
NAFTA	North American Free Trade Agreement
NGO	Non-governmental organization
OECD	Organization for Economic Cooperation and Development
PAH	Polycyclic aromatic hydrocarbon
SFM	Sustainable forest management
UNECE	United Nations Economic Commission for Europe

UNEP	United National Environment Program
US	United States
WDI	World Development Indicators
WHO	World Health Organization
WTO	World Trade Organization
ZINB	Zero-inflated negative binominal model

ENVIRONMENTAL POLICY CHANGE IN EMERGING MARKET DEMOCRACIES

Central and Eastern Europe and Latin America Compared

1 Introduction

The last four decades have been characterized by two central changes in the political and economic systems of industrializing countries. First, an ever-growing number of them have introduced democratic polities. This "third wave" of democratization (Huntington 1991) started in Southern Europe in the mid-1970s, before spreading to Latin America, Central and Eastern Europe, Asia, and Africa (see Haerpfer et al. 2009). Second, several industrializing countries introduced market economic structures and participated in an unprecedented "rush to free trade" (Rodrik 1992). The launch of multilateral trade regimes such as the General Agreement on Tariffs and Trade (GATT) and the World Trade Organization (WTO), and the proliferation of regional economic integration, such as the North American Free Trade Agreement (NAFTA) or the Southern Common Market (Mercosur), has further intensified economic interactions between countries of different socio-economic development levels (Ayres 1998: 9).[1] The financial crisis that posed a serious threat to the global economic order between 2007 and 2009 provided evidence of how interdependent the national economies have become (Teeple and McBride 2011: ix).

Industrializing countries that have been affected by "the end of the Cold War, the "third wave" of democratization, and economic globalization" are commonly referred to as emerging market democracies (Whitehead 2000: 65). This book examines how changes in the political and economic systems of emerging market democracies have affected policymaking. To this end, it focuses on environmental policy change in two regions that underwent comparatively similar political and economic reforms: Central and Eastern Europe (CEE) and Latin America (LA). Of course, the extent, the timing, and the sequence of the different transformation processes vary from one country to another within each region as well as across the two regions. Moreover, the points of departure for the transformation processes were different. While most LA countries were under military rule before their transition to democracy, the CEE countries and Mexico had hegemonic party systems in place. Concerning the economic dimension, the LA countries experienced import-substitution industrialization, that is, a development strategy designed to stimulate the domestic production of labour-intensive goods that were formerly imported from industrialized countries. The CEE countries' economies were centrally planned, that is, the direction and development of economic activities were defined and administered by the government and inter-country competition was restricted to the members of the Council for Mutual Economic Assistance trade system (see Hewett 2011).

Despite these different initial situations, the countries in both regions have developed democratic polities and market economies that gradually became integrated into the international system. In light of these similarities, with respect to the outcome of the transformation processes, a number of empirical studies compare CEE and LA countries and provide many intriguing insights into the characteristics of policymaking in emerging market democracies (see, e.g., Przeworski 1991; Lijphart and Waisman 1996; Pickvance 1999; Weyland 1999; Anderson, Lewis-Beck, and Stegmaier 2003; Müller 2003). This book aims to contribute to this seminal research strand by extending the analysis of policymaking in CEE and LA to the field of environmental policy.

Environmental issues represent a particularly suitable policy field for the purpose of this study as the theoretical literature suggests that democratization and economic globalization are key determinants of the governments' responses to degradation. Regarding democratization, the literature predominantly argues that there exists a positive relationship between the level of democracy and the stringency of environmental policies (see, e.g., Silva 1996; Cole 1998; Desai 1998; Neumayer 2002; Li and Reuveny 2006). This expectation is straightforward as citizens in democracies are usually better informed about environmental problems and can express demands for regulation, which will, in turn, put pressure on policymakers to respond positively to these demands (Payne 1995). The main expectation with regard to economic globalization is that it is likely to induce a "race to the bottom," in which countries deliberately set environmental protection standards at low levels to avoid a reduction in their competitive position (see, e.g., Sinn 1997; Holzinger and Knill 2004, 2005, 2008; Drezner 2007;

Holzinger, Knill, and Sommerer 2008, 2011). Hence, the two most central dimensions of political and economic transformation, that is, democratization and economic globalization, are associated with different, if not to say contradictory, expectations regarding their respective impact on environmental policy choices. This raises the question of which of these two forces is the dominant one and, more generally, if the theoretical expectations as stated above hold true empirically for a large number of emerging market democracies.

There is an additional aspect of environmental policymaking in emerging market democracies that turns it into an appealing research subject. The literature generally stresses that even if environmental regulations have recently proliferated in these countries, the governmental capacity and willingness to enforce them has lagged behind significantly (Desai 1998; Holzinger and Knoepfel 2000; Andonova 2004; McAllister 2008; McAllister, Van Rooij, and Kagan 2010). In other words, emerging market democracies in CEE and LA are frequently connected with reduced regulatory enforcement efforts. Against this background, it seems promising to investigate to what extent and in which ways processes of political and economic transformation have affected the governments' commitment to enforce environmental protection standards. Again, the general expectation is that the consequences of democratization for enforcement are positive (see, e.g., Earnhart 1997; Cole 1998; Pickvance 2003), whereas economic developments are often associated with the preservation of a lax approach to regulatory enforcement (see, e.g., Porter 1999; Gallagher 2002, 2004; Konisky 2007; Knill, Tosun, and Heichel 2008; Bechtel and Tosun 2009).

These considerations give way to the three core research questions that guide this book: How have the consequences of dual system transformation affected environmental policy arrangements? Have the CEE and LA countries developed similar environmental regulation patterns? How have these processes affected the governments' commitment to enforce the set rules? To account for the dynamic processes underlying political and economic transformation, the study approaches these research questions from an equally dynamic theoretical perspective, namely, the study of policy and institutional change.

Overview of Key Concepts

This book investigates changes in the stringency of environmental policy and the governments' commitment to enforce environmental law. Concerning the term "policy," this study conceives of it as any sort of legally binding rules enacted by elected policymakers in order to solve a particular societal problem like environmental degradation. This definition already refines the subject of analysis by excluding, for instance, people's opinions on environmental issues or public spending for environmental programs. Nevertheless, policy is still a very encompassing term and to be able to elaborate an accurate explanatory model a more precise disaggregation of the various elements of a policy is needed (Howlett and Cashore 2009: 37). The widely accepted typology of Hall (1993) that distinguishes between policy paradigms, policy instruments, and instrument settings represents a useful tool for this purpose. Policy paradigms refer to the goals guiding a policy in a particular field, which also involves how the societal problem in question is perceived. The dimension of policy instruments concerns how or by which means something is regulated. The settings involve the calibration of policy instruments, that is, how stringent they are. In accordance with this taxonomy, the present study conceives of environmental policy dynamics as changes in certain environmental policy instruments and their corresponding settings. It leaves unconsidered changes in policy paradigms since those are difficult to measure and prone to different interpretations.[2]

The second key concept refers to changes in the governments' commitment to enforce environmental protection standards. Most essentially, regulatory enforcement is about monitoring and the imposition of sanctions. Monitoring increases transparency and exposes possible environmental offenders, whereas sanctions raise the costs of non-compliance and turn it into a less attractive option (Becker 1968; see also Gray and Shimshack 2011). The use of public prosecution with environmental offences increases the costs of non-compliance significantly and can therefore be regarded as a particularly consequential form of regulatory enforcement (Strock 1990: 920; Garvie and Keeler 1994: 158).

This study sets changes in the governmental commitment to the enforcement of environmental protection standards as equal to institutional change. More precisely, it focuses on the establishment of an agency or any other type of organizational unit that is authorized to prosecute non-compliance with environmental regulations, also known as an "environmental procuracy" (see McAllister 2008; Abbot 2009; Mueller 2010). Changes in the enforcement commitment are hence defined as changes in the governments' attitude towards strengthening environmental enforcement institutions. Although rather simple and narrow, this definition is more concrete and more functional than most alternatives, thus facilitating data gathering and empirical analysis.

As concerns the conceptualization of policy and institutional dynamics, this book adopts a broad perspective in terms of the scope, the direction, and the reversibility of change (see Capano 2009: 13–18). The scope of policy change is usually characterized as either incremental or radical. The classical policy-analytical literature predominantly conceives of policy change as an incremental process where new elements are added to existing policy arrangements. It was Lindblom (1959) who most prominently argued that incrementalism is the most likely form of policy change as policymakers possess limited information and resources and are often confronted with the disagreement of the other actors involved regarding values and ideas. Events of radical policy change are thought to occur rather seldom and be caused by "exogenous" disturbances (see, e.g., Sabatier and Jenkins-Smith 1993, 1999; Sabatier 1998; Howlett and Ramesh 2002; Sabatier and Weible 2007; Baumgartner and Jones 2009). However, since the interpretation of the scope of policy change depends on the levels of abstraction (Knill and Lenschow 2001: 211), this study does not put forward any theoretical expectations with regard to this dimension. This means that all instances of policy – whether they refer to changes in policy instruments or their settings – are employed for the empirical analysis, but the explanatory model does not associate the independent variables with policy change of different scopes.

This book, however, does contend that it is vital to understand that policy change can occur either as "upward" change or "downward" change (Knill, Tosun, and Bauer 2009). Upward – or "positive" – change entails an increase in the degree to which the environment is protected, which may be achieved through adopting a new policy instrument or tightening the setting of the existing policy arrangements. Downward – or "negative" – change, in contrast, leads to a reduction in the extent to which the environment is protected, which may occur by means of abolishing policy instruments or redefining their settings in such ways that they become less stringent.

Finally, and related to the prior point, this study holds the view that policy change is principally reversible. This means that it explicitly acknowledges a scenario in which a government first adopts stricter protection standards and then relaxes them again and vice versa. Such a back-peddling can have many reasons, such as the recognition of a "wrong" policy decision, the realization of costs emerging from a newly adopted policy, changes in the public's will or changes in the preferences of the policymakers. Hence, the reasons for reversing policies should be no different from those inducing other types of policy change.

Main Arguments in Brief

There are three lines along which this book aims to advance the understanding of policy and institutional change in emerging market democracies. First, it seeks to demonstrate that comparative policy analysis offers a suitable theoretical approach for explaining policymaking in emerging market democracies. Second, the book pursues the objective of combining different methodological approaches to increase confidence in its central findings. The third intention is to identify patterns of stability and change in environmental policymaking and to elucidate the underlying causal factors. These objectives are reflected in the book's theoretical framework, the methodological approach, and the main empirical findings.

Theoretical Framework

At the theoretical level, the book is located within the resurging academic debate about the patterns and determinants of policy and institutional change (see, e.g., Bennett and Howlett 1992; Hall 1993; Sabatier and Jenkins-Smith 1993; Knill and Lenschow 2001; Howlett and Ramesh 2002; Héritier 2007; Baumgartner and Jones 2009; Baumgartner et al. 2009). Despite the increasing popularity of this research perspective, there are many theoretical ambiguities that need to be assessed and resolved to ensure empirical and conceptual progress (Capano and Howlett 2009).

In this regard, the book argues that processes of change can be appropriately explained by relying on the framework provided by comparative policy analysis. The objective of this particular research perspective is to explain how policy decisions come about, and to what extent polities (i.e., political institutions) and politics (i.e., political processes) shape them (see, e.g., Schmidt 1996; Roller 2005; Zohlnhöfer 2009). Comparative policy analysis provides a promising framework for the present study since it allows for flexibly focusing on the relevant explanatory factors while establishing causality by means of specific theories for each of them. In this way, changes in the economic and political system can be directly related to incentives for governments to alter existing environmental protection arrangements. Four groups of independent variables are important for explaining changes in environmental policy and enforcement commitment in emerging market democracies: economic integration with international markets, political party competition and participation of environmental groups, integration with international institutions, and increasing response to public demand.

While the analysis of the environmental policy consequences of system transformation clearly addresses a question specific to comparative policy analysis, it also stands at the intersection of three other research perspectives, namely, comparative political economy (see, e.g., Keohane 1984, 2002; Katzenstein 1985; Krasner 1994; Lee and McBride 2007; Teeple and McBride 2011), the study of policy diffusion (see, e.g., Simmons and Elkins 2004; Braun and Gilardi 2006; Gilardi 2008), and cross-national policy convergence (see, e.g., Bennett 1991; Holzinger and Knill 2005; Holzinger, Knill, and Arts 2008; Holzinger, Knill, and Sommerer 2008, 2011; Howlett and Joshi-Koop 2011). The inclusion of these research perspectives is a natural extension in light of the book's analytical focus on economic globalization and other processes of internationalization. Moreover, studies of policy diffusion and cross-national policy are particularly suitable for cross-fertilization as they stress policy dynamics and employ longitudinal data.

Methodological Approach

The book scrutinizes changes in environmental policy and enforcement institutions in twenty-eight countries in CEE and LA between 1990 and 2010. The data are pooled, that is, they consist of repeated observations for each of the countries for multiple years, creating the units of analysis known as "country-years." In this way, the number of observations is increased, which helps to alleviate the "small N" problem experienced by cross-sectional data sets that are based on countries as units of analysis (see Kittel 1999). By increasing the number of observations, quantitative techniques can be employed for analysing the data. Consequently, the first analytical step consists of running different types of quantitative analyses in accordance with the characteristics of the dependent variables in terms of measurement level. In a second step, the quantitative analysis is complemented by a qualitative one in accordance with the logic of "nested analysis" as proposed by Lieberman (2005). The strategy of combining the two methodological approaches aims to improve the quality of conceptualization and measurement.

The two core dependent variables of this study are changes in environmental policy and enforcement institutions. However, as environmental policy spans a multitude of very different areas (see, e.g., Sterner 2002; Holzinger, Knill, and Arts 2008), five indicators – or "policy items" – are selected to take into account the various environmental media. Technically speaking, each of these five indicators represents a dependent variable in the empirical analyses. The first dependent variable is the regulation of water pollution by defining maximum permissible limit values for the concentration of organic material in industrial effluent discharges. A further dependent variable is the definition of limit values for ground-level concentrations of ozone in ambient air. The third dependent variable corresponds to the setting of limit values for polycyclic aromatic hydrocarbon concentrations in agricultural soils. The final two dependent variables refer to restrictions regarding the commercial cultivation of genetically modified (GM) maize and the adoption of the principle of sustainable forest management. As regards the complementary qualitative analysis, it should be noted that it is carried out for the regulation of GM maize as a more fine-grained measurement of this policy item is needed than can be achieved in the context of the quantitative approach. The second core dependent variable measures whether or not the emerging market democracies in CEE and LA established organizations endowed with the competence for prosecuting environmental offences.

The data set used for this study is original and was constructed through the collection of primary and secondary data. Since the study is about policy decisions and legislative outputs, the predominant data sources were legal acts and administrative circulars. The sources used for data gathering were either accessed electronically via the websites of the national environmental ministries or the legislative database FAOLEX. Older legal acts were obtained as hard copies from the International Union for Conservation of Nature (IUCN) Environmental Law Centre in Bonn, Germany. In addition, for cross-checking purposes such secondary sources as academic publications were employed. Furthermore, environmental ministries, procuracies, and a number of practitioners were contacted to clarify data queries.

Empirical Findings

The study provides numerous descriptive and analytical insights. In terms of empirically describing changes in environmental policies and enforcement institutions, the following findings are noteworthy. First, environmental policies are relatively stable over time despite the occurrence of profound changes in the economic and political systems of the CEE and LA countries. Often, the relevant laws changed only once or twice during the observation period of twenty years. In this context, the "maturity" of the different policy items is decisive for the frequency of policy change. For example, water pollution has been regulated since the 1980s in the countries under study and therefore more changes could be observed for this policy item than for those that represent relatively new complements to environmental policy such as the regulation of soil pollution and GM maize.

This picture of relative policy stability stands in marked contrast to studies of policy change that employ budgetary data that vary considerably over time (see, e.g., Baumgartner 2006; Breunig, Koski, and Mortensen 2010). This suggests that data on environmental spending do not adequately reflect the regulatory dynamics of individual policy items, which indicates that these two measurements cannot be regarded as interchangeable. From this it follows that the findings of studies based on budgetary data or other proxies for measuring policy change, for instance, data for the emission of pollutants into the air, may well deviate from the results of the present study, simply because of the different conceptualizations of the dependent variable.

Second, despite the relatively low instances of policy change, on average, environmental policy arrangements became strengthened in both regions over the course of time. This is mainly due to the fact that many events of policy change entailed the adoption of regulatory standards that were previously not in place. However, when the two regions are treated separately, both the frequency of policy change but also the average strictness of environmental protection standards are higher in CEE than in LA. Especially regarding the regulation of air, soil, and water pollution, the CEE countries outperform the LA countries in terms of stringency. Moreover, the CEE countries rather swiftly established environmental procuracies, whereas Bolivia and Uruguay still have not set up such enforcement institutions.

Indeed, numerous LA countries still lack some very basic regulations for combating environmental degradation. The absence of environmental regulations is most visible for the Central American states, but also countries which are generally perceived as being environmentally progressive, such as Chile and Uruguay (see Porter, Schwab, and Lopez-Claros 2005: 611), often do not possess environmental protection standards. Hence, this book challenges the notion that environmental pollution in LA is exclusively an enforcement problem (see, e.g., McAllister 2008). Rather, it suggests that environmental degradation is also likely to stem from absent regulations.

This is clearly different in the CEE countries, which in most cases often had environmental regulations in place before system transformation. Concerning these countries, there exists another problem, namely, that at the beginning of the observation period some of them still set unrealistically strict environmental protection standards in accordance with the regulatory approach practised under state socialism (see, e.g., Earnhart 1997; Klarer and Francis 1997; Cole 1998; Knill and Lenschow 2000; Pavlínek and Pickles 2000; Andonova 2004; Fagan 2004; Carmin and VanDeveer 2005).

Third, and related to the previous observation, the data reveal instances in which policy change entails a relaxation of protection standards. Remarkably, this is predominantly the case with the limit values for ozone concentrations in ambient air and particularly in the CEE countries, which partly results from giving up the regulatory practice of the state-socialist period. However, downward policy change is also observable for limit values of waste-water standards in both CEE and LA, which underlines the argument made above that the maturity of policy items is important for the occurrence and direction of policy change. Further to this, this finding supports the view that policy change is a bidirectional process, including both upward and downward changes (see, e.g., Knill, Tosun, and Bauer 2009; Knill, Schulze, and Tosun 2012).

Turning to the analytical findings, it is important to stress that the explanatory power of the theoretical model varies notably across the different specifications of the dependent variables. The theoretical model explains best changes in the stringency of waste-water and soil pollution standards. It also provides valuable insights into a government's decision to set up an environmental procuracy as well as into changes in the regulation of air quality standards and the adoption of sustainable forest management. The analysis of the regulation of GM maize, however, points to some counterintuitive relationships, which makes it necessary to reanalyse this policy item by means of complementary case studies.

Overall, the empirical analysis shows that public demand and the strength of environmental groups are the most important drivers of a tightening of environmental policy arrangements. Concerning public demand, it is specifically the intensity of environmental degradation that leads to environmental policy change. This lends support to the view that an increasing responsiveness to public demand is a major consequence of political transformation (see Duquette 1999: 28). Equally important is the impact of environmental groups on the definition of environmental policies as well as the establishment of environmental prosecution units. This finding is even more remarkable as the literature tends to posit that environmental groups in CEE and LA have been declining over the course of system transformation (see, e.g., Pickvance 1999). In this context, the qualitative analysis of GM maize contributes greatly to understanding that not only environmental groups are important for inducing governments to set stricter regulations, but that also other civil society groups, such as farmers' associations or indigenous organizations, can be crucial if they feel affected by them.

In addition, economic integration represents an important determinant, but not in the way it was suggested above. Even though it is theoretically plausible to expect that competitive pressures induce governments of emerging market democracies to keep their environmental protection standards at a comparatively low level, the analyses of the regulation of air, soil, and water pollution reveal that economic integration actually helps to tighten the legal provisions. Likewise, economic integration is also the main determinant of the governments' strengthened commitment to enforcing environmental protection standards. Therefore, economic globalization can be mostly associated with positive stimuli for environmental policymaking (see also Hoberg 1991, 2001; Vogel 1995, 1997; Prakash and Potoski 2006, 2007; Holzinger, Knill, and Arts 2008; Holzinger, Knill, and Sommerer 2008, 2011; Perkins and Neumayer 2012).

Finally, integration with the European Union (EU) has important consequences for environmental policymaking in the CEE countries. In this context, an interesting observation is that the EU predominantly triggers environmental policy change through the candidate countries' need to transpose the environmental acquis (see Holzinger and Knoepfel 2000; Schimmelfennig and Sedelmeier 2004; Knill, Tosun, and Heichel 2008). On this occasion, however, the countries often do not only reform those policies that are directly affected by EU requirements, but also undertake additional reforms that aim to strengthen environmental protection arrangements. From this it follows that accession to and membership within the EU yields both direct and indirect impacts on environmental policy change.

Altogether, this study advances the current state of research in three ways. The first contribution is to provide a detailed description of environmental policy developments and the spread of environmental procuracies throughout CEE and LA. To be fair, there have already been some efforts to uncover patterns of environmental policy change for large country samples, which also include some emerging market democracies (see, e.g., Holzinger, Knill, and Arts 2008). Yet, most studies focusing on CEE and LA rely on in-depth analyses of a limited number of cases (see, e.g., Desai 1998; Pavlínek and Pickles 2000; Andonova 2004; Fagan 2004; Carmin and VanDeveer 2005; Knill, Tosun, and Heichel 2008; Fagan and Carmin 2011). In this regard, the body of empirical research on environmental enforcement in CEE and LA is even much smaller (see, e.g., Earnhart 1997; Gallagher 2002, 2004; Andonova 2004; McAllister 2008; McAllister, Van Rooij, and Kagan 2010). This strand of research deserves credit for providing valuable insights into certain interesting cases. However, this literature is less suitable for identifying broad empirical patterns, which this study seeks to accomplish. Therefore, in light of the state of research, the provision of data for a large number of emerging market democracies regarding changes in environmental policies and enforcement institutions can be regarded as progress and may serve as a starting point for future studies.

The second contribution to the literature refers to a transparent measurement of policy and institutional change. Many studies dealing with events of change remain implicit about how they measure them. As a consequence, no scholarly debate about the advantages and disadvantages of certain approaches to the operationalization of policy and institutional change can take place, which also impedes cumulative research. There cannot be any doubt that empirically assessing policy and institutional change is a challenging task (see Capano 2009; Howlett and Cashore 2009) and perhaps the most essential finding of this book is that this claim holds true. To be sure, there are many issues to deal with when one tries to empirically assess policy and institutional change that cannot be fully resolved. Yet, this study spells out the measurement of the central analytical concepts, and although there are certainly aspects related to the approach adopted by the present study that can be criticized, it should be kept in mind that only through debate can veritable scientific progress be achieved. This book accepts this and seeks to stimulate a more intense debate about the opportunities and pitfalls of empirically assessing policy and institutional change.

The third contribution of this book relates to the application of a multi-method design by adopting the logic of nested analysis. This proceeding allows for explaining general patterns of cross-country variation and shedding light on specific cases which initially seem to contradict the theoretical expectations. Combining the virtues of different research designs enhances the consistency of the findings, provides a better understanding of the causal mechanisms underlying the processes of change, and avoids the problem of adopting an overtly reductionist analytical perspective. There are, in principle, many ways of combining quantitative and qualitative methods. The approach adopted here refers to a complementary analysis of one particular policy item, which might be equally suitable for other research contexts.

Organization of the Book

This book primarily aims to shed light on the factors facilitating or impeding the occurrence of policy and institutional change in the field of environmental policy. As a result, theoretical considerations are central to this study and are addressed here and in the next chapter. Of these, chapter 2 is more abstract and aims to provide a general overview of the rich body of theoretical literature on policy and institutional change. Chapter 3 introduces the study's theoretical framework, which follows the approach of comparative policy analysis. The explanatory factors incorporated into the model reflect the most important consequences of political and economic transformation.

Chapter 4 prepares the empirical examination of the theoretical arguments. It outlines the study's research design and explains how changes in the stringency of environmental regulations and enforcement commitment can be accurately measured. Moreover, this chapter sheds light on the operationalization of the explanatory variables and provides an overview of the most appropriate techniques of analysis. The actual empirical analysis begins with chapter 5, which describes in detail the characteristics of the dependent variables. It first sketches the development of the five environmental policy items over time. Next, the chapter illustrates the diffusion of environmental procuracies throughout CEE and LA. Most essentially, this chapter demonstrates the variety in the occurrence and forms of policy and institutional change. In so doing, it underscores that these are demanding analytical concepts that require careful theorizing and analysis.

While chapter 5 offers some suggestive explanations for the observed patterns of change, these cannot substitute for a more rigorous testing of hypotheses, which is done in chapter 6. To this end, different quantitative estimation techniques are employed, which perform well for five of the six dependent variables. An important exception is the regulation of GM maize, which cannot be accurately explained by the quantitative analysis. Consequently, this particular policy item is re-examined in chapter 7 by adopting a qualitative approach. As a result, this chapter is composed of a number of case studies that are later tied together to learn about the factors inducing changes in the regulation of GM maize and to better understand why the quantitative analysis could not provide consistent insights.

The book concludes with some thoughts on the lessons learned from studying environmental policy and institutional change in the emerging market democracies of CEE and LA. Subsequently, this chapter discusses the book's empirical and theoretical limitations and, as well, points to open questions, thus setting the stage for future research. All in all, the concluding chapter encourages a more intense academic discussion of the various forms and causes of policy and institutional change in both advanced and emerging market democracies.

2 Theories of Policy and Institutional Change

This book investigates the patterns and determinants of policy and institutional change in emerging market democracies. To this end, it adopts the approach of comparative policy analysis, which is based on the combination of separate explanatory factors originating from independent theories(Roller 2005). Accordingly, a theoretical framework will be elaborated that is composed of specific empirical elements of the political and economic transformation processes experienced by these countries serving as explanatory variables. However, there also exist various theoretical approaches that explicitly address phenomena of policy and institutional change (for an overview, see John 2003; Héritier 2007; Capano 2009; Mahoney and Thelen 2010), which have already guided many insightful empirical studies.

For example, Kübler (2001) relies on the advocacy coalition framework to explain why the originally prohibitionist Swiss drug policy has moved towards a more liberal model. The punctuated equilibrium framework guides Givel's (2006) study of changes to US tobacco policy as well as Princen's (2010) investigation of modifications to the EU's fisheries policies. Further, Hanisch and Schlüter (2000) examine Bulgarian land reform from the perspective of economic theories of institutional change. In a similar vein, Prado and Trebilcock (2009) employ path dependency theory to explain why recent rule of law and property rights reforms in emerging market democracies mostly produced disappointing results. All of these studies, which clearly only represent a very small portion of the relevant literature, have in common that they only focus on one particular theoretical perspective for explaining events of change.

Why does this study not follow their example by relying on one specific theory in order to explain policy and institutional change? To what extent can these specific theories serve for developing a micro-foundation for the explanatory model to be set up in chapter 3? These are the two main questions guiding this chapter. To address them effectively, the first section presents the most important theories of policy change and discusses their appropriateness for the purpose of this study. The next section provides an introduction to the multifaceted body of literature on institutional change. A more encompassing evaluation and a comparison of these theories from the approach of comparative policy analysis are presented in the concluding section. In this context, it should be noted that this chapter does not attempt an exhaustive criticism of the specific theories of policy and institutional change. Instead, it seeks to explain why the adoption of a broader theoretical lens as provided by comparative policy analysis represents a more suitable approach for achieving the study's research objectives.

Theories of Policy Change:
The Role of Actors and Institutions

The analysis of what governments decide to do and why has always been at the centre of political science. This holds particularly true for the sub-discipline of policy analysis, where events of policy change and the conditions facilitating or constraining them constitute a major area of study. It is hence hardly surprising that there is an ongoing and in recent years intensified debate on how to explain the occurrence of policy change. All the numerous theoretical approaches originating from this fruitful debate have in common that they consider policy change to be a complex phenomenon and (implicitly) emphasize policy resilience and incremental changes as the most likely outcomes.

The different theoretical approaches can be assigned to two major analytical perspectives. The first perspective focuses on the formation and modification of actors' beliefs and preferences in light of a variety of endogenous and exogenous factors. It aims to pinpoint the causal mechanisms underlying the actors' judgments of existing policy arrangements and new policy options. The second perspective also recognizes the vital role of actors, but predominantly sheds light on the system level, that is, the institutional structures facilitating or impeding policy change(see Knill and Tosun 2012).

Actor-Level Theories of Policy Change

There are three interrelated research strands that rely on the preferences and characteristics of policy actors for explaining policy change. The first research perspective refers to policy-oriented learning, which also represents an important component of the other two theoretical approaches, namely, the advocacy coalition framework and the policy-subsystem adjustment framework. There are numerous explanations of policy change that are based on different notions of learning. In this context, the concept of lesson drawing introduced by Rose (1991) has received considerable attention. Lesson drawing refers to situations in which governments rationally utilize policy experience from elsewhere to solve domestic problems. It is a voluntary process whereby one government learns from another government's solution to a common problem, what to do (i.e., it draws a "positive lesson") or what not to do (i.e., it draws a "negative lesson"). In the case of a government drawing a negative lesson, policy change is, however, unlikely to occur (Holzinger and Knill 2008: 44).

An advancement of the lesson-drawing approach is represented by the more recently developed concepts of rational learning and Bayesian learning (see Holzinger and Knill 2005, 2008; Meseguer Yebra 2009; Knill and Tosun 2012: chapter 11). Akin to lesson drawing, these concepts conceive of governments as rational actors looking for appropriate policy solutions that work well abroad. In the case of Bayesian learning, governments update their beliefs on the consequences of policies with all available information about policy designs and choose the one that is expected to yield the best results. This form of rational updating is assumed to correspond to a calculation process based on Bayes's theorem, which also explains the term "Bayesian learning." Hence, with either of these concepts – be it lesson drawing, rational learning, or Bayesian learning – policy change would occur if modifications to the existing policy arrangements promised more effective solutions to public problems than current ones. As concerns the effectiveness of policy-oriented learning, this crucially depends on a country's policy analysis capacity (Howlett and Joshi-Koop 2011).

More refined theoretical expectations about the impact of learning are provided by Hall (1993), who differentiates between three possible types of policy change: First-order change is about modifications to the precise setting or calibration of a policy instrument. Second-order change refers to a variation in policy instruments. Third-order change is about changes in the overarching goal of a policy in a particular field. According to Hall, policy change is most likely for the policy setting (i.e., first-order change), but it becomes more difficult with regard to policy instruments (i.e., second-order change) and even more so with policy goals (i.e., third-order change). Changes in settings are considered as rather unproblematic, since they can be achieved within existing instruments and goals. In a similar way, instrumental changes are considered to be more likely than goal changes, as the latter imply the departure from dominant and institutionally strongly entrenched ideas of how to perceive and resolve certain societal problems.

The advocacy coalition framework (Sabatier and Jenkins-Smith 1993, 1999; Sabatier 1998; Sabatier and Weible 2007; Weible, Sabatier, and McQueen 2009) is one of the most influential approaches to policy change (for an application, see also, e.g., Sotirov and Memmler 2012). Essentially, it views policymaking as the result of the competition between coalitions of actors who advocate beliefs about certain policy options. This competition between advocacy groups takes place within policy subsystems, that is, semi-autonomous networks of policy participants that focus on a particular policy issue and aim to affect public policy in such ways that the issue becomes addressed. The framework further argues that actors process information according to a variety of cognitive heuristics that provide guidance in complex decision-making situations. In this regard, belief systems give guidance about how a social problem is structured, and how it could be remedied. The belief systems consist of deep-core beliefs, that is, ontological and normative world views, a policy core, that is, causal perceptions for achieving deep-core beliefs in a given policy subsystem, and a set of secondary beliefs comprising instrumental considerations on how to implement the policy core. A central assumption of the framework is that these structural categories of belief systems show decreasing resistance to change. The framework predicts that secondary beliefs, compared to deep-core and policy-core beliefs, are most likely to change over time (Weible, Sabatier, and McQueen 2009: 123).

To attain their policy goals, advocacy coalitions try to make governmental institutions behave in accordance with their policy cores by using venues provided by the institutional structure. Against this background, policy change may principally result from two sources. First, policy change can occur due to learning processes, which induce a hegemonic advocacy coalition to transform its behavioural intentions concerning the attainment of policy objectives as a result of experience or new information. Second, non-cognitive events occurring outside the policy subsystem may lead to changes in the power distribution among advocacy coalitions. These kinds of perturbations in non-cognitive factors can include single, extraordinary events, such as disasters, or repeating and less drastic events, such as critical elections (Howlett, Ramesh, and Perl 2009: 205). What matters is that these kinds of external events or shocks entail profound changes in public opinion, socio-economic conditions, governing coalitions, and other subsystems. In fact, depending on the intensity of these external events, major policy change – defined as modifications to the policy core – becomes likely, whereas with policy-oriented learning only minor policy change is expected, since in this case the policy core remains mostly intact.

The revision of the advocacy coalition framework by Sabatier and Weible (2007) identifies two more sources of policy change. One source refers to internal events that occur within the subsystem and are conceived to highlight failures in current subsystem practices. The other source is represented by cross-coalition learning, where professional forums provide an institutional setting that allows coalitions to safely negotiate and implement agreements.

The policy-subsystem adjustment model put forward by Howlett and Ramesh (2002) builds on the critique that the advocacy coalition framework treats endogenous factors (i.e., the advocacy coalitions per se) and exogenous factors (i.e., the non-cognitive factors) separately. As a result of this strict distinction, thus the authors contend, there is little in the way of integrating exogenous processes and endogenous ones for sufficiently explaining the nature of policy change. In response to this flaw, they propose bringing together systemic perturbations and policy spillovers as exogenous factors, with policy learning and venue change as endogenous processes. The basic idea of the model is that actors that are susceptible to endogenous processes use exogenous factors to pursue their desired policy goals. This means that actors can be in favour of policy change due to the reception of new ideas as a consequence of policy-oriented learning. To realize this new idea the actors may change their strategies by practising venue change, which involves the redefinition of a policy issue to facilitate alternation of the locations where policy deliberation occurs (see also Baumgartner and Jones 2009). Yet, policy learning and venue change can more effectively lead to policy change if systemic perturbations, that is, exogenous events that draw new attention to a policy sector, take place. Systemic perturbations bring new actors or new ideas to the forefront and can hence trigger policy change. Finally, subsystem spillovers that promote the merging or integration of previously separate subsystems into a single policy domain can induce policy change through the introduction of new actors and ideas into otherwise stable policy regimes (Howlett, Ramesh, and Perl 2009: 206).

System-Level Theories of Policy Change

One of the best known theoretical approaches towards understanding patterns of policy change is the punctuated equilibrium framework elaborated by Baumgartner and Jones (2009) and True, Jones, and Baumgartner (2007). Essentially, the punctuated equilibrium framework seeks to explain why political processes are generally characterized by stability and incrementalism, that is, minimal adjustments to existing policy arrangements, but occasionally produce fundamental shifts from the past, that is, policy punctuations. According to this approach, both policy stability and change are mostly determined by the presence of policy venues and policy images. Policy venues are institutional arenas in which decision making takes place. Policy images are the shared views of policy communities about the characteristic of a given public problem and ways of solving it. As a rule, policy change happens when a new policy image is received well by the actors of a new policy venue. Thus, institutional shifts open the previously constrained decision-making domain to other actors and ideas, allowing for a reframing of the issue that undermines the previous policy justification and therewith triggers change.

The emergence of large-scale changes, that is, policy punctuations, additionally depends on negative and positive feedback. Negative feedback ensures that when a given policy is affected by change, forces emerge that drive it back to its original position. In contrast, positive feedback reinforces change and makes policies move even further from their initial position. According to the punctuated equilibrium framework, institutions are strictly conservative. Thus, major policy change can only happen if exogenous challenges and transformations help the advocates of change to create new policy images or manage to accomplish venue shifting, that is, shifting decision making on a certain issue to a new venue that is susceptible to different kinds of arguments than the venue that originally dealt with it. Policy punctuations can be initiated by several external factors, one of which is a so-called focusing event, that is, an external shock highlighting policy deficiencies. They may directly challenge the existing policy image and the venue promoting it (Walgrave and Varone 2008: 368).

Institutional arrangements are also central to the concepts of veto points and veto players. Veto points refer to the fact that policy decisions need agreement of several institutional points in a chain of decisions (Immergut 1990; Immergut and Anderson 2007). The adoption of legislative proposals depends upon the number and location of opportunities for a formal veto along this decision-making chain. The more veto points in a political system, the more difficult it becomes to gain approval for a policy proposal, thus reducing the chances of policy change. While this perspective already elucidates how institutional settings can facilitate or impede policy change, some scholars (e.g., Weaver and Rockman 1993) have argued that a more complete explanation would require tackling the question of why veto points are willing to use their formal power.

This question guides a refinement of the veto point perspective, namely, the veto player theory (Tsebelis 1995, 2002). This approach holds that the occurrence of policy change can be explained by the institutions governing the decision-making process and the preferences of the actors involved in it. Veto players are defined as "individual or collective actors whose agreement is necessary for a change of the *status quo*" (Tsebelis 2002: 19). There are two types of veto players: institutional and partisan. Institutional veto players are those established by a country's constitution. Following this definition, the executive and the legislature form the key veto players in any political system, but there are additional institutions that can impede the adoption of a policy, for example, constitutional courts. Partisan veto players correspond to those veto players formed in the course of decision making (see, e.g., Zohlnhöfer 2009; Ganghof 2011).

For analysing veto players and their impact on policy adoption, three types of information are necessary. First, one has to determine the number of veto players. It generally holds that greater numbers of veto players reduce the odds of policy adoption. Second, one has to assess the ideological distance between the actors possessing formal veto power. This dimension generally refers to the veto players' partisan composition and is calculated as the distance between the most extreme veto player on the left and the most extreme veto player on the right side of the policy continuum. The larger the distance between veto players' ideal policy points, the less likely policy change will occur. Finally, as veto players are often collective actors, it is important to assess how cohesive they are concerning their policy interests. A high cohesion implies that all actors constituting this veto player speak with "one voice" (Knill and Tosun 2012: 135–6). Hence, the higher the internal cohesion, the more powerful the collective veto players and the less likely is policy change. In addition, for predicting the likelihood and direction of policy change, it is important to take into consideration the actors' formal agenda-setting powers.

Likewise, the multiple stream approach developed by Kingdon (2002) underscores the possibility of policy change through agenda setting. Moving an idea onto or higher up on the agenda involves three processes: "problems," "proposals," and "politics." The first process – that is, problems – relates to persuading policymakers to pay more attention to one problem over others. Because a policy proposal's chances of rising on the agenda are better if the associated problem is perceived as serious, problem recognition is critical. It can be influenced by how problems are learned about or defined. The next process – proposals – is about how policy proposals are generated, debated, revised, and adopted for serious consideration. Because competing proposals can be attached to the same problem, getting a proposal on the "short list" typically takes time and the willingness to pursue it by using many tactics. The political process refers to political factors that influence agendas such as changes in elected officials. These three elements operate largely independently, although the actors in each can overlap. Successful agenda setting requires that at least two elements come together at a critical time. If this occurs, a "policy window" opens and change becomes feasible (Knill and Tosun 2012: 112).

Theories of Policy Change: Strengths and Limitations

All theoretical approaches presented in this section deserve credit for advancing our understanding of the patterns and determinants of policy change. The actor-level approaches are useful for grasping policy change from a micro-perspective that takes into account the changes in policy-specific beliefs and interests. In addition, the theories of learning provide answers to the question of where new policy ideas come from. In a complementary vein, the system-level approaches shed light on the role of (political) institutions for structuring the interaction of the policy actors and draw attention to the importance of agenda setting for inducing policy change. Despite these analytical strengths, the theoretical approaches presented in this section are of limited suitability for the analytical purpose of this study, which stems from incompatibility with respect to the levels of analysis, problems related to measurement, and conceptual vagueness.

Most of the above approaches require fine-grained research designs such as in-depth studies in order for one to test their explanatory power. This point can be aptly illustrated by the example of the advocacy coalition framework. To evaluate whether environmental policy change in emerging market democracies can be explained by this theoretical approach would entail the identification of all relevant advocacy coalitions, possible instances of policy-oriented learning, events of external and internal systemic perturbations, and cross-coalition learning in professional forums. While such analytical efforts have indeed produced valuable insights into processes of policy change (see, e.g., Albright 2011; Sotirov and Memmler 2012), such a proceeding is not practicable given the empirical scope of the present study. Empirical challenges also await researchers aiming to test the implications of the veto player theory. Notwithstanding some insightful quantitative studies (see, e.g., Jahn and Müller-Rommel 2010), there are numerous pitfalls inherent in a rigorous (macro-quantitative) testing of the veto player theory (see Ganghof 2003). While in abstract terms it is plausible to argue that actors with formal veto power do matter for policy change, it is difficult to identify all relevant veto players and to assess their preferences for a whole policy area or subarea. This becomes even more challenging when one considers that in many political systems formal veto players coexist with informal ones, who can equally affect policy decisions (see, e.g., Obinger 2001). Thus, in light of this study's setup as a macro-level analysis of patterns of environmental policy change in a large number of emerging market democracies, the analytical and methodological requirements of the theoretical approaches outlined above must be regarded as too demanding to be implemented accurately.

Further, there are more general measurement problems with some of the theoretical approaches. This problem particularly applies to the empirical assessment of learning, which is central to many theories of policy change. How can learning be measured? The major challenge is that learning processes cannot be directly observed. One can, for instance, observe that an increasing number of countries are adopting a policy innovation and then conclude that this is the result of learning. However, such a proceeding would still not address the question of whether policy adoption is based on rational considerations, as argued by the various theories of learning, or, for instance, represents emu-latory behaviour driven by the desire of governments "not to be left behind" (Holzinger and Knill 2008: 46). An alternative measurement strategy would be to directly ask policymakers whether policy choices are based on learning. With such a proceeding, however, Radaelli (2009: 1147) cautions that policymakers tend to overestimate the role of learning as opposed to other stimuli. Radaelli further explains that sometimes interviewees make reference to learning merely to protect their organization from criticism. All this does not mean that learning is generally immeasurable or even irrelevant for policy choices. Rather, it should be acknowledged that learning is a methodologically demand-ing concept that warrants particular measurement efforts and therefore cannot be addressed in a satisfactory way in the context of this study (see, e.g., Gilardi 2010).

Finally, the bulk of the theories of policy change are remarkably implicit about the nature of exogenous factors. The corollary of the advocacy coalition framework, for instance, is that major policy change principally arises from transformations that occur outside of the policy subsystem. However, the framework does not specify which kind of events would possess the potential of modifying an advocacy coali-tion's belief system (Capano 2009: 24). The same criticism applies to the punctuated equilibrium framework, which puts forward a fully plau-sible argument about the relevance of policy venues and images for bringing about change. Yet again, it only makes general reference to possible exogenous factors without specifying which of these are more relevant or under which conditions they become particularly effective. A similar vagueness about the exact nature of exogenous factors can be observed for many other theoretical approaches.

It is not the objective of this section to bluntly criticize the theories of policy change presented above, but to highlight that they do not pro-vide for a fully specified explanatory model. The theoretical approaches perform well in elaborating the causal mechanisms underlying policy change. What they do not do – and arguably also do not aim to do – is to provide an extensive discussion of all potential exogenous factors. In fact, this is something that cannot reasonably be expected from such general theoretical approaches. Hence, the conclusion of this discus-sion is that the specific theories of policy change do not substitute for identifying the exogenous drivers of environmental policy change in emerging market democracies on the basis of empirical accounts.

Theories of Institutional Change: Interests, History, and Legitimacy

This book conceives of changes in enforcement commitment as modifications to existing institutional arrangements. More precisely, it concentrates on the creation of units within public prosecution services that are in charge of enforcing compliance with environmental protection standards. As public prosecution services represent organizations, modifications to the tasks they carry out could be explained by theories of institutional change. How suitable are such theories for the empirical subject of this study? For a more straightforward presentation of this vast and diverse body of literature, this section follows Gilley's (2008) distinction between economic, sociopolitical, historical, and legitimacy-based theories of institutional change.

Economic Theories of Institutional Change

Economic theories explain institutional changes in light of competing interests in accordance with rational choice theory, and are, as a consequence, also known as rational choice theories of institutional change. Although rational choice theory is based on a universally valid set of considerations about costs and benefits, there are several theoretical ways in which institutions are interpreted (see Shepsle 2008). These different views can roughly be divided into a functional approach, an evolutionary approach, and a power-based political bargaining approach (Héritier 2007: 10).

The functional approach conceives of institutional change as the outcome of an attempt to solve a collective action problem (see, e.g., Keohane 1984; Weingast and Marshall 1988; Libecap 1989; Crawford and Ostrom 1995). Against this background, institutional change is seen as a centralized process in which rules are explicitly specified by a collective political entity. Individuals and organizations engage in collective action in order to try to change these rules for their own benefit. The outcome of the strategic interaction is an institutional solution which for the actors involved represents an equilibrium. This means that once such a solution has been reached, all players are interested in maintaining the institution.

From this perspective, institutional change occurs through strategic interactions implying either bargaining or negotiations. Most often, however, institutional change is triggered by exogenous parameter shifts. An attempt to endogenize the explanation of institutional change within the functionalist approach represents the work of Greif and Laitin (2004). The authors first establish under which conditions institutions are stable or self-enforcing. They argue that they are self-enforcing when the actual and expected behaviour of all concerned actors generates the institutional rules that motivate other individuals to follow the behaviour associated with the rule. This equilibrium situation suggests that institutional change occurs if one of the parameters defined ex ante are changed (Héritier 2007: 26). According to this view, the most important mechanisms of reinforcement are of a social nature (i.e., through habitual action and ideology), a political nature (i.e., laws and regulations), and an economic nature (i.e., through increasing returns of existing capabilities and learning). The endogenization is achieved by means of the concept of so-called quasi-parameters (i.e., features of a game that are exogenous in the short run, but become endogenous in the long run) and by processes of institutional reinforcement and undermining.

Institutional rules, the argument goes, may persistently influence the given parameters of the rules of the game, such as actors' information. Marginal changes in these parameters do not necessarily lead to a change in the institutional rules and the expected behaviour associated with these rules. If the value of a relevant parameter only marginally changes, the behaviour associated with a stable institution is unlikely to change, because in such an instance actors are likely to rely on past institutions to guide them. Indeed, this argument is closely related to the notion of path dependency (see, e.g., Pierson 2001), which states that even if the environment changes institutions will not necessarily be altered; on the contrary, existing institutions may be reinforced. Changes in quasi-parameters may either broaden the range of situations in which the existing institutional pattern is an equilibrium, or may undermine the existing institution, leading to an impetus for institutional change. Put in this way, the model displays similarities with the punctuated equilibrium framework as well as the advocacy coalition framework and the policy-subsystem adjustment model. The difference, however, stems from the notion of gradual changes in quasi-parameters that occasionally lead to an institutional change when it becomes clear that existing patterns of behaviour no longer constitute an equilibrium (Kingston and Caballero 2009: 172).

The functional rational choice model has been expanded by the notion of transaction costs, that is, costs related to the gathering and processing of information. The incorporation of transaction costs into the theoretical reasoning gives way to an evolutionary approach to institutional change. The main difference between the evolutionary approach and the functional approach is about the selection process determining which rules ultimately emerge. The evolutionary approach is based on the assumption of non-intentionality, that is, institutional rules originate from the uncoordinated choices of many individuals rather than representing a process of collective choice with rational actors intentionally choosing institutional rules. Moreover, the evolutionary perspective is primarily interested in the long-term evolution of institutions in terms of dynamics and stability (Nelson 1995; Witt 2004).

The evolutionary approach has been predominantly established by Nelson and Winter (1982, 2002), who depict firms as non-optimizing organizations that have to learn about institutional rules through the trial and error of experimental searches. The authors argue that instead of profit maximization, firms base their decisions on a continual process of searching for satisfactory but sustainable profits (see also Witt 2003). In this context, Cantwell, Dunning, and Lundan (2010: 574) state that the goal of profit maximization might only be applicable if the innovations are left out of the theoretical considerations. However, in the more realistic modelling of institutional processes with the occurrence of innovations, the notion of an experimental and uncertain search for higher profits is more appropriate.

Transaction costs arise due to bounded rationality and opportunism of the interacting actors. Against this background, North (1990) views processes of institutional change as occurring in repeated interactions. Information is deepened and learning takes place that predominantly leads to incremental institutional change. Institutional change will therefore only happen if expected benefits of the new institutional structure minus bargaining and information costs, as well as the costs of securing compliance with the new structures, exceed the benefits of the existing institution (Héritier 2007: 15). This third economic approach does not only compare the overall outcomes produced by an institution with the outcomes produced if there were no institution, but makes assumptions about the social context in which the interaction takes place and relates them to the pay-offs of the interaction. The argument is that institutions have different distributional consequences for the involved actors and that institutional rules are compared under this perspective. In this regard, Knight (1992) argues that if some actors have greater bargaining power than others, this will possibly affect the kind of rule that ultimately becomes used by the society overall.

Unlike the first perspective, the power-based political bargaining approach does not stress the shared concern with achieving joint gains or efficiency through cooperation, but emphasizes political conflict and strategic bargaining among actors. Principally, it identifies the altered preferences of the involved actors or an increasing power of particular actors or actor coalitions as the main source of institutional change. The reasons why these preferences have changed and why some actors have gained power are not systematically addressed by this approach.

Sociopolitical Institutionalism

The sociopolitical approach to institutional change is similar to the economic approach, but it emphasizes social or political power rather than economic interests (Gilley 2008: 260). The principal difference relates to the view that politics is more than self-interested bargaining over private benefits, and that there is an independent role for state action as well as for reasoned debate on ideological and ethical grounds. A first formulation of this principle can be found in Ruttan and Hayami's (1984) theory of institutional change, which distinguishes between the demand for and the supply of institutional innovations. Exogenous changes in technology, resource endowments, or consumer demand create a disequilibrium in markets, where factors of production are exchanged. The demand for institutional change arises out of this disequilibrium. By the same token, institutional innovations are supplied to the extent dictated by the private returns accruing to political entrepreneurs. Since the private returns may be different from the social ones, institutional supply may be socially inefficient. The authors additionally stress the role of cultural and ideological factors and the current state of knowledge as important determinants of supply. Ruttan (2006) presents a more systematic account of how resource endowments, technology, cultural endowments, and institutions may all mutually affect each other. The framework specifies that new institutions may evolve spontaneously as well as emerge in response to demand for institutional change. In the latter case, new institutions are supplied by political entrepreneurs who mobilize political and bureaucratic resources to change the rules. At the same time, however, Ruttan stresses that cultural endowment such as ideology may represent an impediment to institutional change (Kingston and Caballero 2009: 169).

The study by Migdal (1988) adds a new perspective to the sociopolitical approaches. He contends that not all political action is goal seeking, and the process of political participation may be valued as much as its outcome. The state is not passive, but is a direct agent of socio-economic change, and there is a dialectic between the state and social groups defining their relative positions as well as the arena for political action. In this regard, individuals in societies seek to safeguard their survival by finding a way to satisfy their basic needs. Along the same lines, political elites seek to stay in power, which might be accomplished through inducing institutional change.

A similar logic underlies the seminal book *The Logic of Political Survival* by Bueno de Mesquita et al. (2003), in which the authors link institutional change to democratic institutions through the elaboration of the "selectorate" theory. In a nutshell, the book argues that all political systems have two institutional characteristics that describe how they retain and select leaders: the selectorate and the winning coalition. The selectorate is the set of people in the political system who can take part in choosing a leader. The winning coalition is the quantity of selectors whose support the leader must retain to remain in office. Leaders hold the loyalty of their winning coalition by producing both public goods and private benefits through making decisions about policy and institutional arrangements. It is the mix of the two that varies with selected institutional arrangements (Morrow et al. 2008: 393). As the size of the winning coalition increases, for instance, due to democratization, leaders will shift that mix away from private benefits and towards public goods to ensure their political survival. To achieve this, modifications to existing institutional arrangements might be necessary.

Historical Institutionalism

Historical institutionalism represents a complement to the arguments made above by suggesting that factors responsible for the creation of a political institution may not be the same as those that sustain it over time (Stinchcombe 1968). Put in other words, existing institutional rules may not have been created by the political groups that now benefit from those institutions. Although at its point of creation its substance may have reflected the balance of power among the creators of the rule, over time the institutional rule may undergo a change that shifts the balance of costs and benefits (Thelen 2003). The main implication of this is that "certain courses of political development, once initiated, are hard to reverse" (Pierson 2001: 414). The question that emerges then is what the underlying mechanisms of transformation are to which the institutional rule is subject once it has been created. In this context, the path dependency argument predicts institutional stability due to institutional "lock-ins," that is, a development difficult to deviate from (North 1990: 94; for a discussion, see Howlett and Rayner 2006). Thus, once institutions are created, they often only change in subtle and gradual ways over time (Mahoney and Thelen 2010: 1).

Thelen (2003) elaborates a more dynamic variant of this argument by putting emphasis on the ongoing political contestation, definition, and redefinition of these established institutional structures. A critical juncture (i.e., a situation in which the structural influences on policy choices are notably relaxed for a short period) in institutional development should not be accounted for through external events, her argument goes, but endogenously on the basis of given historical structures and the limits they set for actors as they respond to new opportunities and challenges in their political and economic environment. Even more convincing is Hall and Thelen's (2009) fusion of historical institutionalism with rational-choice arguments. The authors explain that institutional change is difficult and institutions are stable not only for path dependency but due to rationalist uncertainties about new institutions serving interests better, difficulties in shifting to new coordinating institutions, complexities of institutional interactions that might require new strategies, and institutionalized power relations. They emphasize two routes to institutional change: defection and reinterpretation. Defection refers to strategies that deviate from the behaviours associated with a cooperative outcome. In other words, actors who have been following certain practices prescribed by an institution stop doing so. In instances of reinterpretation, by contrast, the actors associated with an institution gradually change their interpretation of its rules without defecting from the formal institution itself.

Legitimacy-Based Institutionalism

The legitimacy-based approach concentrates on the role of popular preferences based on the common goods demands of the political community. In this context, legitimacy relates to the extent to which the citizens regard the government as rightfully exercising political power (Gilley 2008: 260). The concept of legitimacy is also strongly related to sociological institutionalism. At the heart of sociological institutionalism is a broad understanding of institutions, incorporating symbol systems, cognitive scripts, and moral templates that provide meaning to action (Hall and Taylor 1996; Knill and Tosun 2012: 41). Accordingly, sociological institutionalism has a distinctive understanding of the relationship between institutions and individual action. It stresses the way in which institutions influence behaviour by providing the cognitive concepts. In this way, the relationship is between institutions and individual action is thought to be interactive and mutually constitutive. The behavioural assumption is that actors shape and comply with institutions not as a result of cost-benefit calculations, but because they think that following particular norms of behaviour and societal values is legitimate. The actors' behaviour is hence determined by the "logic of appropriateness" and not the "logic of consequences" (see March and Olsen 2008: 7–9). According to the logic of consequences, institutional change can be driven by sanctions and rewards that alter the cost-benefit calculations of the actors, whereas the logic of appropriateness would interpret institutional change as an outcome of social learning. Therefore, according to sociological institutionalism, institutional change is regarded as an outcome of changes in dominant social and cultural codes (Lecours 2005: 13).

The concept of normative isomorphism as defined by DiMaggio and Powell (1991) even argues that considerations about legitimacy may cause institutional convergence, that is, institutions in a similar policy domain become more alike whatever the differences in their immediate environment. The mechanism through which institutional convergence occurs refers to processes of joint socialization of firm managers. In marked contrast to economic theories, these homogenization processes are not based on efficiency considerations, but on the desire to be perceived as legitimate. In the logic of this approach, institutional change would occur when a more legitimate alternative emerges. The arising conflicts and strategies among actors would be mediated by normative persuasions (see, e.g., Henisz and Zelner 2005).

Theories of Institutional Change: Strengths and Limitations

This section has revealed that there is a rich theoretical literature to build on when examining the patterns and causes of institutional change. How useful are the different perspectives for explaining the creation of environmental prosecution units in emerging market democracies? Before addressing this question, it is worthwhile to evaluate the theoretical approaches more generally. A promising way of doing this is provided by Harty (2005: 63), who argues that any theorizing of institutional change should be based on the following two guiding questions: Why would certain actors seek institutional change? When are actors most likely to demand institutional change?

The first question addresses the actors' motivation for institutional change. This dimension is sufficiently addressed by the economic, sociopolitical, and legitimacy-based theories of institutional change. From the perspective of economic theories, actors are likely to seek institutional change in response to repeated interactions and learning as well as altered preferences or modifications to the distribution of political power. From the sociopolitical perspective, decision makers would essentially seek institutional change in response to public demands in order to ensure their political survival. Finally, the actors' motivation for demanding institutional change might stem from the emergence of a new institutional model that is perceived to be more legitimate.

In marked contrast, historical institutionalism is less appropriate for addressing this question. This theoretical perspective predominantly emphasizes the various types of constraints on institutional change and therefore primarily serves to predict the magnitude of institutional reforms. Due to the presence of institutional lock-ins and path dependency, it will generally predict the occurrence of minor institutional reforms. While there cannot be any doubt that path dependency matters for explaining the scope of institutional change in emerging market democracies (see, e.g., Cirtautas and Schimmelfennig 2010), historical institutionalism is of limited use for explaining the establishment of environmental procuracies, as the analytical focus is on the adoption process, which lies outside its purview. It is not the degree to which existing environmental procuracies become modified that is of interest to this study but the creation of such institutions, as they are unlikely to have been in place before the beginning of the observation in 1990.

The second question is basically about the sufficient conditions for institutional change. Addressing this question on the basis of the theories outlined in this section is more difficult. The economic theories contend that a sufficient condition for institutional change to happen is that the expected benefits exceed the costs, but they introduce these parameters in generic terms only and do not specify what kinds of cost and benefit parameters exist. With the sociopolitical perspective again the same problem occurs; it does not specify under which conditions the demand for institutional change is sufficiently high. Similarly, the legitimacy-based approaches do not define how much loss in a given institution's legitimacy is tolerated before it becomes too much and demands for reform grow. Moreover, neither the sociopolitical nor the legitimacy-based perspectives adequately address the causes of increased demand for institutional change or the reasons leading to a delegitimization of institutions. Thus, despite the compelling way in which they illustrate the causal mechanisms underlying institutional change, the theories discussed here do not allow for pinpointing the relevant domestic and international triggers. So, again, these theories do not substitute for the identification of more specific explanatory factors.

Another issue that constrains the suitability of most theoretical approaches for the purpose of the present study is an incompatibility concerning the analytical perspectives. Particularly with the economic and legitimacy-based approaches it became apparent that they conceive of institutional change as a process that is stimulated by the very members of the institutions. This comes as no surprise, especially with the economic theories, as they were often developed in the context of firms. In such cases, it makes perfect sense to model institutional change as an internal reform process characterized by cost-benefit calculus and power distribution. The view of institutional change as the outcome of internal processes, however, contradicts the study's assumption that the creation of environmental enforcement units is the consequence of decisions taken by policymakers, that is, actors external to the organization. From this it follows that only the political reasons for institutional reforms are of interest.

Does this imply that institutional theories are generally inappropriate for this study? In fact, there is one approach that offers a truly exogenous perspective on institutional change, namely, sociopolitical institutionalism. The suitability of this approach becomes particularly apparent with the theoretical model put forward by Bueno de Mesquita et al. (2003) and Morrow et al. (2008), who convincingly link institutional change to changes in public demand. While the precise causes for the changes in the demand for institutional change still need to be identified on the basis of empirical accounts, the sociopolitical approach surely provides an appropriate micro-foundation for the explanatory model to be formulated in the next chapter.

Conclusion

This chapter has presented various strands of theoretical work on policy and institutional change and discussed their suitability for the research objectives of this study. In so doing, it has pursued the objective of explaining why this study does not rely on the frameworks provided by the literature, but adopts the broader theoretical approach of comparative policy analysis. The main reason for this is that most of these theories are remarkably implicit about the nature of exogenous factors, which they, however, often deem to be central for triggering events of change. Is an increasingly competitive political system more important for inducing environmental policy change than economic developments? How much does a drastic deterioration of environmental quality matter for triggering more rigorous enforcement activities relative to other factors? These questions cannot be answered on the basis of the theories presented in this chapter.

Furthermore, there is often a certain incompatibility with respect to the levels of analysis. Many of the theoretical approaches to policy and institutional change are based on a micro-perspective. To test them accurately, one would need to characterize each and every policymaking process in detail, such as by identifying the relevant advocacy coalitions and shedding light on how their beliefs might have become modified. While this fine-grained analytical perspective clearly represents the theories' analytical strength, it hampers their application to a macro-quantitative analysis with a broad empirical focus. A similar observation was made concerning theories of institutional change that tend to concentrate on internal processes. Again, such a perspective contradicts this study's assumption that institutional reform is the consequence of decisions made by policymakers and therewith determined by actors external to the organizations.

In light of these shortcomings, a more promising approach is to identify the main explanatory factors associated with system transformation and to link changes in these to changes at the policy and institutional level through adequate theories of policymaking. This approach corresponds exactly to that of comparative policy analysis, which has developed numerous theories and hypotheses to better explain variation between countries. However, most of these theories have not been explicitly applied to policy change (Zohlnhöfer 2009: 97) – a research gap that this study seeks to fill. Comparative policy analysis yields several analytical advantages. First, it allows for exploring whether variations in certain aspects of the political or economic structure, such as the party system, systematically relate to the behaviour of governments. Second, it enables the use of more specific theories for understanding the causal relationship between the dependent and the independent variables, which also makes it possible to make explicit and – even more important – to test the importance of exogenous factors. Yet, the adoption of the comparative policy-analysis perspective does not exclude the possibility that some of the specific theories of policy and institutional change can serve as a micro-foundation for the explanatory model. Indeed, as concerns sociopolitical institutionalism and some theories of policy change, there is room for seminally integrating them into the explanatory model.

3 Explaining Changes in Environmental Policies and Institutions in Emerging Market Democracies

This chapter introduces possible explanations for why governments in emerging market democracies may change environmental policies and enforcement institutions. To this end, it focuses on the consequences of transformation processes for the CEE and LA countries' political and economic systems. These primarily consist of economic integration with international markets, increased party competition, and participation of environmental groups, as well as integration with international institutions and an enhanced responsiveness to public demand. Each of these major explanatory factors is part of an independent theory on the basis of which hypotheses will be deducted (see Roller 2005: 81).

As concerns the impact of political parties, environmental groups, and institutional integration, some of the theories discussed in chapter 2 will be employed for linking them to policy change. Additional theories are needed to be able to explain how the other independent variables affect governmental decision making on environmental issues in emerging market democracies. These theories are derived from environmental economics, comparative political economy as well as the study of policy diffusion and cross-national policy convergence. To establish a causal relationship between the independent variables and the creation of environmental procuracies, this chapter follows the basic reasoning of sociopolitical institutionalism. This theoretical perspective focuses on the structural conditions – mostly those related to social or political power – that shape institutional change (Gilley 2008: 260). It is the aim of the theoretical discussion to shed light on how different forms of such structural conditions affect public demand for and governmental provision of institutional change in emerging market democracies.

Key Assumptions

This section introduces the assumptions underlying the theoretical framework. The first and most central assumption is that national governments are conceived as the main actors in bringing about changes in environmental policies and enforcement institutions. This assumption entails that this study is interested in changes in the actual policies adopted by government, not in changes of environmental quality as it is often the case with macro-quantitative studies (see, e.g., Neumayer 2003; Scruggs 2003; Wälti 2004; Sigman 2005; Earnhart and Lizal 2008; Perkins and Neumayer 2009; Bernauer and Koubi 2009; Bernauer and Kuhn 2010; Cao and Prakash 2010; Rudra 2011; Knill, Schulze, and Tosun 2012). Consequently, the causal relationships to be established in this chapter depend on how governments perceive of and respond to the various stimuli stemming from system transformation.

Second, national governments are assumed to act as rational actors who seek to maximize their expected utility. The argument is that governments compare their behavioural options, rank these options in accordance with their preferences, and finally choose the outcome that appears most desirable to them. In terms of this study, "most desirable" means securing political survival through re-election.[1] Hence, the third assumption is that political actors seek to secure government office. Since the emergence of a competitive polity represents one central characteristic of political transformation, making this assumption about the importance of re-election seems justified and even necessary. In fact, in strong contrast to the situation under state-socialist or military rule, in the newly democratized systems of CEE and LA "a policy maker is constantly kept on his or her toes to work for re-election" (Dai 2006: 697).

When re-election concerns drive policymaking, parties that form the government must be certain that their policy choices will maximize their electoral advantage, which incites a fourth assumption, namely, that environmental protection is a salient issue to the voters in CEE and LA. This view can be justified on the basis of polling data from the World Values Survey. Table 3.1 shows the reactions of respondents in CEE and LA countries, averaged over five survey waves (1981–2008), to the following statement: "I would give part of my income if I were certain that the money would be used to prevent environmental pollution." One can infer from the table that the majority of respondents (strongly) agreed with this statement. From this it can be concluded that if the citizens are even willing to bear the cost of pollution prevention,

Table 3.1 Attitudes towards the prevention of environmental pollution (1981–2008)

	Central and Eastern Europe valid %	Latin America valid %
(Strongly) Agree	60.2	70.8
(Strongly) Disagree	39.8	29.2

Remarks: Elaboration based on the World Values Survey's online data analysis tool: http://www.wvsevsdb.com/wvs/WVSIntegratedEVSWVS.jsp?Idioma=I.

they should also somehow take environmental issues into consideration when making their electoral decisions (see Ready, Malzubris, and Senkane 2002).

However, it would be unrealistic to claim that citizens – especially in the two regions under scrutiny – vote on the basis of environmental factors alone (Esty 1996: 598). This assumption would not even hold for countries belonging to the Organization for Economic Co-operation and Development (OECD). There are surely several other factors, such as economic considerations, which are more important for voters' electoral decisions (see, e.g., Anderson, Lewis-Beck, and Stegmaier 2003; Lewis-Beck and Stegmaier 2008). Thus, it is only claimed here that environmental concerns represent one – though surely not the dominant – dimension of issues on which the electorate in CEE and LA votes. This indicates that a government reluctant to address the environmental concerns of voters will probably be confronted with electoral costs.

Towards a Theoretical Framework

Chapter 2 outlined theories that explicitly address policy and institutional change. The evaluation of these theories revealed that they can indeed provide an improved understanding of the causal mechanisms underlying events of change, that is, the micro level, but in order to test them empirically in a macro-quantitative design they need to be linked to macro-level independent variables. Since this study's principal research interest lies in exploring the impact of transformation-related changes in political and economic systems on environmental policymaking in emerging market democracies, the identification of the relevant independent variables represents a straightforward task. What are the most relevant changes in the political and economic systems of CEE and LA countries that might have induced reforms in their environmental policy arrangements and enforcement institutions?

First, the CEE and LA countries adopted market economic structures and became increasingly integrated with global markets. Second, they introduced more democratic political systems, which are expected to increase the decision-making power of political parties and the influence of environmental groups. Third, the CEE countries became economically and politically integrated into the EU and are affected by its policy-shaping powers in the field of environmental policy. Finally, both CEE and LA countries are perceived to have experienced socio-economic changes that should entail an enhanced public demand for environmental protection, to which the government is likely to respond in order to ensure re-election. In what follows, the causal mechanisms underlying these four groups of variables are discussed in order to derive hypotheses about their impact on changes in environmental policy setting and the creation of environmental procuracies.

Economic Integration

Until the mid-1980s, LA countries experienced import-substitution industrialization, that is, they produced goods that were formerly imported from industrialized countries (Wiarda and Kline 2007: 94). In subsequent years they gradually began to adopt market-oriented economic reforms in accordance with the so-called Washington Consensus, which refers to economic policy prescriptions promoted by the International Monetary Fund (IMF), the World Bank, and the US Treasury Department. The scheme included five broad sets of recommendations involving macroeconomic stabilization, privatization, fiscal reforms, trade liberalization, and the liberalization of inward foreign direct investments (FDI) (see, e.g., Duquette 1999; Gallagher, K.P. 2008).

The collapse of the centrally planned economies in CEE happened in a more concentrated and radical manner. Until 1989, CEE countries were characterized by an economic system in which the means of production were controlled by the state through either state ownership or regulation. As a consequence, there was only limited economic competition. Trade only occurred through the Council for Mutual Economic Assistance, within which state orders for imports and exports were bilaterally negotiated in a complex barter system (Hillman 1994: 210; for an overview, see Hewett 2011).

The focus of this study is on two dimensions only of economic transformation as prescribed by the Washington Consensus, namely, the liberalization of trade and inward FDI, which represent the most drastic changes in the economic systems. Economic integration through liberalizing trade and inward FDI are likely to yield incentives for governments of emerging market democracies to reform existing public policies. Which kind of pressures arise from increased importance of investment and trade? This section addresses this question for each of the two dimensions of economic integration.

CONSEQUENCES OF INVESTMENT LIBERALIZATION
FOR ENVIRONMENTAL POLICYMAKING

The theories of policy change introduced in chapter 2 primarily focus on the actors' preferences and the policymaking process. In this regard, they argue that the actors' policy preferences may change, but they do not provide a sufficiently well developed explanation for how, for instance, economic integration may affect them. Consequently, a different theoretical approach is needed for better understanding in which ways investment liberalization may induce environmental policy change. Essentially, liberalizing inward investment means that individuals and firms would be allowed to move their resources into an emerging market democracy without encountering substantial restrictions. Many studies associate investment liberalization with two economic theories: the competitiveness hypothesis and the pollution haven hypothesis (Copeland and Taylor 2004).

The competitiveness hypothesis regards the trade policy of a country as given and asks what happens if environmental policy arrangements in that country become stricter. It predicts that stricter regulations will shift some pollution-intensive production away from the country that tightens its environmental policy. The research interest of the pollution haven hypothesis is slightly different as it takes environmental policy differences across countries as given and asks what happens if barriers to investment and trade become reduced. It anticipates that this will cause the production of pollution-intensive goods to shift to countries with relatively weak environmental policy arrangements (Copeland 2008: 61–4). In empirical terms, there is thin evidence only for the pollution haven hypothesis, which led several scholars to the conclusion that "environmental compliance costs are relatively insignificant as compared with the other potential benefits of moving to developing countries, such as substantially lower labor costs" (Gallagher,

K.S. 2008: 148; see also Sorsa 1994). There is, however, some empirical evidence supporting the competitiveness hypothesis (see, e.g., Ederington and Minier 2003). This suggests that environmental regulations do affect plant location and production decisions, at least to a certain extent. This may make the governments of emerging market democracies likely to attract industries by offering them comparatively weaker environmental standards (see, e.g., Copeland and Gulati 2006; Spatareanu 2007; Levinson and Taylor 2008).

While these two economic perspectives are helpful for understanding the behaviour of economic actors, they are less appropriate for making testable statements about how competition for FDI affects environmental policy choices in emerging market democracies. More suitable for addressing the governments' behaviour is the theory of regulatory competition. Essentially, the theory of regulatory competition posits that in a world where the mobility of capital cannot be limited, it will seek the location where it can earn the highest return (Tiebout 1956; Goodman and Pauly 1993; Sinn 1997). Since environmental regulations are presumed to lower profit rates by raising the costs of production – and this has been shown by the research on the competitiveness hypothesis (see, e.g., Copeland 2008) – capital is expected to move to countries with the lowest regulatory standards. Hence, the general expectation is that all countries will adjust their environmental protection standards in a manner that avoids regulatory burdens for their industries, which should incite a race to the bottom.

While the theory of regulatory competition is logically compelling, for industrialized countries there is solid evidence that no such races to the bottom have occurred (see, e.g., Hoberg 1991, 2001; Vogel 1995, 1997; Vogel and Kagan 2004; Drezner 2007; Holzinger, Knill and Arts 2008; Holzinger, Knill, and Sommerer 2008, 2011). However, the picture looks more ambivalent for industrializing countries. For instance, Andonova, Mansfield, and Milner (2007) demonstrate that enhanced exposure to competition for trade and investment did indeed have a negative impact on environmental funds in the countries of CEE and the Commonwealth of Independent States.

A plausible explanation for the behaviour of emerging market democracies is provided by K.S. Gallagher (2006), who contends that such countries do not raise environmental standards for fear that domestic industries cannot compete with the foreign-invested firms due to a lack of technology. As a result, the governments are expected to postpone raising environmental standards to minimize the risk of putting domestic firms out of business. In the meantime, however, foreign firms will further innovate to meet ever more stringent standards abroad, with the result that the environmental-technological gap continues to widen between domestic firms and their foreign counterparts (Gallagher, K.S. 2008: 148). The outcome of this will be that the imposition of stricter environmental protection standards is delayed as the theory of "regulatory chill" predicts (Zarsky 1999). In accordance with this theoretical perspective, this study argues that the emerging market democracies' desire to attract more FDI together with their fear of losing FDI to other industrializing countries will induce their governments either to preserve weak environmental protection standards or to lower them even further.

Preserving weak environmental policy is only one way of increasing a country's attractiveness for FDI. Another way is to offer a weak enforcement of environmental regulations (Rauscher 2005: 1409). In this context, Konisky (2007), for instance, posits that governments could be motivated to attract investment through their enforcement of pollution control regulations. Using a panel dataset of state-level enforcement of US federal air and water pollution control regulations, the author shows that a state's choice about its level of environmental enforcement is a function of similar choices in states with which it competes for economic investment. This finding provides support for the existence of race to the bottom-type dynamics affecting the environmental enforcement behaviour of some US states. The consequences of such a behaviour for water quality are illustrated by Sigman (2005).

Similar dynamics are observed for the relationship between environmental rule setting and actual enforcement efforts in Hungary and Mexico (see Mumme 1998; Gallagher 2002, 2004; Knill, Tosun, and Heichel 2008). Along these lines, Angel et al. (2000) and Brown (2007) show that "flexible" enforcement approaches have in fact attracted foreign firms to Poland. Such a strategic behaviour is intuitive since the costs of stricter environmental protection standards mainly emerge during the implementation stage. Thus, it can make a difference to an investor whether regulations are also put into practice or are only introduced for symbolic reasons (see Zarsky 2008: 88). Therefore, weak regulatory enforcement may persist if there is no public demand for changing this practice. In this context, the literature points out that the domestic firms rather than the foreign-based ones demand a lax enforcement approach. To be sure, the foreign firms principally possess the capacity to comply with local environmental regulations (see, e.g., Garcia-Johnson

2000; Prakash 2000). Domestic firms, by contrast, often lack this capacity and are therefore even less likely to demand stricter regulatory enforcement (see, e.g., Gallagher 2006; Knill, Tosun, and Heichel 2008). Based on this reasoning, it is hypothesized that an increasing importance of inward investment reduces the odds of a government establishing an environmental procuracy.

Hypothesis 1.1: Regulatory competition

Environmental regulations will remain weak or will be weakened further with an increasing importance of inward investment. The commitment to enforce environmental regulations will remain weak or will be weakened further with an increasing importance of inward investment.

CONSEQUENCES OF TRADE LIBERALIZATION
FOR ENVIRONMENTAL POLICYMAKING

The theories of regulatory competition and regulatory chill represent the classical approaches to the impact of economic integration on environmental policymaking. There is, however, another dimension of economic integration, that is, trade, which can influence environmental standards in a markedly different way. In this regard, the seminal work by Vogel (1995, 1997) suggests that under certain circumstances the benefits for firms from raising environmental standards to levels found in high-regulating countries may actually outweigh the costs and create incentives for these actors to lobby for stricter regulations. This scenario is most likely to take place if emerging market democracies mainly export their products to jurisdictions that have more stringent environmental standards in place. Vogel refers to them as "green" jurisdictions and primarily sets them equal with the EU and the United States.

In this context, Drezner (2007: 55–8) stresses that the benefits of adopting the high-regulating countries' environmental protection standards depend upon the size of the newly opened market. Accordingly, it should make a difference to an emerging market democracy whether it seeks to enter, for instance, the huge EU or US markets or a comparatively smaller one, such as Japan. As a rule, the larger the importing market the larger are the benefits of adopting stricter environmental standards corresponding to those of the importing green jurisdiction. The idea underlying this scenario is that these green markets can act as "price makers" (Esty 1996: 630). This implies that the costs of not increasing the environmental protection level are likely to exceed the costs stemming from actually tightening environmental regulations. In this way, trade liberalization can function as a vehicle for transmitting the importing (high-regulating) countries' environmental protection standards to the exporting (low-regulating) countries. Given that the American state of California has been a pacesetter for national and international environmental regulations, this mechanism is called the "California effect." Alternatively, this mechanism is discussed under the heading of "trading-up."

While the California effect is mostly expected to occur with product standards, there is also increasing evidence that it also holds true for production-process standards (see, e.g., Ederington and Minier 2003). Chilean environmental policy provides an ideal case in point. During the early 1990s, eleven US copper producers asked the US International Trade Commission to launch quotas for Chilean copper, arguing that the lenient environmental regulations in Chile could be conceived of as some sort of subsidy. The repeated pressure by the US government to introduce more appropriate environmental regulations had an effect. After the US government had decided to decrease imports of copper products because of low production-process standards, companies operating in Chile independently adopted standards compatible with those of the US Environmental Protection Agency (EPA). The Chilean regulatory authority subsequently turned these voluntary standards into legally binding ones (Borregaard et al. 1999: 34). Likewise, Andonova (2004) shows that Bulgaria, the Czech Republic, and Poland introduced EU chemical policies even before applying for membership to facilitate their access to the attractive EU market. Based on a large country sample, Prakash and Potoski (2006, 2007) demonstrate that trade creates incentives for firms in industrializing countries to introduce the – relatively costly – ISO 14001 management system. Along the same lines, Perkins and Neumayer (2012) highlight that exports of automobiles and related components from industrializing countries to industrialized ones have a positive impact on domestic emission standards in the first.

This study adopts the theoretical reasoning of the California effect and anticipates that emerging market democracies' governments will tighten their environmental protection standards if they rely on exports to high-regulating jurisdictions such as the EU or the United States.

What are the implications of the theoretical approach of the California effect for changes in regulatory enforcement? Principally, it is conceivable that the positive implications of the California effect are restricted to the level of policy setting. For example, Bechtel and Tosun (2009) develop a game-theoretic model of imperfect information to analyse under which conditions low-regulating countries enforce stricter environmental policy standards in exchange for a free trade agreement with a high-regulating country. They show that in situations in which low-regulating countries face high enforcement costs but low reputation costs and a low detection probability, the introduction of environmental standards that are more stringent yet without enforcement is a possible outcome. Similar theoretical arguments have been elaborated by Porter (1999), Gallagher (2002, 2004), Konisky (2007) as well as Knill, Tosun, and Heichel (2008).

While it is logically feasible to argue that regulatory costs only emerge during the implementation stage and that this may entail strategic action as suggested above, the California effect presumes that lax enforcement practices will be targeted by the powerful green trading partners, for instance, through erecting trade restrictions. In fact, there are some hints in the literature that support this view. The United States, for instance, has a number of laws – although of questionable WTO-legality – that authorize the use of unilateral sanctions to force its trading partners to adopt US-style process standards and to ensure compliance with them (DeSombre 2000). If high-regulating countries can monitor and target insufficient enforcement in emerging market democracies, there should, in principle, be an explicit demand by exporting firms to increase regulatory enforcement, as they might otherwise be faced with trade barriers. Consequently, it is expected that the more emerging market democracies depend on exports to high-regulating jurisdictions, the more they should also be willing to tighten their enforcement efforts.

Hypothesis 1.2: California effect

Environmental regulations will be strengthened with an increasing importance of exports to high-regulating countries. The commitment to enforce environmental regulations will be strengthened with an increasing importance of exports to high-regulating countries.

Domestic Politics

At a very basic level, political transformation involves the introduction of institutions that foster political competition and participation (Dahl 1971). Political competition is defined as the extent to which political power is freely contested by political parties, pressure groups, or other organized factions within a political structure. The right of citizens to participate in the selection of their government refers to the second dimension, that is, political participation. Overall, democratic institutions should be responsive to the needs of individual actors and capable of providing collective goods to society.

In the period from 1978 to 1992 virtually all LA countries modified their political systems in order to enhance political competition and participation. While most of them were under military rule before democratization, authoritarian rule in Mexico resulted from a hegemonic party system in which the Institutional Revolutionary Party unceasingly held office for seventy years (Diez 2006: 13; Close 2010: 176). The political changes in the post-socialist countries of CEE in the late 1980s and early 1990s also mainly involved the demise of the one-party system in which the single national communist/socialist parties controlled all existing political, economic, and social structures, eliminating virtually all non-governmental organizations (NGOs).

In the cases under consideration, the most relevant changes due to political transformation relate to politics, that is, the process by which actors make collective decisions. In this context, two dimensions appear particularly worthwhile to be examined in detail. The first dimension concerns the development of a competitive party system and the increasing importance of political parties and their specific policy goals. The second dimension refers to the participation of NGOs in the policymaking process, which represents a core aspect of CEE and LA democratization (see, e.g., Botcheva 1996; Mumme and Korzetz 1997; Lewis 2001; Fagan 2004; Diez 2006; Fagan and Carmin 2011).

CONSEQUENCES OF PARTISANSHIP FOR ENVIRONMENTAL POLICYMAKING

Free and competitive elections are the main mechanism of translating rule by the people over the people into a system of government (Sartori 1997: 144). This stems from the fact that competitive elections give political parties the chance to be voted into government and thus signals to them that their contributions to the policy agenda are likely to have a greater impact. Accordingly, in competitive electoral systems political parties are the central vehicles for transforming public demand into public policies, which highlights the relevance of partisan theory for policy consequences.

Partisan theory dates back to Hibbs (1977), whose so-called party difference hypothesis originally intended to explain macroeconomic policies, notably the trade-off between inflation and unemployment. The basic argument is that left-wing parties would solve this trade-off by preferring lower unemployment over inflation, whereas right-wing parties would tend to keep inflation at the lowest possible level. Rational voters should hence support left-wing parties when high unemployment is expected and right-wing parties when high inflation is expected. According to more recent concepts of partisan theory (see, e.g., Schmidt 1996; Zohlnhöfer 2009), parties matter for all areas of policymaking.

How can parties bring about policy change? Most of the theories presented in chapter 2 pay scant attention only to the role of political parties for triggering policy change. In this regard, Walgrave and Varone (2008), for instance, argue that the punctuated equilibrium framework could benefit from taking into account the crucial role of political parties as they act as issue entrepreneurs or veto players. In fact, of these specific approaches to policy change, it is mainly the veto player theory as put forward by Tsebelis (1995, 2002) that includes considerations about partisanship. However, veto player theory is not the most appropriate theoretical framework to rely on in the context of this study, since it is more concerned about policies in the presence of different or even opposing actors' preferences.

A theoretical argument for assessing the "isolated" effect of political parties on policy change is put forward by Zohlnhöfer (2009), who argues that policy change should most likely occur after a change in the partisan composition of a government. It should be greater in scope the further the legislative status quo is located away from the policy-specific ideal points of the incoming government. Thus, policy change should be more drastic if competing political parties are programmatically far apart. This reasoning is based on the idea that political parties are willing to make a difference in a large number of policy areas, which also stems from their motivation to maximize electoral votes and to ensure re-election. More precisely, political parties compete for electoral votes by offering different policy options and once they are voted into government, responsible political parties implement those policy options as they want to ensure their re-election. From these arguments it can be derived that the entering into office of a pro-environment party should entail an increase in the stringency of environmental policy. In contrast, an incoming government consisting of an anti-environment party is expected to preserve the regulatory status quo or even lower the regulatory level. This outcome is particularly likely if the previous government had a pro-environment position.

Which parties have pro- and anti-environment positions in CEE and LA? Ideally, party positions on environmental issues would be measured on the basis of their election manifestos. This is the way the Manifesto Research Group and the Comparative Manifesto Project measure parties' policy positions (Budge et al. 2001). Most unfortunately, however, such estimates of party positions are only available for members of the EU, the OECD, and some CEE countries (Klingemann et al. 2006). Since LA countries are not included, this study must adopt an indirect approach to identifying the political parties with explicitly positive and negative stances on environmental issues. Focusing on these extreme positions reduces the uncertainty related to the construction of environmental-policy-specific ideal positions of the CEE and LA political parties.

One of the most commonly employed approaches to the classification of political parties is based on the concept of party families. It takes up the idea of core cleavage structures and argues that they have stabilized in a manner to give way to a limited range of types of parties with relatively fixed policy positions (see Lipset and Rokkan 1967; Rokkan 1970; Mair and Mudde 1998). Identifying the party family with the presumably most positive stance on environmental protection is straightforward: green or ecological parties tend to give most prominence to environmental issues (see, e.g., Müller-Rommel and Poguntke 2002; Neumayer 2003, 2004).[2] Although primarily a Western European phenomenon, ecological parties have also emerged in CEE and LA (see, e.g., Hajba 1994; Bugajski 2002; Fagan 2004; Nohlen 2005; Close 2010). In fact, in the CEE countries ecological parties have also participated in coalition governments, and Latvia was the first country in Europe to have a green party prime minister (see Galbreath and Auers 2009). Likewise, the Green Ecological Party of Mexico has established itself as a political force in the country (see, e.g., Diez 2006).

More challenging is to determine political parties with a presumably negative stance on environmental issues. Empirical studies emphasize that CEE and LA parties can be categorized along an economic left-right dimension (see, e.g., Pennings and Lane 1998; Rosas 2005). From this it can be concluded that, analogously to Western Europe, a party family exists that is particularly in favour of economic issues, namely, economically liberal parties. These parties are generally supportive of minimal government intervention into the economy. Since environmental regulations, however, clearly represent such an intervention that may burden industry, economically liberal parties should have a more negative stance on environmental protection than any other non-radical and non-extremist party family.

It is therefore expected that environmental policy change most likely happens if either green parties (i.e., the party family with the presumably most progressive position on environmental protection) or economically liberal parties (i.e., the party family with the presumably least favourable position on environmental protection) are voted into government.[3]

There is one characteristic about many LA and some CEE countries that must be taken into consideration, that is, they have presidential or semi-presidential systems in place.[4] Therefore, focusing merely on the partisan composition of the government would imply a misspecification with regard to the far-reaching political agenda-setting powers of the presidents. In CEE, the presidents of Latvia, Lithuania, and Ukraine have considerable amendatory powers that require either simple or qualified majorities to be overturned (Tsebelis and Rizova 2007). Similarly, the presidents of Argentina, Bolivia, Brazil, Chile, Costa Rica, Ecuador, El Salvador, Mexico, Nicaragua, Peru, Uruguay, and Venezuela are particularly influential in policymaking (Tsebelis and Alemán 2005). Consequently, the party affiliation of the presidents must also be taken into consideration. Another important point here is that there has never been a green president elected in the countries under scrutiny – or in industrialized countries. From this it follows that no hypothesis can be formulated for this specific case. As a result, this study formulates only one theoretical expectation with regard to the partisan affiliation of the president, namely, that a president belonging to an economically liberal party should have a negative impact on the stringency of environmental policy.

Having clarified the relevance of partisanship for environmental policy setting, now the question emerges as to whether political parties also matter for environmental enforcement. To be sure, political parties are primarily involved in policy setting and are not directly responsible for enforcement. However, Atlas (2007: 944) introduces an interesting thought by arguing that both the executive and the legislative branch could – through control over appropriations for an agency or other tactics – also influence the enforcement level. Essentially, this theory asserts that agency bureaucrats implement policy in a manner responsive to the preferences of elected officials. That political parties indeed matter for enforcement decisions is illustrated by Scholz, Twombly, and Headrick (1991) as well as Konisky (2007). Both studies demonstrate that US states with Democratic governors tend to conduct more environmental enforcement actions than states with Republican governors.

In view of the study's conceptualization of enforcement commitment, the impact of political parties should be even more manifest, since the elected officials themselves decide directly about whether to create environmental prosecution institutions or not. Therefore, governments consisting of a green party are more likely to strengthen regulatory enforcement since their electorate should demand that they do this. By the same token, governments consisting of economically liberal parties can be expected to pay less attention to this issue, since their electorate is unlikely to ask them to strengthen the enforcement of environmental regulations. It is thus hypothesized that green parties in government are more likely to create powerful enforcement institutions, whereas economically liberal governments and presidents are likely to keep the enforcement commitment low.

Hypothesis 2.1: Party difference – government participation green party

Environmental regulations will be strengthened with the governmental participation of a green party. The commitment to enforce environmental regulations will be strengthened with the government participation of a green party.

Hypothesis 2.2: Party difference – government participation economically liberal party

Environmental regulations will remain weak or will be weakened further with the governmental participation of an economically liberal party. The commitment to enforce environmental regulations will remain weak or will be weakened further with the government participation of an economically liberal party.

Hypothesis 2.3: Party difference – president from an economically liberal party

Environmental regulations will remain weak or will be weakened further with a president of an economically liberal party. The commitment to enforce environmental regulations will remain weak or will be weakened further with a president of an economically liberal party.

CONSEQUENCES OF ENVIRONMENTAL GROUPS
FOR ENVIRONMENTAL POLICYMAKING

In the event of democratization, not only was party competition introduced or intensified, but also social movements received the freedom to organize and influence policymaking. Especially in the early stages of democratic transformation in post-socialist CEE, social movements grew in number and were more popular than political parties (Lewis 2001: 546; see also Fagan 2004; Carmin and VanDeveer 2005; Fagan and Carmin 2011).[5] Similarly, environmental groups have been mushrooming in LA (see, e.g., Mumme and Korzetz 1997; Assetto, Hajba, and Mumme 2003; Diez 2006). Therefore, it can be expected that the growth of environmental groups in both CEE and LA has entailed changes in environmental policies and their enforcement.

In the literature, the political lobbying model outlined by Hillman and Ursprung (1988) is the dominant perspective on the impact of interest groups. Competing lobby groups – typically environmentalists and the industry – have different preferences regarding the strictness of environmental regulations (see, e.g., Dai 2006). Allied to each of these lobby groups is a political party that formulates its environmental policy choices to maximize the probability of being elected to office. This probability is assumed to depend upon the level of resources available for electoral campaigning. For influencing the strictness of environmental regulations each lobby group makes campaign contributions to a single party. Therefore, the party associated with environmentalists formulates its policies to maximize contributions from environmentalists. In contrast, the industrialists' party designs its policies to maximize contributions from industry.

Despite its plausibility, this approach has attracted criticism, since environmental groups generally do not make campaign contributions to political parties, and if they do make them they are dwarfed by those of industry (Yu 2005: 270). In this sense, environmental lobby groups would always appear weak vis-à-vis the "privileged position" of business lobbies in politics (Lindblom 1977; see also Macdonald 2007: 47–56). However, empirical studies show that environmental groups indeed matter for policymaking. For example, Bernhagen (2008) finds that greater participation by environmental groups and corporatist forms of interest mediation contribute to higher compliance with international environmental agreements (see also Frank, Hironaka, and Schofer 2000; Fagan 2004; Carmin and VanDeveer 2005; Fagan and Carmin 2011).

A more compelling view on the role of interest groups for inducing policy change – at least for the context of this study – is provided by Baumgartner and Jones (2009). As already outlined in chapter 2, the authors generally expect that incremental policy changes occur more often than major changes. This view is based on the importance they attach to "policy monopolies," which represent a particular way of perceiving a policy issue (see Albaek, Green-Pedersen, and Nielsen 2007: 5). In order to facilitate policy change, this monopoly must be destroyed by means of "conflict expansion" (Schattschneider 1960). Put differently, a given societal problem must be perceived as such by those who are responsible for policymaking. The politicization of an issue facilitates its inclusion in the policy agenda, which represents a necessary condition for policy change. To achieve this, the opponents of the prevalent issue image must mobilize and increase the scope of conflict to include actors outside of the policy monopoly. If the mobilization efforts are successful, they entail an alteration of the dominant policy image and incite policy change.

Cashore and Howlett (2006), for instance, apply this logic to the analysis of changes in management and harvesting practices in the forests of the US Pacific Northwest. For decades, the US Forest Service held the policy monopoly, which was characterized by a strong rent-seeking bond with the timber industry. The policy change was precipitated by a venue change and the reframing of the issue from one of commodity supply to one of endangered species protection, which was achieved by environmental lobbying. The result of this mobilization process was a major policy shift towards ecosystem-based forest management.

In this regard, Baumgartner et al. (2009) distinguish between three forms of lobbying. The first one is done by inside advocacy, in which information is supplied to those involved in the policymaking process. This can, for instance, happen through (in)formal meetings with civil servants or ministers, contacts with local government authorities, participation in commissions and government advisory committees, contacts with members of parliament or parliamentary committees, as well as contacts with officials of political parties (Dalton, Recchia, and Rohrschneider 2003: 751). For example, Greenpeace Argentina was very successful in using inside advocacy, which resulted in the enactment of a law on renewable wind-power energy generation (Aguilar 2002: 228).

The second strategy is outside advocacy, whereby information is communicated to actors outside the policymaking process such as through press conferences. The third form refers to grassroots advocacy, and entails the mobilization of masses.

Regardless of which particular strategy is chosen, the growing strength of environmental groups is likely to increase their capacity for conflict expansion and therewith to trigger policy change. Following the reasoning of the punctuated equilibrium framework, this study hypothesizes that the growth in the number of environmental groups increases the odds of governments in emerging market democracies adopting stricter environmental protection standards.

As with environmental policy setting, it is reasonable to expect that environmental groups can affect enforcement activities through their function as "watchdogs" (Vogel and Kessler 1998: 33). However, this theoretical argument needs some refinement. Generally, environmental groups in emerging market democracies do not address enforcement issues. Most are involved in information dissemination activities (Carmin 2010). Issues related to enforcement are predominantly discussed in transnational networks such as the International Network for Environmental Compliance and Enforcement (INECE). Therefore, mainly those environmental NGOs that are actively involved in transnational communication with other national or international NGOs, such as Greenpeace or Friends of the Earth, can be presumed to be effective in integrating enforcement topics into their agendas (Jancar-Webster 1997: 230; Zaelke, Kaniaru, and Kružíková 2005: 554). For example, both Ayres (1998) and Hogenboom (1998) show that during the NAFTA negotiations, increased transnational communication with Canadian and US interest groups occurred, which induced Mexican environmental NGOs to criticize the weak enforcement of environmental policy. Before the NAFTA preparations and the accompanying processes of transnational communication, environmental policy enforcement was not on the agendas of Mexican environmental NGOs. For this reason, it is argued that it is usually the environmental groups that are in exchange with national or international NGOs in high-regulating countries who ask the government to increase its enforcement efforts.

Another aspect related to this argument is that those environmental groups that are internationally linked have particular organizational characteristics. Most important, they are more professionally organized and have more funding and personnel than environmental groups that only operate at the local level (see McCormick 1993). As a result, they can be expected to be able to devote more resources to mobilization efforts and therefore pose a greater "risk" for governments that are unwilling to improve the enforcement of environmental standards. Consequently, it is hypothesized that the growth of internationally linked environmental groups in emerging market democracies positively influences the enforcement efforts of governments in emerging market democracies.

Hypothesis 2.4: Lobbying

Environmental regulations will be strengthened with the growth of environmental groups. The commitment to enforce environmental regulations will be strengthened with the growth of internationally linked environmental groups.

Institutional Integration

The introduction of democratic political systems and market economies established the foundation for the CEE and LA countries to achieve full participation in international cooperation. Shortly after their transition to democracy, Bulgaria, the Czech Republic, Estonia, Hungary, Latvia, Lithuania, Poland, Romania, Slovakia, and Slovenia declared that EU membership would be their foremost goal (Andonova 2004: 1). The EU is an international organization sui generis that has developed a common market through a standardized system of laws applying to all member states. The economic and political integration of the majority of CEE countries with the EU, without question, represents the main difference vis-à-vis the LA states.

In fact, two regional economic-integration processes exist in LA that originally also aimed to address the issue of environmental protection. In this regard, NAFTA deserves particular attention as it was the first integration project comprising two high-regulating states, that is, Canada and the United States, and Mexico as a low-regulating one. While environmental concerns did play a role in the NAFTA negotiations, they were mostly confined to the very early stage when political support for the project was vanishing in the United States (see, e.g., Ayres 1998; Hogenboom 1998; Deere and Esty 2002; Knill, Tosun, and Heichel 2008; Bechtel and Tosun 2009). In this context, it was indeed intensely argued that the inclusion of Mexico could trigger race to the bottom – like dynamics (see, e.g., Gallagher 2004). The environment-related public concerns in Canada and the United States led to the formulation of what the US EPA administrator William Reilly regarded as "the most environmentally sensitive, the greenest free trade agreement ever negotiated anywhere" (quoted by Bailey 1993: 839). One of the key concessions made to the environmental movement was the citizen submission process, permitting individuals and NGOs in the three constituent countries of NAFTA to file complaints when they believed that any of the three governments were failing to effectively enforce their own environmental laws (Blair 2003: 296).

Despite the inclusion of some environmental policy elements into NAFTA, it does not reduce the signatory states' deliberative power concerning the setting of domestic environmental regulations. Neither can the NAFTA organizations command the formulation of mutual standards. Instead, environmental improvements shall be achieved by strengthening compliance with domestic laws (Stevis and Mumme 2000; see also Hoberg, Banting, and Simeon 2002). The same applies to the Mercosur, which includes Argentina, Brazil, Paraguay, and Uruguay as full members, and Bolivia, Chile, Colombia, Ecuador, and Peru as associate members. While the Mercosur agreement includes some weak environmental components (Hochstetler 2003), its implementation has not induced modifications in the existing environmental regulatory frameworks of these member states (Gobbi 2009). Since the environmental policy-shaping powers of both Mercosur and NAFTA have to be judged as limited, the theoretical considerations in this section concentrate on the CEE states that applied for EU membership.

Generally, the EU is conceived to trigger policy change through two causal mechanisms, namely, international cooperation and harmonization (Holzinger and Knill 2004, 2005, 2008). Both mechanisms presuppose the existence of interdependencies or externalities pushing governments to resolve common problems through cooperation within international institutions (see, e.g., Simmons 2010). The harmonization potential of the EU is provided by a broad range of environmental policies to which the member states adjust the content of their national regulations, policy instruments, and even administrative structures (see, e.g., Knill 2001; Holzinger and Sommerer 2011). To be sure, the main reason for the establishment of environmental policy action at the European level can be seen in anxieties that different environmental standards, for instance, for automobile emissions, would have led to trade barriers and competitive distortions of the common market (Knill and Liefferink 2007: 3).

However, the EU does not regulate every aspect of national environmental policies. Therefore, the EU can affect environmental policies in the member states not only through international harmonization, but also through international cooperation. Thus, environmental policies that are not regulated at the EU level are subject to international cooperation, whereas international harmonization should be effective with those environmental policies that have been regulated at the supranational level. In the case of international cooperation, the EU merely serves as an instrument for enabling transnational communication, which may lead to environmental policy change by means of policy-oriented learning. The implications of learning for policy change were already outlined in chapter 2. For example, according to the subsystem adjustment model elaborated by Howlett and Ramesh (2002), learning can lead to a reception of new ideas about policy, and if these ideas can be brought into the policymaking process they can effectively trigger policy change. With regard to learning-induced environmental policy change in the EU, Holzinger and Knill (2008: 57–8) argue that policy-oriented learning should require governments to adjust their policies to pioneer models (see also Simmons and Elkins 2004). Therefore, the CEE countries engaged in international cooperation within the context of the EU are expected to strengthen their environmental protection standards in accordance with more progressive regulatory models.

Regarding international harmonization, the direct effect and supremacy of European law arising from EU membership is at the centre of attention. When an environmental issue is harmonized at the European level, policy change will occur through compliance with supranational law. As concerns the direction of policy change, the most likely outcome is an increase in the strictness of environmental policy arrangements, at least from the perspective of emerging market democracies. This view is based on the observation that countries preferring stricter environmental regulations are more influential when formulating EU policies (Jänicke 2006: 15). Moreover, it is important to note that the EU mainly defines minimum standards with which it is possible for member states with a preference for higher regulatory levels to enact standards beyond the minimum level (Holzinger and Knill 2004: 35).

International harmonization is expected to be particularly effective in the case of CEE countries, since in order to become EU members they were exposed to considerable acquis conditionality, that is, they had to adopt the entire body of European legislation, also known as the acquis communautaire, within a short period of time and with considerable scrutiny directed at them (Schimmelfennig and Sedelmeier 2004; Börzel and Buzogány 2010; Tosun 2011). Environmental policy forms an important and extensive part of the acquis communautaire and therefore it is reasonable to conceive of acquis conditionality as a major trigger of environmental policy change, at least with regard to those policy items that are regulated at the supranational level.

To sum up, it is argued that both international cooperation and harmonization are likely to stimulate an increase in the strictness of environmental protection standards in those CEE states that applied for EU membership. In this sense, EU integration should lead to higher environmental protection standards for those environmental policies that are not regulated at the supranational level via international cooperation. Likewise, EU integration should lead to higher environmental protection standards for those environmental policies that are regulated at the supranational level by means of international harmonization.

In terms of enforcement commitment, the theoretical discussion only refers to international cooperation, since there is no EU obligation to establish environmental procuracies and therefore international harmonization cannot be effective. To be able to formulate a theoretical expectation, the importance of acquis conditionality and monitoring must be highlighted again. In fact, the EU exerted considerable pressure on the CEE countries not only to strengthen their environmental policy arrangements, but also to ensure their effective enforcement. For example, the EU used the instrument of selective invitations to accession negotiations in 1997 and 1999 to lend the accession conditionality high credibility (Schimmelfennig and Trauner 2009: 2). Therefore, it can be argued that the CEE countries signalled their commitment to proper enforcement to the EU by establishing environmental prosecution units.

An alternative explanation would be that institutional change is motivated by learning as a consequence of transnational communication. The theories of institutional change presented in chapter 2 did not explicitly mention this possibility, but this argument can be connected to Ruttan and Hayami's (1984) model of the demand for and supply of institutional innovations. Put in this way, one can contend that transnational communication between the EU member states promoted environmental procuracies as an institutional innovation and motivated governments of CEE countries to establish similar institutional arrangements. The theoretical expectation to be derived from this reasoning is that international cooperation is likely to increase the CEE governments' enforcement efforts.

Hypothesis 3.1: Learning

Environmental regulations will be strengthened with the application for EU membership. The commitment to enforce environmental regulations will be strengthened with the application for EU membership.

Hypothesis 3.2: Compliance

For harmonized environmental policy items, environmental regulations will be strengthened with the application for EU membership.

Public Demand

In addition to the three previous groups of variables, the research literature suggests more factors that are expected to exert pressure on governments in emerging market democracies to increase the strictness of environmental protection standards and their enforcement. In this context, changes in per capita income and the salience of issues represent the most important factors (see, e.g., Weidner and Jänicke 2002). Together they are expected to affect the level of public demand for policy and institutional change.

CONSEQUENCES OF INCOME
FOR ENVIRONMENTAL POLICYMAKING

A number of non-institutional factors have often been suggested in the literature to have an influence on environmental policy choices. Many of these are based on broad economic and structural changes in industrial societies (see, e.g., John 2003: 484–5). Of these factors, levels of income and income growth have received the most attention. The relationship between income and the environment has predominantly been discussed by the economic literature on the environmental Kuznets curve (Grossman and Krueger 1995). The environmental Kuznets curve posits an inverted U-shaped relationship between pollution intensity and economic growth. The underlying logic can be summarized as follows. In an emerging market economy, little priority is given to environmental concerns, which increases environmental pollution. After attaining a certain standard of living from the industrial production system and when environmental pollution is at its greatest, the focus changes from self-interest to social interest. The social interests give greater weight to a clean environment by reversing the environmental pollution trend from industrialization (van Alstine and Neumayer 2008).

Much of the environmental Kuznets curve literature has focused on testing this basic hypothesis and estimating the turning-point level of development at which the per capita pollution – growth relationship changes sign (see, e.g., Copeland and Taylor 2004; Gallagher 2004; Aubourg, Good, and Krutilla 2008; for an overview, see Van Alstine and Neumayer 2008). While the environmental Kuznets curve provides a compelling way of thinking about the economy-ecology nexus, it is of limited help for this study since it is mainly interested in shedding light on changes in environmental quality by taking environmental policy arrangements as given. A more appropriate way of thinking about how raising income may affect environmental policymaking is put forward by Magnani (2001: 163), who argues that in democratic political systems, economic growth affects policy decisions by changing the median voter's willingness to pay for the environment. In other words, income growth may shift the median voter's preferences away from higher consumption of private goods and towards environmental quality.

Here Inglehart's (1997) argument about post-materialism also comes into play. Improvements in individuals' socio-economic environment, the argument goes, results in shifting their attention from issues of physical sustenance to concerns related to quality of life. Materialist values are the concern of those who have experienced insecurity, leading them to give priority to political stability and economic strength. Those who have post-materialist values have been exposed to greater security and are oriented towards satisfying other needs, including environmental protection. This causal statement is supported by the empirical work of Ready, Malzubris, and Senkane (2002), who find that with rising income Latvian citizens increasingly expressed their demand for stricter environmental protection standards. Based on these considerations, this study expects that there is a linear relationship between increasing income and demand for stricter environmental regulations.

Along the same theoretical lines, that is, changes in the preferences of the median voter, it can be expected that raising income does not only enhance the demand for a higher level of formal regulation, but even more for an actual improvement of environmental quality. Accordingly, higher national incomes should generate political pressure for more rigorous environmental policy enforcement. In fact, several empirical studies have shown a strong association between per capita income and regulatory monitoring as well as enforcement (see, e.g., Copeland and Taylor 2004; Esty and Porter 2005). For this reason, income growth is likely to induce governments of emerging market democracies to demonstrate a stronger commitment to regulatory enforcement.

Hypothesis 4.1: Functional response – income

> Environmental regulations will be strengthened with increasing per capita income. The commitment to enforcing environmental regulations will be strengthened with increasing per capita income.

CONSEQUENCES OF ISSUE SALIENCE
FOR ENVIRONMENTAL POLICYMAKING

Environmental policy change can be the result of a functional response to certain challenges such as high pollution levels. In fact, enhanced productive activities due to enhanced export rates could worsen environmental degradation to such an extent that the government must react to this problem. To give an example, pressing environmental problems as a legacy of the state-socialist regime stimulated the development of more stringent environmental policies in Slovakia and the Czech Republic (Albrecht 1998; Fagan 2004). In a similar vein, environmental policy reforms in Mexico must be seen against the background of environmental degradation caused by an expansion of industrial activities (Mumme 1998).

Yet, it is not only the accumulation of industry-generated pollution that pushes governments to tighten environmental protection standards. Indeed, what actually matters is whether a certain environmental issue is salient, that is, whether there is public awareness and debate about it. This represents an important aspect of transformation-related consequences for environmental policymaking since access to information is critical for an issue to become salient. Access to information, in turn, is strongly related to democratization (see, e.g., Payne 1995; Neumayer 2002). An environmental issue can be salient mostly for two reasons. The first one is the visibility of the degradation of environmental resources. Hence, this form of salience is closely related to the concept of environmental problem pressure (see, e.g., Holzinger and Knill 2005, 2008). Another source of salience involves the general value citizens attach to certain environmental resources, like forests.

This study argues that salience affects environmental policy change through increasing the public attention paid to environmental conditions and therewith raising the electoral costs for policymakers who are unwilling to tighten regulations. Following this logic, a highly salient environmental issue should entail the adoption of more stringent environmental protection standards.

The salience of environmental issues can also be expected to affect the governmental approach to regulatory enforcement (Vogel and Kessler 1998: 31). If there is sufficiently high public concern with certain environmental problems, not addressing them in an effective way could threaten re-election. The intuitiveness of this argument is reflected by several empirical studies that have underscored the importance of the salience of environmental problems for improved environmental quality (see, e.g., Wälti 2004: 601). Therefore, the higher the salience of an environmental issue the higher is the related public concern and, in turn, the more likely policymakers in emerging market democracies should be to address them by strengthening enforcement institutions.

Hypothesis 4.2: Functional response – salience

Environmental regulations will be strengthened with a high salience of environmental issues. The commitment to enforcing environmental regulations will be strengthened with a high salience of environmental issues.

Conclusion

The aim of this chapter was to disaggregate the complex variables underlying the dual system transformation in CEE and LA in order to elaborate an encompassing explanatory framework. Four sets of independent variables were found to be relevant for changes in environmental policies and enforcement institutions: economic integration with international markets, partisan characteristics of those in power and participation of environmental groups as well as integration with international institutions, and issue salience. The theoretical considerations led to the formulation of ten hypotheses on the likelihood and direction of policy and institutional change. Table 3.2 summarizes the main

Table 3.2 Summary of hypotheses

Analytical categories	Hypotheses	Variables	Mechanisms	Policies	Institutions
Economic integration	1.1	FDI	Regulatory competition	Status quo / laxer	Status quo / laxer
	1.2	Trade with industrialized countries	California effect	Stricter	Stricter
Domestic politics	2.1	Green government	Party difference	Stricter	Stricter
	2.2	Liberal government	Party difference	Status quo / laxer	Status quo / laxer
	2.3	Liberal president	Party difference	Status quo / laxer	Status quo / laxer
	2.4	NGOs	Lobbying	Stricter	Stricter
Institutional integration	3.1	Cooperation	Learning	Stricter	Stricter
	3.2	Harmonization*	Compliance	Stricter	–
Public demand	4.1	Income	Functional response	Stricter	Stricter
	4.2	Salience*	Functional response	Stricter	Stricter

* The theoretical expectations deviate from the ones stated in the table for GM maize.

explanatory variables, outlines the underlying causal mechanisms, and points to the expectations with regard to the direction of change.

Based on the theoretical discussion, most consequences of political and economic transformation suggest an increase in the strictness of environmental policy setting and an enhanced commitment to enforce the policies set. Only enhanced competition for inward investment and the ascension to power of a government that is composed of an economically liberal political party or a president with such a party affiliation are associated with negative change. Consequently, the overall expectation for the empirical analysis is that changes in environmental policies and enforcement institutions are likely to occur and that they should predominantly entail the establishment of a more stringent environmental protection regime.

As concerns the identification of causal mechanisms, this chapter has shown that the approach of comparative policy analysis can indeed be fruitfully combined with the more specific theories of policy and institutional change. This worked particularly well for the elaboration of the causal mechanism underlying the relationship between the growth of environmental groups and policy change. The role of environmental groups as it is modelled by the punctuated equilibrium framework was indeed found to be more suitable for providing an explanation for the present research subject than economic theories of lobbying. Likewise, policy-oriented learning offers a compelling theoretical perspective for understanding why and in which ways international cooperation might trigger processes of environmental policy change. Moreover, the basic reasoning of the sociopolitical theories of institutional change – and in the case of international cooperation, economic and legitimacy-based theories as well – facilitated the connection of the individual explanatory factors to changes in enforcement institutions. While these perspectives are theoretically compelling, however, the next chapters presenting the empirical analysis will determine the actual explanatory power of the model.

4 Research Design and the Measurement of Change

The previous chapter concluded that in terms of theory, the emergence of globally integrated market economies and democratic polities are likely to trigger an increase in the stringency of environmental protection standards and governments' commitment to enforce them. The following chapters consider these theoretical arguments empirically. To this end, they shed light on the development of environmental regulations and the decisions of governments to strengthen their enforcement in twenty-eight CEE and LA countries over a period of two decades. Before turning to the main empirical analysis, though, this chapter gives a number of conceptual and methodological clarifications. In what follows, it first discusses the study's research design, including the motivation for the selection of countries and time frame. Next, it explains how changes in the stringency of environmental regulations and enforcement commitment can be accurately measured. In this context, the data sources and the coding decisions are also outlined. Subsequently, the chapter turns to the operationalization of the explanatory variables. The final section then discusses which analysis techniques to employ in view of the data structure and how to complement the quantitative analyses with a qualitative evaluation of a limited number of cases.

Introducing the Overall Research Design

This book is based on a comparison of the development of environmental policy arrangements and enforcement commitment in two geographic regions that experienced shifts in their economic and political systems. Due to this broad empirical focus, the study predominantly relies on a quantitative approach. Designing a quantitative study may, however, be more demanding than subsequently executing it. Once data are collected, it may prove difficult to correct for problems of poor model specification, omitted variables, and low data quality (Sprinz 1999: 43). Therefore, sources of uncertainty must be minimized during the very early stages of the research process. To this end, a quasi-experimental quantitative design is employed here, which is expected to increase the analytical confidence through the inclusion of additional controls. Practically speaking, a quasi-experimental design involves the selection of groups upon which a variable is tested without any random preselection processes. In this sense, quasi-experimental designs parallel the logic of "strategic" case selection in qualitative methods (see De Vaus 2001: 238).

There is a multitude of quasi-experimental designs to choose from. This study employs a design that is closely related to the so-called repeated-treatment design, which according to Shadish, Cook, and Campbell (2002: 113) is particularly suitable for scrutinizing transient effects. It is based on the comparison of two treatment groups, which have both experienced the relevant stimuli, that is, political and economic transformation, albeit to varying extents. Moreover, the groups differ with regard to the potential impact of EU integration, which can only affect the CEE countries. The focus of the present design is primarily on the post-test stage, namely, instances of policy and institutional change after the beginning of system transformation. Nevertheless, the pre-test stage is implicitly modelled through varying starting and ending points of system transformation. For instance, according to the Freedom House Index, Chile was evaluated as a free democratic polity for the first time in 1990, while Ukraine just reached this status in 2005 after a series of protests and political events that became known as the Orange Revolution.[1] From this it follows that in the case of Ukraine, the pre-test stage with regard to democratization is explicitly measured until 2004, that is, the year predating the democratic transition.

Motivation for Country Selection

This book investigates decisions regarding environmental policies and enforcement measures taken by governments of emerging market democracies. The level of analysis is hence the nation state, which attributes high importance to the selection of countries that form the empirical basis. As noted earlier, here the sampling of countries is accomplished by purposeful selection based on theoretical considerations.

Table 4.1 Countries included in the analysis

Central and Eastern European countries (N = 11)	Latin American countries (N = 17)	
• Bulgaria	• Argentina	• Nicaragua
• Czech Republic	• Bolivia	• Panama
• Estonia	• Brazil	• Paraguay
• Hungary	• Chile	• Peru
• Latvia	• Colombia	• Uruguay
• Lithuania	• Costa Rica	• Venezuela
• Poland	• Ecuador	
• Romania	• El Salvador	
• Slovakia	• Guatemala	
• Slovenia	• Honduras	
• Ukraine	• Mexico	

Several studies point out that a systematic comparison of CEE and LA emerging market democracies is instructive as the regions share the experience of economic and political system shifts (see, e.g., Przeworski 1991; Lijphart and Waisman 1996; Pickvance 1999; Weyland 1999; Anderson, Lewis-Beck, and Stegmaier 2003; Müller 2003). At the same time, however, CEE and LA countries are dissimilar in many important ways. They are geographically distant, have different levels of socio-economic development, and different relationships with the EU and the United States. The latter aspect is expected to be particularly important for the possible effects of trade relationships on environmental policy change, as the EU and United States represent two different regulatory poles (Skogstad 2006; Drezner 2007; Pollack and Shaffer 2009). In view of all these differences, a joint analysis of CEE and LA countries affords a critical test of "most different systems" (Przeworski and Teune 1970), which seeks to demonstrate that an observed causal relationship holds in a range of contrasting settings (see Anderson, Lewis-Beck, and Stegmaier 2003: 471).

Table 4.1 presents the individual countries forming the sample. It consists of the entire continental area of Latin America except for Guyana, Suriname, and French Guiana. These three countries were excluded due to their very low population density, and, in the case of French Guiana, because of its status as a French overseas department. The countries selected from CEE represent a smaller subsample of the geographic area mainly consisting of the "new" EU member states plus Ukraine as a non-EU member state. Both the Czech Republic and Slovakia are included in the country sample as two different observatory units. Although the Czech Republic and Slovakia were one state until 1993, the inclusion of both countries poses no problem to the analysis since the bulk of relevant environmental legislation was promulgated after their formal separation.

Generally, the methodological literature recommends that quantitative analyses use random sampling to ensure that the selection criteria do not correlate with the dependent variable. Valid inferences are, however, possible from any sample selected in a way that it does not result in a set of cases clustered at one end of the outcome continuum (Geddes 2003: 97). Therefore, the present country sample is chosen in a manner so as to have sufficient variation in the values of the explanatory variables, that is, economic and political transformation.

In the last three decades, LA has become more democratic and its economies more open, but these developments occurred to different degrees and with varying performance across the individual countries (see, e.g., Mainwaring and Hagopian 2005; Wiarda and Kline 2007; Oelsner and Bain 2009). Likewise, the CEE countries returned to democratic rule and opened their markets after 1989. Yet, there are also considerable differences in how these countries dealt with the dissolution of state-controlled economies and authoritarianism (see, e.g., Voszka 1996; Pollack et al. 2003; Haerpfer 2009). Consequently, there should be sufficient variation in the main explanatory variables for making valid causal inferences.

Motivation for the Selection of the Time Frame

As noted above, the book's principal research interest is in policy and institutional change. In this case, the variables must necessarily be related to a time axis consisting at least of two points in time. To accurately assess the occurrence of change, the present study annually repeats the observations for a period of twenty years, starting in 1990 and ending in 2010. The resulting pooled time-series cross-section data (hereafter: pooled data) is widely used in comparative political economy (see, e.g., Beck and Katz 1995; Kittel 1999; Kittel and Winner 2005; Baum 2006; Cameron and Trivedi 2010). The main advantage of pooled data is that it increases the number of observations (albeit not cases) due to its two-dimensional composition, that is, observations for countries over years, also known as country-years.

When measuring change, there is the risk of misspecification stemming from the exclusion of important empirical information. One specific form of longitudinal quantitative research, that is, event history analysis, refers to this problem as censoring, that is, an incomplete recording of information at the beginning and ending of certain events of interest (see Blossfeld, Golsch, and Rohwer 2007: 38). If censoring occurs at the beginning of a certain event, it is censored on the "left." If it refers to the ending of a certain event, it is censored on the "right."

Censoring can occur at varying intensities: First, an observation might be completely censored on the left, implying that all instances of change occurred before the beginning of the observation. Hence, the researcher would merely observe the prevalence of the status quo and miss the actual event of change. Second, an observation can be partially censored on the left, so that the researcher merely observes one moment of change instead of two or more. This may lead to an incorrect assessment of the intensity of change due to absent information about previous levels. Third, an observation can be completely censored on the right, implying that the starting and ending time of the episode of change is located after the conclusion of the observation. Again, the researcher would wrongly conclude that no change has occurred. Finally, an observation can be partially censored on the right, which would incorrectly suggest that the status quo is prevailing, although in reality change has occurred after the end of the observation period (Knill and Tosun 2012: 258–9).

Recognizing the importance of the temporal dimension, what is needed is a time frame that allows for observing the entire episode of potential change. Of course, it is impossible to completely eliminate the risk of censoring. Nevertheless, appropriate theoretical considerations can be helpful for reducing this particular threat to valid measurement. To achieve this, the analysis starts in 1990, which corresponds to the fall of the Iron Curtain and the disintegration of the Eastern Bloc. Before this year, some of the countries currently forming CEE did not exist, which represents another motivation for selecting 1990 as the starting point of the observation.[2] While in CEE political transformation coincided with economic transformation, these developments occurred separately in LA. It can generally be stated that democratization began earlier in LA, namely, around the late 1970s and early 1980s (Mainwaring and Hagopian 2005: 3). By contrast, however, economic transformation processes were strongly affected by the Washington Consensus of 1990 and thus mostly took place from the 1990s onwards

(Tondl 2008: 17). In this regard, only Chile represents an exception as it had already implemented economic reforms in the mid-1970s (see Meseguer Yebra 2009).

Concerning the selection of 2010 as the ending year, this decision must be seen against the background of practical constraints, as it represents the last year for which at the time of writing the most complete data for the dependent and independent variables is available. However, with regard to the coding of the dependent variables, it should be noted that if legislative changes started in 2010, but were only completed in 2011, these data points were still included to avoid an inaccurate measurement due to right censoring. Indeed, deciding when to end an observation certainly represents one of the major challenges when working with longitudinal data.

Introducing the Dependent Variables

So far, the concepts of policy and institutional change have been discussed in abstract terms only. For the empirical analysis, however, important decisions regarding conceptual specification and measurement must be taken. It is thus the objective of this section to illustrate the principal coding decisions with respect to the empirical assessment of changes in environmental policy and enforcement commitment.

Measuring Environmental Policy Change

Quantifying environmental policy change across countries is a challenging endeavour. The first problem in measuring environmental policy is that it spans a multitude of very different areas. It includes topics such as air and water pollution, forest protection, soil degradation and waste management, as well as the protection of biodiversity, and climate change – just to name a few. In addition, it is strongly related to neighbouring policy fields, such as agriculture, consumer protection, health, transportation, and energy. The second problem relates to the comparability of data when exploring the characteristics of change. In fact, most CEE countries possessed quite comprehensive, but largely ineffective, environmental legislation during the state-socialist period (see, e.g., Earnhart 1997; Klarer and Francis 1997; Cole 1998; Knill and Lenschow 2000; Pavlínek and Pickles 2000; Andonova 2004; Fagan 2004; Carmin and VanDeveer 2005). The LA countries' point of departure is markedly different; many of them completely lacked environmental protection standards. It is a demanding task to construct a measure that provides comparable data on environmental policy change and simultaneously reflects the large range of environmental policies.

To handle this challenge, the study relies on the selection of so-called policy items, that is, precisely defined rules within legal acts (see, e.g., Fredriksson et al. 2005; Andonova, Mansfield, and Milner 2007; Holzinger, Knill, and Arts 2008; Holzinger, Knill, and Sommerer 2008, 2011). While this approach represents the most direct measurement of governmental decisions, the process of data collection is challenging, since environmental regulations are not systematically compiled and accessible for all countries. Although the database FAOLEX provides some legal acts, one must still contact national environmental ministries to get a copy of the relevant legal acts, especially when these date back in time. Also, the information drawn from the legal acts must be coded and adjusted before it can be used for quantitative research. All this entails the need to make a considerable number of conceptual decisions.

Which environmental policy items are appropriate for the analysis? The policy items to be chosen should fulfil three criteria. First, they should cover a wide range of environmental media to achieve some degree of representativeness. Second, they should ideally relate to issues that are equally salient for both regions. Third, as a consequence of the theoretical model elaborated in chapter 3, the policy items should possess some relevance for economic actors. These considerations give way to the following five environmental policy items:

- *Standards for biological oxygen demand*: The item is measured by means of maximum permissible limit values for biological oxygen demand (BOD) concentrations in industrial waste-water discharged into continental surface waters (mostly rivers and lakes)
- *Ozone standards*: The item corresponds to the definition of limit values for ground-level concentrations of ozone in ambient air.
- *Standards for polycyclic aromatic hydrocarbons*: The item corresponds to the setting of limit values for polycyclic aromatic hydrocarbon (PAH) concentration in agricultural soils.
- *Regulation of GM maize*: The item is about imposing legal restrictions on the commercial cultivation of the GM maize line MON810 developed by the Monsanto Company.
- *Sustainable Forest Management (SFM)*: The item is about the adoption of a particular practice of forestry.

The first three policy items represent typical examples of "command and control" instruments, that is, the most common form of environmental policies in both industrialized and industrializing countries (see Sterner 2002: chapter 6). The "command" aspect inherent in this type of instrument relates to the setting of limit values, that is, the maximum level of permissible pollution, whereas the "control" aspect is about monitoring and enforcing them. There are two principal types of environmental command and control instruments, namely, emission standards (here: the regulation of water and soil pollution) and ambient standards (here: air quality standards). An emission standard specifies the maximum level of permitted emissions, whereas ambient standards set the minimum desired level of air or water quality that must be maintained. In terms of measurement, emission and ambient standards yield the advantage that they provide interval-scaled numerical values, which facilitates their quantification and the subsequent analysis.

The regulation of GM maize also belongs to the group of command and control instruments, albeit in this case no numerical limit values are defined. Instead, the cultivation of GM maize can be regulated in a manner to constrain or entirely ban this activity. SFM, by contrast, defines an abstract goal and leaves the specification of the means by which this goal should be reached to the individual governments. This gives them considerable leeway in the interpretation of this principle.

Combating water pollution is an important area of environmental policy as it may have a plethora of harmful effects. For example, the concentration of bacteria and viruses in polluted water can lead to health problems. Moreover, water pollution may adversely affect the flora and fauna of water bodies. In this context, the definition of limit values for BOD represents a main instrument for regulating organic water pollution. In fact, BOD is among the most important water pollutants emitted by numerous production processes (Tietenberg 2006: 447). It indicates the amount of oxygen demanded for the decomposition of organic material in effluents. Often, the limit values refer to the amount of dissolved oxygen consumed in five days by biological processes breaking down organic matter. Limiting the BOD content of water is important since organic pollution can lead to eutrophication, that is, an excessive growth of water plants such as algae, which reduces dissolved oxygen in the water and can cause other organisms to die. The main sources of organic waste in surface waters are domestic sewage, municipal waste, and agro-industrial effluents. It is a salient environmental problem in both CEE and LA and is clearly related to industrial production processes.

Ozone is a naturally occurring greenhouse gas formed as a product of photochemical reactions with the following precursors: nitrogen oxides, methane, carbon dioxide, and volatile organic compounds. Ozone is hence not emitted directly into the air, but is formed by reaction with other substances in the presence of heat and sunlight. These substances are emitted by a variety of sources, including motor vehicles, electric power plants, chemical plants, and refineries. In this way, they are directly related to industrial activities and are likely to affect the overall costs related to environmental regulations. Together with the other greenhouse gases, ozone in various ways contributes to climate change. For example, Sitch et al. (2007) argue that ozone causes cellular damage in plants, which leads to reduced rates of photosynthesis and requires increased resource allocation to detoxify and repair leaves. As increases in ozone concentrations adversely affect plant production, more carbon dioxide accumulates in the atmosphere, thus contributing to global warming. In addition to the implications for climate change, high ozone concentrations have some directly noticeable harmful impacts on human health. In response to the serious impact of ozone on human health and the environment, the EU harmonized limit values for ozone concentrations in ambient air through the Directives 92/72/EEC, 2002/3/EC, and 2008/50/EC (see Knill and Liefferink 2007: 50). This is a desired difference vis-à-vis the other policy items, since it allows for testing the effectiveness of international harmonization for triggering policy change.

Soil is a largely non-renewable natural resource. Once contaminated, it is very difficult and cost-intensive to purify it, a fact increasingly realized by policymakers. Generally, soil degradation includes pollution by heavy metals, acidification, over-fertilization, and organic contaminants such as PAHs, which are a class of organic chemicals consisting of two or more fused-benzene rings. They are primarily formed as by-products of the incomplete combustion of organic materials. PAHs have been identified in many emission sources, such as vehicle exhaust, power plants, and urban sewage. Some of the PAHs like benzo(a) pyrene are also carcinogenic. Several studies indicate that industrial sites throughout CEE show high concentrations of PAHs (see, e.g., Miroshnichenko 2008). In LA, a major source of PAHs is the import and production of crude oil (see, e.g., Iturbe et al. 2007).

The selection of MON810 maize for this analysis results from the fact that it is one of few genetically modified organisms (GMOs) that can be legally cultivated in the EU (Pollack and Shaffer 2010: 351; Skogstad 2011: 905). The regulation of GM maize – or rather GM crops in general – is mostly a matter of agriculture and consumer protection policy, but due to its multiple ecological impacts it is also an important component of environmental policy (see Skogstad 2006: 228). To give an example, the widespread use of GM crops may cause a shift in weed populations and thus lower weeds' diversity and ecosystem complexity in agricultural habitats (Dale et al. 2002: 571). However, there is also another dimension to GM crops, which complicates the evaluation of their environmental consequences. Recent empirical studies have shown that the use of GM crops can reduce pesticide and insecticide spraying and, as a result, decrease the environmental impact associated with the use of these substances (see, e.g., Brookes and Barfoot 2007). Thus, from this perspective GM crops might also have a positive impact on the environment. This ambivalence in terms of their environmental effects turns GM crops – or more precisely, MON810 maize – into a rewarding subject of analysis.

Finally, SFM has been chosen due to the fact that forests are a valuable environmental and economic resource in both regions. LA forests, especially, have a global importance due to their size. For centuries, forest management has been based on the principle of sustained yield, meaning that the volume of wood harvested should not exceed the volume of growth gained over a given period of time. However, in recent years, and particularly since the 1992 Rio Earth Summit, there has been growing recognition of the importance of SFM (Hickey 2008; Wijewardana 2008; Gulbrandsen 2010).

Each of these five policy items will be treated as a dependent variable in the analyses to be carried out in chapters 5 and 6. This approach has two advantages. First, problems related to the construction of additive or multiplicative indices, like weighing decisions, are circumvented. Second, with each policy item treated as a separate dependent variable the robustness of the estimation findings can be submitted to an additional check.

How do the selected policy items reflect change? There are three ways of using empirical information on the policy items for assessing the occurrence and direction of policy change. First, concerning the policy items on water, air, and soil pollution, the assessment of regulatory change is straightforward, as it corresponds to changes in the numerical values of the limit values. In this regard, lower limit values indicate a higher protection level. Hence, the adoption of limit values in general or the replacement of existing limit values by lower ones corresponds to an increase in regulatory stringency. By the same token, the abolition of limit values or the replacement of existing limit values by higher ones would equal a reduced stringency.

This reasoning gives way to a bidirectional concept of policy change: positive or upward change on the one side, and negative or downward change on the other. Positive change implies that limit values are lowered and therewith become stricter, whereas negative change relates to higher limit values, characterizing a more lenient regulatory approach. Also, no change might occur at all if during the entire observation period no limit values are defined or the limit values introduced before the observation period remain unchanged. This scenario corresponds to the prevalence of the regulatory status quo.

Regarding the regulation of GM maize, policy change corresponds to one direction only, namely, positive change through restricting the commercial cultivation of MON810 maize. The regulatory point of departure is that there are no cultivation restrictions. Therefore, the item is coded as a binary variable, which takes on the value 1 if any restriction of MON810 maize cultivation is passed by the legislative bodies. Conversely, if the initial legal status of unrestricted cultivation prevails, the variable takes on the value 0. Repeals of cultivation restrictions should be unlikely during the observation period, since it is a new policy area that just received attention in the 1990s, and if restrictions are imposed, they should, at least in principle, last for a while. This expectation will be revisited in detail in chapters 5 and 7.

The coding of SFM is similar to that of GM maize and generates a binary variable. As there exist various criteria and indicators for SFM which are difficult to compare (see, e.g., (Hickey 2008; Wijewardana 2008; Gulbrandsen 2010), in this study a country is perceived to have the SFM principle in place if there is a national legal act explicitly stating that forests shall be managed in a manner that ensures their sustainability. Any other term that might parallel the idea underlying SFM, such as a "rational" use of forests, has not been taken into consideration for two reasons. First, the term "sustainable" mainly appeared after the publication of the Brundtland Report in 1987 (Silva 1997: 369) and therefore represents a rather new concept, which should reduce the risk of leaving out empirical information predating the beginning of the observation period. Second, alternative forest management principles do not always directly correspond to SFM. As a result, the evaluation of the legal acts would entail a lot of leeway for interpretation, which in turn may threaten the validity of the measurement.

Again, the coding procedure assumes that only positive change occurs, which is, however, fully in line with the existing empirical accounts – there exist no cases in which SFM after being adopted was terminated afterwards (see, e.g., Schmithüsen, Herbst, and Le Master 2000; Gallardo and Schmithüsen 2005). This perspective becomes even more intuitive when one considers the interpretative leeway in applying this principle, which should hardly motivate legislators to eliminate it altogether.

Measuring Changes in Enforcement Commitment

The second main dependent variable aims to assess changes in the governments' commitment to regulatory enforcement. The purpose of enforcement is to ensure that preventative or remedial action is taken to secure compliance with environmental protection standards. The powers available to the enforcement authority include formal legal mechanisms such as prosecution, which is characterized by a process in which the courts impose a sanction for violating environmental regulations. Further, enforcement involves the use of administrative mechanisms, including prohibition notices, suspension of licences, the imposition of monetary administrative penalties, and the launch of formal civil proceeding with a view to, inter alia, ceasing environmentally harmful activities and carrying out remedial works. These formal mechanisms are completed by informal ones such as the provision of information, negotiation, and persuasion (Abbot 2009: 9; see also Blanc 2013). Most essentially, however, enforcement is about monitoring and the imposition of sanctions (Becker 1968). Monitoring increases the likelihood of exposing possible environmental offenders, whereas sanctions raise the costs of non-compliance and turn it into a less attractive action.

Gathering reliable cross-country data on environmental policy enforcement is challenging, which explains why relatively little comparative research has been carried out (see McAllister et al. 2010: 2). Therefore, hardly any data exist to build on for measuring enforcement efforts in a nuanced manner. Instead, this book approaches the issue of changes in enforcement in a pragmatic way by focusing on governments' visible commitment to increase monitoring and punishment related to non-compliance through institutional change.

Which institutions are adequate for achieving a more rigorous enforcement? Or in other words, which is the most consequential form of enforcement? Environmental enforcement is mostly associated with

administrative institutions that are in charge of monitoring and imposing sanctions when they determine that non-compliance with environmental laws has occurred. In most countries, this task is carried out by
environmental inspectorates (see, e.g., Cole 1998; Pickvance 2003; Abbot
2009; Blanc 2013). Certainly more consequential is, however, the use of
criminal instruments that aim to punish wrongdoing, to avoid a recur-
rence, and to act as a deterrent to others. In this context, the involvement of public prosecutors with environmental offences is important
(Strock 1990: 920; Garvie and Keeler 1994: 158). In fact, many industrialized countries operate special environmental prosecution units.

In Canada, for instance, the Public Prosecution Service is endowed
with the competence to prosecute offences against environmental law.
In exercising its mandate, the Public Prosecution Service collaborates
with the enforcement arms of federal departments and agencies such
as Environment Canada or Fisheries and Oceans Canada (see Abbot
2009: 101–5). In the United States, overall environmental monitoring
and enforcement is carried out by the EPA. However, many inspection
and sanctioning activities are conducted by state-level regulatory agencies, sometimes with the assistance of EPA regional offices (Gray and
Shimshack 2011: 4).

To measure changes in the governmental enforcement commitment, again a binary variable is used, which takes on the value 1 if
an environmental prosecution unit is established and 0 otherwise. The
measure adopted here represents a necessary conceptual simplifica-
tion in response to the data situation. Of course, the mere existence of
an institution does not necessarily imply improvements of regulatory
enforcement. A more appropriate measurement would include data
about organizational resources and information about the frequency
of prosecution-related activities (see, e.g., Pickvance 2003; McAllister
2008; Abbot 2009; Ehrke 2010; Blanc 2013). Despite considerable efforts,
however, this kind of information could not be gathered for the country
sample due to the lack of willingness of the national authorities to provide access to data. More generally, the data situation on enforcement
activities can only be judged as satisfactory for the United States. Even
for many industrialized countries there are serious constraints concerning data availability (Gray and Shimshack 2011: 18–19).

Changes in enforcement actions and the creation of enforcement
institutions are not the same, but there are still a number of reasons why
data on the latter are a sufficiently good proxy. First, the establishment
of an institution in charge of prosecuting environmental offences is a

decision taken by the government, indicating that this concept is in line with the study's objective of explaining the behaviour of policymakers.

Second, while it cannot be questioned that the creation of institutions does not necessarily translate into concrete actions, it must be stressed that this analysis is merely interested in the decision a government takes and not in the impact of the institution concerned. That being said, the obvious increase in monitoring and the severity of punishment related to legal prosecution should entail costs for the governments, as they impose additional burdens on those regulated. Due to the signalling power of establishing a prosecution unit, a rational government would not opt for this step if it were not willing to bear the risk of political opposition from the regulated community.

Third, the bulk of the small number of existing comparative enforcement studies equally tends to focus on the institutional dimension. This holds true not only for studies that directly address environmental enforcement (see, e.g., Abbot 2009), but also for studies of regulatory enforcement in related areas (see, e.g., Versluis 2007). The prominence of the institutional dimension mainly stems from the assumption that institutions are a necessary – albeit certainly not a sufficient – condition for achieving legal compliance.

Fourth, empirical studies indeed show that the involvement of public prosecutors with environmental policy enforcement can make a difference. For example, Mauri (2002) demonstrates that Costa Rican prosecutors played a vital role in gathering evidence on violations of environmental law, which eventually led to a criminal tribunal sentencing a property owner to a fine and five years in jail. Likewise, Mueller (2010) shows that public prosecutors yield a positive impact on environmental quality in Brazil, even after controlling for a number of intervening factors.

Finally, there is another measurement-related advantage with regard to the chosen conceptualization, namely, that environmental prosecution is a relatively recent empirical phenomenon. As a consequence, focusing on environmental procuracies can be expected to reduce the risk of left-censored data.

Details on Data Sources and Coding Decisions

The data for the dependent variables were collected between February 2007 and November 2011. The sources used for gathering the data were predominantly legal documents accessed electronically via either the websites of the national environmental ministries or the legislative database FAOLEX. Older legal acts were received from the IUCN Environmental Law Center in Bonn, Germany. The empirical information was coded by the author herself, although in some instances student assistants with relevant language skills helped to translate information regarding CEE countries. Generally, however, despite multiple languages, the coding process was a relatively straightforward process as limit values for air, soil, and water were often displayed by tables incorporated into the legal acts and could be easily identified through the chemical abbreviations of the substances and the corresponding measurement units. The numerical values were adopted as they were displayed in the legal acts. The data on cultivation restrictions for GM maize were also easy to code by screening the relevant legislation. Again, the technical label of MON810 maize turned out to be helpful in identifying the necessary information. The availability of comprehensive secondary literature (Schmithüsen et al. 2000; Gallardo and Schmithüsen 2005) and information on the environmental ministries' websites turned the coding of SFM into an equally easy undertaking.

Empirical information on the establishment of prosecution units specialized in environmental offences was taken from various sources. For the LA countries, the most important document was an overview of organs specialized in environmental crime provided by the United Nations Environment Program (UNEP) (2008). This information was cross-validated by employing information that LA environmental ministries and public prosecutors' offices provided on their websites. A similar overview document could not be found for the CEE countries. As a result, the data had to be gathered separately for each country on the basis of the relevant governmental organizations' websites and secondary sources. In this context, the country-specific overviews of the *International Comparative Legal Guide to Environmental Law* served as the main point of reference.[3] Furthermore, in some countries the prosecution units were established through a legal act. Accordingly, these legal acts were also used to determine the dates when prosecution units were created.

The entirety of the coded legal acts and secondary sources along with a thorough description of the data are presented at length in chapter 5. In addition, the chapter supplies information regarding minor modifications to the data for a more plausible interpretation, particularly in the case of the limit values for air and water pollution. Accordingly, for replication purposes one would simply need to consult the listed legal acts or secondary sources and follow the clarifications on the presentation of the data.

Concerning the starting values, for LA countries legislation predating 1990 was also included in order to reconstruct change in the most accurate way and to avoid problems of left-censoring. Of course, this refers only to legal acts with direct implications for the interpretation of policy change during the observation period. For CEE countries, by contrast, legislation predating 1990 was omitted. This approach is based on explanations in the literature that, while CEE countries under state socialism possessed very strict written environmental standards, those were, however, technically infeasible and therefore never intended to be enforced (see, e.g., Earnhart 1997; Klarer and Francis 1997; Cole 1998; Knill and Lenschow 2000; Pavlínek and Pickles 2000; Andonova 2004; Fagan 2004; Carmin and VanDeveer 2005). Consequently, the inclusion of the pre-transformation legislation could be seen as a more virulent source of bias than setting this legislation equal to "no regulation," since this reflects the reality more accurately.

Introducing the Explanatory Variables

This section gives an overview of the operationalization of the explanatory variables. The corresponding summary statistics are presented in appendix A1. All missing values were imputed in accordance with the "last observation carried forward" approach (see Gelman and Hill 2007: 533). This strategy utilizes the temporally closest empirical information (i.e., the last year for which data were available) and treats them as constant values for the missing observations. Overall, however, only few variables needed to be imputed.

Measuring Economic Integration

There are several conceptions of international economic integration, which generally imply that economic activities make boundaries between nation states less discontinuous, leading instead to the formation of more interconnected systems (Jovanović 2006: 15). For the sake of analytical simplicity, this study focuses on only two aspects of economic integration. The first concerns economic integration as rising investment flows. The second aspect takes up the idea underlying the California effect and thus draws attention to the direction of international trade. These considerations give way to two variables for examining the impact of economic integration on policy and institutional change: *FDI* and *Exports*. Data for these variables come from two sources. FDISTAT offered the most complete data on *FDI* stocks. The Direction of Trade Statistics (DOTS) published by the IMF turned out to be the most reliable data source for *Exports*.

The variable *FDI* assesses a country's structural dependence on investment based on the argument that, irrespective of the *FDI's* source, higher levels of *FDI* discourage the adoption of more stringent protection standards. As *FDI* accumulates over time, the potential influence multinational companies exercise in host economies depends not only on the *FDI* inflow in a given year t, but even more so on the multinational companies' accumulated inward *FDI* stock (Prakash and Potoski 2007: 730). The variable *FDI* is therefore calculated as a country i's total inward FDI stock as a proportion of Gross Domestic Product (GDP) in year t.

Exports are calculated as a country i's exports to industrialized countries as a share of its total exports in year t. This measure gauges each country's dependence on exports to industrialized countries and therewith indicates the "regulatory leverage" that these have over emerging market democracies.

Measuring Domestic Politics

The politics dimension refers to the impact of political parties and environmental groups. In this regard, *Green government* and *Liberal government* are binary variables, taking the value 1 if a green or economically liberal party participates in a (coalition) government. Likewise, the variable *Liberal president* takes the value 1 if an economically liberal president enters office. Considering the empirical literature, this is a very simple operationalization of political party impact (see, e.g., Knill, Debus, and Heichel 2010), which is again a consequence of restricted data availability. Obtaining reliable electoral data for CEE and LA countries is a difficult undertaking. Especially in CEE countries, party coalitions rather than individual parties fight elections (Lewis 2000: 88). As a result, official election data only provide information on the entire electoral coalition, which cannot be disaggregated in a reliable manner. Therefore, receiving data on vote shares of green and economically liberal parties in all countries of interest is not feasible. The most appealing type of data is given by the policy-specific positions of political parties. However, the Comparative Manifesto Project's data (Klingemann et al.

2006), which indeed provides this kind of information, is available for CEE but not LA countries. As a consequence, the use of party dummies represents the only practicable measurement option.

When applying such an operationalization, the assignment of political parties to the party families of interest is a crucial aspect. To this end, the political parties were coded on the basis of a multitude of authoritative sources. For CEE parties, the publications by Lewis (2000) and Bugajski (2002), the codebooks of the Comparative Manifesto Project, and the Comparative Political Data Set II (Armingeon and Careja 2007) served for data coding. The coding of LA parties followed the classifications put forward by Coppedge (1997), Alcántara and Freidenberg (2001a, 2001b), Freidenberg and Alcántara (2001), and Huber et al. (2008).[4]

The variable *NGOs* measures the cumulative number of environmental groups founded in country i in year t divided by population. The data were taken from the Environment Encyclopedia and Directory (Europa Publications 2005). Nevertheless, the completeness of information provided by the compilation varies strongly from one country to another. This aspect also affected this study due to incomplete information about the founding dates of the *NGOs*. Information was only complete for the environmental groups in Honduras, Nicaragua, and Panama. In contrast, the percentage of entries with founding dates lay between 16 and 18 per cent for Latvia, Romania, and Slovenia. The missing information was gathered via internet investigation, email requests, and phone calls. Yet, if the contact details turned out be wrong or if no replies were received, the corresponding organization was omitted.

The IUCN members complemented the empirical information received from the Environment Encyclopedia and Directory. This second source also guaranteed the identification of environmental groups that were established after 2005. Merging both sources turned out to be fruitful. For example, in the case of Paraguay, the Environment Encyclopedia and Directory indicated that no environmental groups exist. This information was proved wrong by the IUCN source.

The IUCN members' database also served as the basis for creating the variable *INGOs* (international non-governmental organizations) measuring the cumulative number of internationally linked environmental groups founded in country i in year t divided by population. This subgroup of environmental groups is also used separately, since IUCN members are significantly different from other domestic environmental groups in terms of funding and personnel, but also with regard to the extent to which they participate in processes of transnational communication. To recall, chapter 3 formulated the expectation that internationally linked environmental groups influence a government's decision to set up specific prosecution units for environmental offences.

Measuring Institutional Integration

The indicators *EU accession* and *EU membership* measure the impact of international institutional integration. The first variable, *EU accession*, focuses on the date when the official accession talks began with the ten CEE countries that applied for membership. This operationalization allows for directly measuring accession effects. In contrast, *EU membership* focuses on the post-accession stage when the former candidates had already become EU members. A differentiation between these two effects is important for clarifying whether a change in membership status also makes a difference in terms of policy and institutional change. As will be shown in chapter 6 when analysing SFM, the variables *EU accession* and *EU membership* cause collinearity problems and are therefore replaced by *EU application*. It starts measuring the impact of the EU from the date of the CEE countries' application for membership. While this measurement still mirrors the theoretical construct of interest, namely, international institutional integration, the drawback is that the separate effects of candidacy and membership status can no longer be discerned.

    EU accession, *EU membership*, and *EU application* are binary variables taking on the value 1 if a given CEE country receives the status of an accession candidate or a member state. Otherwise, the value of the binary variable remains 0. The accession talks began in the late 1990s, whereas eight CEE countries became EU members in 2004 and Bulgaria and Romania in 2007. The data for these variables come from the European Commission's website on enlargements.

Measurement of Public Demand

The variable *Income* refers to the GDP per capita at purchasing power parity (in constant 2005 international dollars) as provided by the World Bank's World Development Indicators (WDI) online database. This exchange rate equalizes the purchasing power of different currencies in their home countries for a given basket of goods. Using such an adjusted measure is arguably more insightful when comparing values across countries and over time since the concept of purchasing power parity takes into account the inflation rates of different countries, which the nominal GDP does not.

The second set of variables addressing public demand refers to the salience of environmental issues. Since the items for measuring policy change address different environmental media – that is, water, air, soil, crops, and forests – the indicators for measuring issue salience should ideally also somehow reflect the regulated medium. The following five indicators are selected to fulfil this condition. The first indicator, *Water*, reports the total renewable water resources per capita as provided by the AQUASTAT database of the Food and Agriculture Organization of the United Nations (FAO). *Water* adequately reflects problem pressure when evaluating the determinants of changes in the regulation of water pollution. In this context, lower values of *Water* signal a higher degree of problem pressure and therewith issue salience.

With regard to air quality standards for ozone, the variable CO_2 represents an appropriate indicator for air-related problem pressure. The variable reports the carbon dioxide emissions (CO_2) in metric tons per capita as provided by the WDI. Higher emission levels are associated with a higher extent of problem pressure. To avoid associating this measure with endogeneity problems, all explanatory variables will be incorporated into estimation models with a timelag of one year.

The variable *Land* measures the area of arable land as expressed in hectares per person. Since hydrocarbon-compound pollution results in a decrease of arable land (Krüger and Carius 2001: 23), it represents a suitable measure of problem pressure for the model addressing the determinants of soil pollution regulations. Larger areas of arable land imply a higher level of problem pressure due to the relative importance of agricultural production for the respective economy.

The variable *Insecticides* refers to the analysis of GM maize and measures the insecticide consumption per capita. The data were taken from the online GEO Data Portal of UNEP. The higher the use of *Insecticides*, the higher is the issue salience. However, in the case of this indicator, it is expected that a higher use of *Insecticides* makes it rather unlikely to expect a cultivation ban for GM maize, since MON810 maize possesses built-in insecticides, which should make its use more appealing (see Brookes and Barfoot 2007; Brookes 2008).

To measure forest-related problem pressure, the variable *Forest* is employed. It indicates the percentage of each country's land area covered by forest. It relates salience to the presence of forest areas.

Accordingly, the salience should be higher in countries with large shares of area covered by forest. The data for *Forest* were taken from the website of the United Nations Millennium Development Goals Indicators.

For testing the impact of environmental problem pressure on the governments' decision to establish environmental prosecution units a very general measure is needed. The literature considers *Energy* use to be such an indicator. This variable reports the per capita consumption of energy (in kg of oil equivalent) as reported by the WDI. Several studies confirm that there is a direct relationship between industrial and other energy-consuming activities and pollution intensity (see, e.g., Tapiero 2009). In this sense, higher levels of energy consumption indicate a greater extent of environmental problem pressure.

Presentation of Techniques of Analysis

This book employs both quantitative and qualitative techniques of analysis. This multi-methods design allows for more accurately testing hypotheses. Generally, when examining policy and institutional change the focus can be on either the process or the outcome (Capano 2009; Howlett and Cashore 2009). The choice of the analysis technique depends on this basic decision. Here the focus lies on the outcome of change entailing the question whether and why environmental protection standards became modified over time. Along the same lines, the study seeks to explain which causes motivate or impede governments to enhance their enforcement commitment.

The discussion about the most appropriate techniques of analysis begins with the three binary dependent variables, that is, the regulation of GM maize, the SFM principle, and the creation of environmental procuracies. In light of the particular characteristics of these three variables, the analysis will be based on event history models (see, e.g., Box-Steffensmeier and Jones 2004; Blossfeld et al. 2007; Cleves et al. 2008). Event history models estimate the probability of the occurrence of events. An event is a transition from one state to another, that is, from an original state to a destination state. For the purpose of this study, events relate to the enactment of legislation that implies a restriction of the cultivation of MON810 maize, the adoption of a forest law that launches the SFM principle, and the establishment of a unit endowed with the task of prosecuting environmental offences.

As concerns the other dependent variables, that is, the regulation of water and soil pollution as well as air quality standards for ozone, estimation techniques for pooled data must be applied. The particular structure of pooled data, that is, the repeated observation of cross-sections, permits researchers to accurately study the dynamics of change. To be sure, the combination of these two dimensions can enhance both the quality and quantity of data in ways that would be impossible using only one of these two dimensions. These advantages, however, come at a price. Pooled data are confronted with several problems, such as heterogeneity bias. Consequently, model selection and specification warrant particular attention. Therefore, chapter 6 will explain the application of the estimation models for pooled data in detail after we have gained a better impression of the data structure in chapter 5.

In a next step, chapter 7 will present in-depth analyses of interesting cases. Which cases shall be chosen for this purpose? Following Lieberman (2005), the results of the quantitative analysis are an appropriate starting point for selecting "instructive" cases. The idea of this approach is to compare the predicted values of the dependent variable with the actual values. Against this background, deviant cases, which have not been accurately predicted by the theoretical model, appear particularly useful for learning more about alternative explanations (see Gilardi 2008: 126–34). When practising such a deliberative case selection, it is, however, important to avoid using the specific cases that informed the initial development of the theoretical model as the basis for testing the model (Lieberman 2005: 446). In the case of this study, the deviant case is represented by the regulation of GM maize, which did not inform the development of the theoretical model. Thus, the conditions for nested analysis are met. Chapter 6 will outline why this policy item represents a deviant case that is worthy of being studied in detail by employing qualitative methods.

Conclusion

This chapter provided an overview of the research design and measurement of the variables. To empirically assess environmental policy change, this study concentrates on the regulation of air, water, and soil pollution. These three items are complemented by changes in the regulations concerning the cultivation of GM maize and the incorporation of the principle of sustainable forestry into the body of national legislation. These five policy items only represent a small selection of a plethora of measures summarized by the term environmental policy.

This chapter explained that restricting the empirical focus is indispensable for measuring and comparing instances of policy change in a large number of countries. It outlined that to address changes in the governments' commitment to environmental law enforcement this study needs to employ a pragmatic measurement concept. To this end, it concentrates on the establishment of units within the public prosecutor's office endowed with the task of prosecuting environmental offences. While far from perfect, this measurement yields some advantages. Most important, it enables a comparative assessment of changes in the institutional characteristics of enforcement. Furthermore, there are some hints in the research literature that the involvement of public prosecutors with environmental law enforcement might be consequential indeed.

More generally, this chapter demonstrated that operationalizing policy and institutional change is anything but trivial. Numerous conceptual and methodological decisions must be made that have important repercussions on the findings. Key challenges not only involve the selection of appropriate policy items, but also decisions regarding the starting and ending of the observation period. In addition, the composition of the country sample has to satisfy certain criteria in order for the study to make valid causal inferences. Furthermore, there is the difficulty of systematically linking the methodological discussion with theoretical considerations. After all, it is the theoretical approach that can help in encountering the various methodological challenges emerging from the study of policy and institutional change.

5 Descriptive Analysis of Policy and Institutional Change

This chapter explores the characteristics of environmental policy and institutional change in CEE and LA between 1990 and 2010. In doing so, it poses three questions: Have environmental regulatory standards become stricter over time? Have the countries established environmental procuracies? Are there notable differences between the two regions? To address these questions effectively, this chapter outlines the legislative history of five environmental policy items and examines the diffusion of environmental procuracies throughout the two regions.

The empirical information is presented in two different ways. As explained in chapter 4, the items on air, soil, and water pollution are measured on an interval scale. This allows for making statements not only about the existence of regulations in a given country, but also about their numerical settings. Therefore, the sections on these policy items provide a particularly nuanced overview of regulatory changes, facilitating the identification of both increases and decreases in regulatory stringency. The regulation of GM maize, sustainable forestry, and changes in the enforcement commitment, in contrast, are coded as binary variables. Consequently, the empirical information presented in these sections is less differentiated, thus primarily enabling the presentation of events of upward change and the prevalence of the status quo.

The structure of this chapter is straightforward: it illustrates how the policies related to waste-water, air and soil pollution, GM maize, and forest management have changed over time. In a next step, the patterns of institutional change with respect to the creation of environmental procuracies are outlined. Finally, in the concluding section, the major findings of the descriptive empirical analysis are discussed.

Changes in Environmental Regulations

This section sheds light on changes in the stringency of regulations targeting water, air, and soil pollution as well as GM maize and forest management. To increase the consistency of the presentation of the empirical information, all subsections are organized in an identical manner: They first provide a general entry into the main characteristics of the policy items and, where necessary, give details on data transformation procedures. Next, the subsections present the legislative developments, starting with the CEE countries and then moving on to the LA countries. In a final step, the regulatory patterns of each region are contrasted with one another by focusing on the occurrence, direction, and, whenever possible, intensity of change.

The empirical analysis is generally restricted to environmental legislation promulgated at the national level. The only exception from this approach is Brazil, where certain pollution parameters are left completely unspecified by the national standards and must be defined at the state level (von Sperling 2007: 130–1). Therefore, in cases where no national protection standards are defined, the study relies on the state environmental legislation of São Paulo in accordance with the approach adopted by other empirical research (see, e.g., McAllister 2008).

Changes in the Regulation of Water Pollution

To recall, the regulation of water pollution is based on the definition of limit values for BOD concentrations in industrial waste-waters discharged into water bodies. Limit values for BOD concentrations can be validly compared across countries after making a few adjustments to them. Some countries define universal discharge standards that specify a unique value for BOD concentrations in waste-water discharges. Other countries define industry-specific effluent standards or limit values that vary with the types of the receiving water bodies. Further, in some cases the national regulatory approaches change over time; that is, at the beginning of the observation period they have universal effluent standards in place, which subsequently become replaced by industry-specific ones. To make the regulatory approaches comparable across different jurisdictions, the universal effluent standards are employed along with the arithmetic mean of limit values that vary with the industry sectors or receiving water bodies.[1]

Although limit values possess a numeric character that facilitates comparing their regulatory stringency, their interpretation is counterintuitive as lower values indicate that they are stricter and vice versa. Furthermore, the absence of regulation does not correspond to the value of 0, but to a very high hypothetical limit value. As all this is not very intuitive, the limit values for BOD are transformed in accordance with equation 5.1. This simple transformation reverses the ordering of the limit values and therewith facilitates their interpretation. In addition, it allows for assigning 0 to any state characterized by the absence of limit values. This is possible since the insertion of a very large fictive value in the denominator makes the term become infinitesimally smaller, thus approximating 0.

$$1 \text{ regulatory unit} = \frac{1}{1000 \text{ mg/l}} \times 1000 \qquad (5.1)$$

Since the collapse of state socialism, the CEE countries have increasingly strengthened their effluent standards (see, e.g., Buzogány 2009a, b). Table 5.1 shows that by the year 2002 all countries had adopted limit values for BOD concentrations in industrial waste-water discharges. As outlined in chapter 4, standards that existed before 1990 are excluded here, since regulations predating the transformation process were excessively stringent and, in view of the technological possibilities of that time, not practically implementable (Klarer and Francis 1997: 9). The inclusion of those values would have simulated a drastic relaxation of regulatory stringency, which has actually not occurred. Keeping this important qualification in mind, the "first" country to introduce limit values for BOD concentrations was Poland, whereas Hungary and Latvia just adopted them in 2002.

The majority of the CEE countries introduced a sophisticated system of industry-specific waste-water standards. Exceptions are the Romanian and Ukrainian standards as well as the Polish regulation of 1991. A markedly different approach has been adopted by Estonia and Lithuania, as these states only defined limit values for indirect discharges, that is, the pollutant concentration in waste-water after being treated.[2] Accordingly, the Estonian and Lithuanian limit values correspond to those established by the EU Urban Waste Water Treatment Directive (91 / 271 / EEC), which harmonizes the requirements for discharges from urban waste-water treatment plants. Limit values for direct discharges do not exist in these two countries.

Seven CEE countries modified the limit values at least once during the observation period. However, it should be noted that not all reforms of effluent standards affected the limit values for BOD. In some cases,

Table 5.1 Standards for biological oxygen demand in Central and Eastern Europe

States	Legal acts	Limits	Direction
Bulgaria	Regulation 6 (2000)	25.3	+
Czech Republic	Decree 171 (1992); Decree 185 (1996); Decree 82 (1999)	16.9	+
	Order 61 (2003)	19.3	+
	Decree 229 (2007)	19.9	+
Estonia	Regulation 464 (1994); Regulation 201 (1995) Regulation 11 (1998)	57.5	+
	Regulation 269 (2001); Regulation 327	52.9	−
	(2003); Regulation 46 (2006)	76.9	+
Hungary	Joint Decree 9 (2002); Decree 28 (2004)	33.3	+
Latvia	Regulation 34 (2002)	40	+
Lithuania	Standard LAND 10-6 (1997)	33.4	+
	Regulation D1-36 (2006)	50	+
Poland	Regulation 116 / 503 (1991)	33.3*	+
	Regulation 212 / 117 (2002)	26.7	−
	Regulation 168 / 1763 (2004); Regulation 137 / 984 (2006)	28.6	+
Romania	Governmental Decision 730 (1997)	50*	+
	Governmental Decision 188 (2002)	40*	−
Slovakia	Order 242 (1993)	20.5	+
	Order 491 (2002); Order 296 (2005)	23.3	+
Slovenia	Various industry-specific decrees (1996)	35.3	+
	Various industry-specific decrees (1999)	41.7	+
	Decree 11 (2002)	45.5	+
	Decree 41 (2007)	42.5	−
Ukraine	Procedures for the Development and Adoption of Maximum Allowable Discharge of Pollutants and List of Pollutants (1996; amended in 2002)	66.7*	+

* Universal values (i.e., independent of industry sectors and receiving water bodies); the direction of change relative to the previous measurement is indicated by + (increase), − (decrease), and 0 (status quo).

multiple legal acts are assigned to one and the same limit value, indicating that regulatory reforms had an impact on other aspects of water-pollution control, but not on the provisions for BOD concentrations in waste-water discharges. The greatest number of regulatory changes affecting BOD limit values can be observed for Slovenia, but the Czech, Estonian, and Polish authorities also made several modifications to the waste-water standards. The countries with the lowest number of changes, that is, with one event of regulatory change, are Bulgaria, Latvia, and Ukraine.

Another important observation is that regulatory standards were not only tightened but also relaxed. In this regard, the Polish case is a particularly interesting one, since the very strict level of the 1991 standard has never been reached again since. In light of the relatively early setting of this standard, it can be interpreted as a "legacy" of policy-making under state socialism (see also Francis, Klarer, and Moldan 1997: 277; Cole 1998; Knill and Lenschow 2000). In other words, at that early stage of system transformation the Polish government appears to have continued setting limit values in accordance with the "old" regulatory approach, namely, defining excessively strict standards. It was only with progressing system transformation that this approach was replaced by the setting of implementable effluent standards. While one must recognize the difficulties in identifying processes of policy-oriented learning (see Radaelli 2009), this alternation in the Polish government's approach to the setting of effluent standards might be interpreted as a specific form of learning.

The lowering of the Slovenian limit value in 2007, in contrast, results from the specific approach to measurement this study adopts when countries have multiple industry-specific BOD standards in place, that is, the calculation of the arithmetic mean of all these different standards. The Slovenian authorities promulgated additional industry-specific BOD limit values addressing pollution-intensive industries, for which less stringent limit values were defined. It is due to this extension of the regulatory scope that the mean regulatory level decreased between 2002 and 2007.

Table 5.2 illustrates the legislative developments in LA. In this context, it should be noted that the Colombian regulatory approach strongly deviates from that of the other countries in the region. Instead of defining fixed limit values, Decree 1.594 demands that 80 per cent of the organic pollutant load must be removed from waste-waters before they can be emitted into any receiving water body. As this specific regulatory approach impedes the identification of one universally valid limit value, the table reports the limit value that many subnational units such as the metropolitan area of Bogotá apply (see Resolution 1.974 of 1997; León-Chaux 2006: 198). This widely applied limit value corresponds to 1000 mg / l or one regulatory unit after being transformed in accordance with equation 5.1, presented above.

Three aspects of the legislative developments in LA are particularly noteworthy. First, there are four countries – Brazil, Colombia,

Table 5.2 Standards for biological oxygen demand in Latin America

States	Legal acts	Limits	Direction
Argentina	Resolution 79.179 (1990)	20*	+
Bolivia	Regulation of Law 1.333 (1995; amended in 2003)	12.5*	+
Brazil	Decree 8.468 (1976; amended in 2009) (São Paulo)	16.7*	0
Chile	Supreme Decree 90 (2001)	9.3	+
Colombia	Decree 1.594 (1984)	1	0
Costa Rica	Decree 24.158-MIRENEM-S (1995)	8.9	+
	Decree 26.042-S / MINAE (1997)	5.2	–
	Decree 33.601-MINAE (2006)	20*	+
Ecuador	Environmental Quality and Waste Water Discharge Standards: Resource Water (2003)	10	+
El Salvador	Standard NSO 134.901 (2006)	5.6	+
Guatemala	Governmental Accord 60 (1990)	4.4	+
	Governmental Accord 66 (2005)	6.25	+
	Governmental Accord 236 (2006)	3.8	–
Honduras	Governmental Accord 058 (1996)	20*	+
Mexico	Technical Standards 026-033 (1991)	10.5	+
	Mexican Standards 001-030 (1993)	8.7	–
	Mexican Standards 063-073 (1994)	8.3	–
	Mexican Standard 001 (1996)	7.1	–
Nicaragua	Decree 33 (1995); Decree 7 (2002)	7.8	+
	Decree 77 (2003)	11.1*	+
Panama	Resolution 351 (2000)	28.6*	+
Paraguay	Resolution 585 (1995); Resolution 222 (2002)	20*	+
Peru	Supreme Decree 033 (2002)	3.4	+
Uruguay	Decree 698 (1989); Decree 195 (1991)	16.7*	0
Venezuela	Resolution 31 (1985); Decree 883 (1995)	16.7*	0

* Universal values (i.e., independent of industry sectors and receiving water bodies); the direction of change relative to the previous measurement is indicated by + (increase), – (decrease), and 0 (status quo).

Uruguay, and Venezuela – in which between 1990 and 2010 no relevant regulatory changes occurred at all. Second, there is considerable variation in the timing of the introduction of effluent standards. While the Brazilian state of São Paulo introduced limit values for BOD back in 1976, the Central American state of El Salvador just promulgated its first effluent standards in 2006. Third, like the situation in CEE, changes in regulatory strictness in LA countries are bidirectional. While most states have continually tightened their effluent standards, Costa Rica,

Guatemala, and Mexico relaxed the strictness of their BOD standards at least once during the observation period. Of these, the Mexican case is certainly the most drastic one, as it represents a steady lowering of the limit values during the observation period. This finding corresponds with other empirical accounts of changes in waste-water policies in Mexico (see, e.g., Tortajada 1998).

What are the most striking differences and parallels between the two regions? First of all, the CEE countries turn out to have experienced more events of policy change than the LA countries. A plausible explanation for the frequency of policy change in the CEE countries would be that these countries had to make various adjustments to their regulations on water pollution in order to adopt the EU's environmental acquis. Even though limit values for BOD are not harmonized at the European level, it is conceivable that they were modified on the occasion of adopting other water-related EU legislation. This is, for instance, hinted at by the case of Romania. In 2002, the Romanian parliament passed legislation to adopt EU directives related to water pollution and management (see Buzogány 2009b: 174), which coincides temporally with the definition of new BOD limit values.

Second, in both regions the direction of change is predominantly positive, meaning that the limit values became stricter. Yet, in Costa Rica, Estonia, Guatemala, Mexico, Poland, Romania, and Slovenia the limit values were also relaxed. Downward changes occurred more often in CEE than in LA. The frequent occurrence of downward changes in the CEE countries might have resulted from the regulatory legacy of state socialism defining unrealistically strict limit values. Policymaking in LA countries is not affected by such a legacy. Instead, in many countries the point of departure for policy change is one where effluent standards are absent.

Third, the average regulatory strictness is notably higher in the CEE countries. Even Panama as the LA state with the most stringent BOD limit value (28.6 regulatory units) clearly falls behind the currently valid limit values in most CEE countries. Only the limit values of Bulgaria (25.2 regulatory units), the Czech Republic (19.9 regulatory units), and Slovakia (23.3 regulatory units) are laxer than the Panamanian standard.

Changes in Air Quality Standards

The focus of this study is on ambient air quality standards, which set legal ceilings on the permissible concentration of ozone. Limit values for ozone concentrations represent an ideal policy item, since the regulatory approaches are very similar across countries, thus increasing the comparability of the empirical data. As air pollution is very likely to cause transborder environmental degradation, the EU has harmonized limit values for ozone concentrations in ambient air. The limit values defined by the EU are identical to those recommended by the air quality guidelines of the World Health Organization (WHO).

Generally, limit values for ozone concentrations in ambient air are averaged over a specific time period. Here, all limit values are converted to reflect the values for the eight-hour average.[3] Further, to enable a more plausible interpretation of the limit values with respect to their ordering, they are inverted and multiplied by 1000 in accordance with equation 5.2. This transformation produces a variable ranging from 0 to 22.2 regulatory units.

$$1 \text{ regulatory unit} = \frac{1}{1000 \ \mu g/m^3} \times 1000 \qquad (5.2)$$

Before the collapse of state socialism, air pollution was one of the most pressing problems in CEE. The deterioration of air quality was a consequence of rapid industrialization, a disproportionate concentration of heavy industry and power production, and inefficient enterprises. After 1990, the newly established democratic governments of the CEE countries faced strong domestic and international pressure to address this particular degradation problem (Fagan 2004: 11–12). Table 5.3 shows that most governments were swift in reacting to this pressure. With the exception of Latvia, Lithuania, and Romania, the CEE countries had already adopted limit values for ozone concentrations in the early 1990s.

The table further reveals that again regulatory change did not exclusively result in the tightening of limit values. On the contrary, the Baltic States, Bulgaria, Poland, Slovakia, and Slovenia are characterized by bidirectional policy change, that is, they not only tightened, but also relaxed, the stringency of the limit values for ozone concentrations. Remarkably, the downward change took place uniformly in the early 2000s in order to exactly meet the EU limit value of 8.3 regulatory units. The remaining countries – the Czech Republic, Hungary, Romania, and Ukraine – exclusively tightened the stringency of their ozone standards. Similarly to the regulation of water pollution, the Ukrainian standard is notably stricter than the EU limit value. In this context, it also becomes apparent that the first limit values defined by the Baltic States, which

Table 5.3 Ozone standards in Central and Eastern Europe

States	Legal acts	Limits	Direction
Bulgaria	Regulation 2 (1992)	6.7	+
	Regulation 8 (1999)	9.1	+
	Ordinance 12 (2010)	8.3	−
Czech Republic	Committee for the Environment Decree to Act 309 (1991)	6.25	+
	Government Order 350 (2002); Government Order 597(2006)	8.3	+
Estonia	Regulation 59 (1994)	22.2	+
	Ambient Air Protection Act (2004)	8.3	−
Hungary	Decree 5 (1990)	6.7	+
	Decree 14 (2001)	8.3	+
Latvia	Law on Chemical Substances (1997)	22.2	+
	Regulation 588 (2003)	8.3	−
Lithuania	Hygienic Norm 35 (1998)	22.2	+
	Order 544 / 508 (2002)	8.3	−
Poland	Executive Order 92 (1990)	22.2	+
	Regulation 87 / 798 (2002)	8.3	−
Romania	Government Order 592 (2002)	8.3	+
Slovakia	Committee for the Environment Decree to Act 309 (1991)	6.25	+
	Government Order 92 (1996)	9.1	+
	Decree 705 (2002)	8.3	−
Slovenia	Decree 74 (1994)	9.1	+
	Decree 8 (2003)	8.3	−
Ukraine	Law on Atmospheric Air Protection (1992); Order 161 (2000)	22.2	+

Note: The direction of change relative to the previous measurement is indicated by + (increase), − (decrease), and 0 (status quo).

previously formed part of the Soviet Union, and the current Ukrainian limit values are identical. The difference between these countries is that Ukraine is keeping these very strict levels, whereas the Baltic States replaced them with the European limit value. This suggests that the Ukrainian government continues to follow the previous regulatory approach, which is characterized by setting excessively strict limit values, which are likely to be implemented imperfectly.

While all CEE countries introduced limit values for ozone concentrations in ambient air, the regulatory situation looks quite different in the LA countries. By 2010, Guatemala, Honduras, Panama, Paraguay, and Uruguay still lacked ozone standards, as highlighted by table 5.4.

Table 5.4 Ozone standards in Latin America

States	Legal acts	Limits	Direction
Argentina	Law 20.284 (1973)	7.7	0
Bolivia	Regulation of Atmospheric Contamination (1995)	6.4	+
Brazil	CONAMA Resolution 3 (1990)	8.3	+
Chile	Resolution 1.215 (1978); Supreme Decree 112 (2002)	8.3	0
Colombia	Decree 2 (1982)	8.8	0
	Resolution 601 (2006)	8.3	–
Costa Rica	Decree 30.221 (1996); Decree 30.221-S (2002)	8.3	+
Ecuador	Regulation Establishing Air Quality Norms and Measurement Methods (1991)	7.5	+
	Ecuadorian Air Quality Standard (2003)	8.3	+
El Salvador	Decree 40 (2000); Norm on Atmospheric Contamination (2003)	8.3	+
Guatemala	–	0	0
Honduras	–	0	0
Mexico	Standard NOM-020-SSA1-1993 (1994; amended in 2002)	6.9	+
Nicaragua	Technical Air Quality Standard (2002)	6.25	+
Panama	–	0	0
Paraguay	–	0	0
Peru	Supreme Decree 074 (2001)	8.3	+
Uruguay	–	0	0
Venezuela	Decree 2.225 (1992); Decree 638 (1995)	6.25	+

Note: The direction of change relative to the previous measurement is indicated by + (increase), – (decrease), and 0 (status quo).

Of these five countries, the environmental authorities in Panama and Uruguay have announced that they are developing such standards, but to date none of the policy proposals has been formally adopted.

Another important observation relates to the fact that there are many instances of policy stability in the region. One source of stability is the ongoing absence of limit values. The other source is legislation that was adopted before 1990 and was not changed during the observation period, such as in Argentina and Chile. This also indicates that the selection of 1990 as the starting point for the observation could not prevent the data from being left-censored for some units of analysis. However, if any regulatory changes occurred in the LA countries, these corresponded to upward changes. Only the Colombian government slightly relaxed the limit value in 2006 to bring it in line with the WHO standard. Related to this is the more general observation that several LA countries (i.e., Brazil, Chile, Colombia, Costa Rica, Ecuador, El Salvador, and Peru) adopted limit values corresponding to WHO standards. The countries that still have limit values in place that are below the international standards are Argentina, Bolivia, Mexico, Nicaragua, and Venezuela.

As the data description above already hinted, the regulatory approaches to limiting ozone concentrations in ambient air markedly differ across the two regions. There are three interesting observations about the occurrence and direction of change as well as the mean stringency of the limit values. To begin with, changes in the strictness of ozone standards occurred more often in CEE. For one, this is most certainly driven by the CEE countries' need to adopt the air-related European legislation that represents a major part of the environmental acquis. That being said, the adoption of EU rules did not lead to upward changes. On the contrary, for many CEE countries (exceptions are the Czech Republic and Hungary) harmonization entailed a downward change. To be sure, the harmonized limit value of 8.3 regulatory units only represents a minimum standard that also could have led to the preservation of the stricter national standards. However, the CEE countries were not willing to keep their stricter regulatory standards. This finding highlights the fact that the environmental consequences of EU accession are not strictly positive. Indeed, this ambivalence is also noted by Andonova (2004: 25), who explains that environmental groups in CEE frequently "pointed out that in some cases EU standards replace stricter (albeit not enforced) domestic requirements."

As compared to the CEE countries, the events of policy change are few in LA, but if policy change occurred it almost always implied an upward adjustment. However, this does not mean that the overall stringency of ozone standards is higher in LA: There are many countries that still have not adopted any ozone standards or have limit values in place that are below the standards internationally agreed upon. Generally, the policy pattern observed for the LA countries is surprising as there is considerable variation within the region. There is one group of countries that have limit values in place that correspond to the international standards. There is a second group that is composed of those countries that possess ozone standards, but which are below the internationally recommended level. The third group consists of those LA countries that still have no regulations in place.

Changes in the Regulation of Soil Pollution

The regulation of organic soil pollution by PAHs is a relatively new policy area, which only began to emerge in the early 1990s. To assess how this policy item has been regulated, a count variable is used that reflects the number of PAHs for which limit values are defined. This approach produces a valid measurement, since PAHs are composed by a group of over one hundred chemicals. Of these, the US EPA declared sixteen to be priority pollutants, hence representing the regulatory benchmark (see Trapido 1999). A strict regulatory approach would comprise these sixteen chemicals belonging to the priority list.[4]

As table 5.5 shows, between 1991 and 2007 all CEE countries adopted soil quality standards defining limit values for PAH concentrations, with Ukraine being the first and Romania the last country to introduce them. Despite being a pioneer in introducing this policy measure, Ukraine's strict standard clearly falls behind that of all the other CEE states, since only one PAH is regulated. Comparatively lax also are the soil quality standards of the Czech Republic, Lithuania, and Poland. In marked contrast, Bulgaria and Hungary regulate the highest number of contaminants. The Hungarian Joint Ministerial Decree 10 even exceeds the regulatory benchmark set by the EPA, as it regulates seventeen PAHs.

In the case of this particular item, regulatory change is unidirectional and strictly positive, that is, all changes entailed a tightening of regulatory stringency. More precisely, policy change solely consists of the first-time adoption of soil quality standards, but it does not involve any further modifications to existing PAH standards. Both observations underscore that this is a comparatively new area of environmental policy. In fact, even though soil pollution was an environmental issue of public concern in the CEE countries, for a long time it was subordinate to the tremendous problem pressure emerging from air pollution (see Fagan 2004: 12). It is hence likely that this environmental issue only received attention after other – arguably more urgent – pollution problems were addressed.

Intensive mining exploitation and enhanced industrial growth, especially of the metallurgy and chemical industry resulted in alarming soil contamination in many LA states. Despite these persisting problems,

Table 5.5 Standards for polycyclic aromatic hydrocarbons in Central and Eastern Europe

States	Legal acts	Number	Direction
Bulgaria	Regulation 3 (2000)	16	+
Czech Republic	Decree 13 (1994)	7	+
Estonia	Regulation 58 (1999)	10	+
Hungary	Joint Ministerial Decree 10 (2000)	17	+
Latvia	Soil Quality Norms (2005)	10	+
Lithuania	Decree V-114 (2004)	8	+
Poland	Decree in Matter of Soil Quality Standards and Earth Quality Standards (2002)	9	+
Romania	Decision 1408 (2007)	11	+
Slovakia	Act 220 (2004)	12	+
Slovenia	Decree on the Limit, Warning and Critical ConcentrationValues of Dangerous Substances in Soil (1996)	10	+
Ukraine	Hygienic Standard 6229 (1991)	1	+

Note: The direction of change relative to the previous measurement is indicated by + (increase), – (decrease), and 0 (status quo).

most countries in the region still lack legislation addressing contaminated land and soil protection issues. As table 5.6 illustrates, only seven of the seventeen LA countries under study have adopted limit values for PAH concentrations in soil.

The table reveals three more interesting pieces of empirical information. First, with the exception of Argentina, the promulgation of soil quality standards represents a notably recent policy action. Most of the LA countries having limit values in place just adopted them in the 2000s. Second, similarly to the CEE countries, the direction of policy change is constrained to upward change. There is not one case in which the protection level has been lowered. Related to this is the observation that there are two cases in which existing standards were further tightened shortly after their first introduction. Hence, the Mexican emergency standard of 2002 was immediately reformed in 2003 by adding one more PAH. In the case of the Brazilian state of São Paulo, the government significantly strengthened the protection level by adding nine more PAHs. Third, it is surprising that Bolivia has the strictest regulation in place, whereas, for instance, Chile, a country that is often perceived as environmentally

Table 5.6 Standards for polycyclic aromatic hydrocarbons in Latin America

States	Legal acts	Number	Direction
Argentina	Decree 831 (1993)	9	+
Bolivia	Supreme Decree 26.171 (2001)	15	+
Brazil	Directorial Decision 14 (2001) (São Paulo)	1	+
	Directional Decision 195 (2005) (São Paulo)	10	+
Chile	–	0	0
Colombia	–	0	0
Costa Rica	Regulation of Maximum Permissible Concentrations of Contaminating Substances in Soils (2010)	6	+
Ecuador	Environmental Quality Norms for the Resource Soil and Criteria for the Remediation of Contaminated Soils (2000)	4	+
El Salvador	–	0	0
Guatemala	–	0	0
Honduras	–	0	0
Mexico	NOM-EM-138-ECOL (2002)	5	+
	NOM-138-SEMARNAT / SS-2003 (2005)	6	+
Nicaragua	–	0	0
Panama	Executive Decree 2 on Environmental Quality Norms for Soils of Different Use (2009)	10	+
Paraguay	–	0	0
Peru	Supreme Decree PCM (2007)	1	+
Uruguay	–	0	0
Venezuela	–	0	0

Note: The direction of change relative to the previous measurement is indicated by + (increase), – (decrease), and 0 (status quo).

progressive (see, e.g., Esty and Porter 2005; Porter, Schwab, and Lopez-Claros 2005: 612), has not defined any standards at all.

What do the two regions have in common concerning the regulation of organic soil pollution? Both have exclusively experienced upward policy change, which is mainly the result of the first-time introduction of regulatory standards. Only the Brazilian state of São Paulo and Mexico strengthened existing standards. In CEE, no country had modified the soil quality standards by 2010. Here, however, the similarities between the regions end. In fact, they differ significantly regarding the share of countries possessing soil quality standards. Not even half of the LA countries have relevant soil legislation in place, whereas all CEE countries have defined limit values for PAHs. The documents scrutinized for this analysis also did not point to the existence of governmental plans in the LA countries having no standards in place for regulating PAHs, even though Chile and Uruguay, for instance, are preparing clean-up and remediation programs for specific contaminated sites.

Changes in the Regulation of Genetically Modified Maize

The regulation of GM maize represents another new area of environmental policy that only emerged with the commercial appearance of GM crops in the early 1990s. Although MON810 maize can be grown for commercial purposes in the EU, by means of a safeguard clause introduced by Article 23 of Directive 2001 / 18 / EC and Article 34 of Regulation 1829 / 2003, member states can unilaterally impose bans. The formal conditions for making use of this clause are, however, quite restrictive. First, according to the text of the safeguard clause, the ban can only be provisional. Next, the member state seeking to impose a ban needs to provide new scientific evidence that succeeds in demonstrating that the planting or consumption of GM maize constitutes a serious risk to human health or the environment (Hristova 2011: 21; see also Pollack and Shaffer 2009: 258–60).

In light of this regulatory background, three CEE countries decided to impose a ban on the commercial cultivation of MON810 maize: Bulgaria, Hungary, and Poland. Hungary managed to install a complete ban in 2005 shortly after becoming an EU member. In a similar vein, Poland imposed a ban on sixteen out of thirty-one MON810 varieties legally allowed to be grown in the EU in 2005 (Pelc 2009: 34), which was extended to a total ban in 2012. In Bulgaria, the process of prohibiting the cultivation of GM maize took longer. In late 2009, the Bulgarian parliamentarians started to work on a cultivation ban of MON810 maize. However, it was the approval of a five-year ban on GMOs in the Environment and Water Committee of the Bulgarian parliament in March 2010 that prepared the ground for the temporally unrestricted ban, which was eventually promulgated in February 2011. Noteworthy also is Latvia, where local governments are authorized to institute cultivation bans.

In LA, seven states have promulgated legally binding acts (temporarily) banning the cultivation of GM maize. However, in two of these countries the bans have since been revoked. In Paraguay, GM maize was prohibited in 1993 by the Environmental Impact Assessment Law 294. Despite the fact that the country currently allows the cultivation of other GM crops such as soybeans, the prohibition of the commercial growing of GM maize is still in effect. In 1998, Mexico imposed a ban on the cultivation of GM maize. Similarly, a federal court ruling prohibited the growing of any kind of GMOs in Brazil between 1999 and 2003 (Nap et al. 2003: 3). In 2005, however, both houses of the Brazilian parliament adopted a bill to legalize the cultivation of GM crops. The other country that is characterized by a U-turn in its biosafety policy is El Salvador. The country originally banned the cultivation of GM maize on the grounds of Article 30 of the 2001 Planting Seed Law. In 2008, the growing of GM maize was legalized by abolishing Article 30.

More recently, Bolivia and Ecuador incorporated articles about GM crops into their constitutions. Thus, Article 401 of the 2008 constitution declares Ecuador free of GM crops and seeds. Even though this represents an important step, the article also states that the Ecuadorian president and the National Assembly could still allow the cultivation of GM crops if this served the national interest. Likewise, Article 255 of the Bolivian constitution of 2009 defines a prohibition of the importation, exportation, production, and marketing of GM crops. In November 2011, after intense debate, Peru's congress adopted a ten-year moratorium on the import and cultivation of GMOs. Although the moratorium was only adopted in 2011, already in June 2009 draft law 3025 was introduced to the Peruvian congress aiming to ban the cultivation of GM maize.

Finally, there is one case in LA that is difficult to interpret. In 2004, Venezuelan president Chávez announced the prohibition of the cultivation of GM crops, but to date no official law or decree has been passed (Altieri 2009: 11; Bravo 2009: 68–9). As there is no legal basis to rely on, Venezuela is not included in table 5.7, which gives an overview of the policy developments in both CEE and LA.

What both regions have in common is that they are relatively heterogeneous with respect to their approval of GM maize. There are some countries in each region that are strongly in favour of GM maize, coexisting with the ones opposing it. In CEE, the Czech and Estonian governments are particularly pro-GM (see Pelc 2009; Sabalza et al. 2011), while in LA the governments of Argentina, Chile, and Uruguay are strong supporters of GM crops (see Newell 2009). Another important observation is that the cultivation ban on GM maize represents the policy item with the lowest number of events of policy change. Of the twenty-eight countries under study, only ten promulgated relevant

Table 5.7 Cultivation bans for genetically modified maize

States	Dates	Legal acts	Lifting of ban
Central and Eastern Europe			
Bulgaria	2010/11	Genetically Modified Organisms Act	–
Hungary	2005	Announcement of the Ministry of Agriculture	–
Poland	2005	Governmental announcement	–
Latin America			
Bolivia	2009	Constitution (art. 255)	–
Brazil	1999	Federal court rulings	2005
Ecuador	2008	Constitution (art. 401)	–
El Salvador	2001	Planting Seed Law (art. 30)	2008
Mexico	1998	Governmental announcement	–
Paraguay	1993	Environmental Impact Assessment Law 294	–
Peru	2011	Moratorium	–

Note: Only (temporary/partial) nationwide bans based on legally binding law or court rulings are reported. Latvia excluded because there only local bans can be instituted.

legislation that prohibits the commercial cultivation of GM maize. This corresponds to a share of about 27 per cent in the CEE countries and about 41 per cent in the LA countries. In fact, for the first time in this study the LA countries turn out to be more susceptible to policy change than the CEE countries. However, the countries in LA are also those that appear more unsteady concerning their regulatory approach to GM maize, as shown by the cases of Brazil and El Salvador. In contrast to the expectation regarding the pattern of policy change presented in chapter 4, the regulation of GM maize is susceptible to a bidirectional dynamics – and this within a relatively short period of time.

Adoption of Sustainable Forest Management

During the 1990s, the CEE countries adopted a variety of forest policy tools, including measures related to the protection, use, and management of forests. The change in forest policy must be seen against the background of the situation under state socialism, which was characterized by the dominant role of the state. In this system, forests were not only state-owned, but forest management was also based on plans elaborated by the central authority (Nordberg 2007). After the collapse of state socialism, it was obvious that the conditions of the forest sector had changed profoundly and that reforms were necessary.

This process was also accelerated by the fact that SFM has an economic dimension, as it yields important implications for the production and trade of lumber products (see Laaksonen-Craig 2004; Nijnik and Oskam 2004). Hence, it comes as no surprise that all the eleven CEE countries under study introduced SFM within a relatively short period of eight years.

The first country to introduce SFM was Poland through the promulgation of the Forest Act in 1991. It was followed by the Slovak Forestry Policy Act and the Slovenian Forest Act (both enacted in 1993) as well as the Lithuanian and Ukrainian Forest Codes of 1994. The Czech Forest Act was launched in 1995. Then, in the period from 1996 to 1998, Hungary, Bulgaria, Estonia, Latvia, and then Romania reformed their forest legislation to include SFM. Some of the forest legislation is remarkably progressive. The Slovak Forestry Policy Act, for instance, is based on both biological and ecological principles and aims at the promotion and fulfilment of the production, protection, and environmental functions of forests. In this respect, it takes into account a wide range of measures to effectively fulfill the principle of SFM (Šulek 2000).

The fact that most countries introduced SFM via general forest acts further indicates that changes in approaches to forest management occurred in the context of more general forest policy reforms. Only Romania represents an exception, as there is not one single piece of legislation prescribing SFM, but an extensive and very explicit set of guidelines, that is, the Forest Management Technical Norms, which were completed in 1998 (Sandulescu et al. 2007). In this context, it is interesting to note that the Romanian government seems to attach high priority to the implementation of SFM, as it exempts companies from paying their contribution to the national environmental fund if they buy their wood from certified forests. Conversely, if they purchase non-certified wood, the companies have to pay a contribution of three per cent of the value of the wood to the national environmental fund (Environmental Technologies Action Plan 2007).

Considering that the LA countries have extended forest areas, the adoption of the SFM principle represents a major issue with regard to both the preservation of biodiversity and long-term timber production. In recent years, legal initiatives to increase the sustainability of forest management have proliferated. In this regard, Venezuela was the first LA country to introduce SFM. In 1988, the Ministry of Environment and Renewable Natural Resources presented the National Plan for the Development of Forest Resources, which already included SFM (see Silva 1997: 381). Eleven countries introduced SFM during the 1990s: Nicaragua (1992), Brazil (1994), Panama (1994), Paraguay (1995), Bolivia (1996), Colombia (1996), Costa Rica (1996), Guatemala (1996), Honduras (1996), Argentina (1997), Mexico (1997), and Peru (1997). The remaining seven countries adopted SFM in the 2000s: Ecuador (2000), El Salvador (2002), Uruguay (2002), and Chile (2007).

Of this latter group of countries, the case of Chile is certainly the most interesting one. Indeed, the Chilean Native Forest Law had been in negotiation for fifteen years before the parliament unanimously approved the law in December 2007. The bill that the administration of Chilean president Patricio Aylwin introduced to the legislature in 1992 included some mild elements of a "grassroots" approach to forest management, including the idea of establishing a fiscal incentive program that would cover most of the costs of native forest management and which was accessible to small and medium-sized landowners, as well as the objective of protecting native forests against clear-cutting by industrial interests. Because of these elements, the bill generated turbulent political conflict and was blocked in the Chilean congress (Silva 1997: 378–9). However, after a long political struggle, some of these elements seem to have survived, as the adopted law not only considers forests as an economic resource, but also establishes funds for forest conservation, recovery, and sustainable management projects. In addition, it aims to strengthen scientific and technological research related to native forests and the protection of its biodiversity.

Figure 5.1 displays the policy adoption patterns for both regions, which were standardized to the number of the LA countries (that is, seventeen) in order to facilitate comparison. The figure shows that all the countries included in the sample had introduced the SFM principle by the end of 2007. The main difference between the two regions is that in LA the inclusion of SFM into the forest legislation took place over a longer period of time. The policy adoption process in the CEE countries, by contrast, was already completed in 1998 with the adoption of the Romanian Forest Management Technical Norms. Hence, it took the CEE countries only eight years to adopt the SFM principle, whereas the LA countries needed about two decades to complete the process. The differentiation in the respective regional adoption paces mainly occurred around 1997. The figure shows that the adoption curve for the LA countries was also very steep in the early 1990s, but then started to level off.

Figure 5.1 Standardized diffusion patterns for sustainable forest management

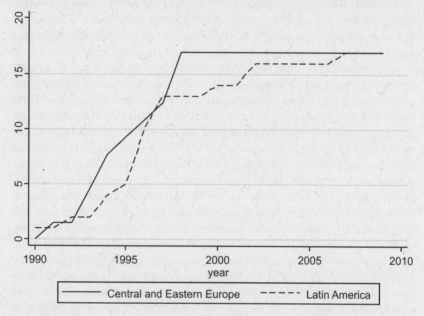

Note: The data for the Central and Eastern European countries were transformed to reflect the same maximum number of policy adoptions as the Latin American countries.

Changes in Environmental Regulations: Summary and Discussion

This section examined whether environmental regulatory standards have become stricter in CEE and LA countries since 1990. In terms of the regulation of soil pollution and SFM, the descriptive analysis demonstrated that there was exclusively upward policy change in both regions. Concerning the regulation of water pollution, there was a trend in the data indicating upward change, although there were also some instances of downward change. Even more difficult to evaluate is the development of air quality standards and the regulation of GM maize. In the case of ozone standards, the CEE countries in particular displayed many instances of downward change. Regarding the regulation of GM maize, the data revealed that this policy area is predominantly marked by the absence of cultivation restrictions. Of the twenty-eight countries under study, only ten have imposed a (temporary/partial) nationwide ban on the cultivation of MON810 maize. Moreover, two LA countries that had previously enacted bans, that is, Brazil and El Salvador, revoked them in the course of the observation period, which further complicates the interpretation of the overall regulatory situation.

Another major finding refers to the legacies of the state-socialist regulatory system in the CEE countries, which, especially in the early transition phase, led to the definition of overtly stringent limit values. While most CEE countries adopted more realistic regulatory standards from the mid-1990s onward, Ukraine still displays a tendency to promulgate excessively strict limit values. This became particularly apparent with the limit values defined for BOD concentrations in waste-water discharges and ozone standards. As concerns the policy items addressing soil pollution, GM maize, and SFM, the empirical data for Ukraine looked, however, quite unremarkable. The legacy of the state-socialist regulatory approach, without question, again complicates the interpretation of the direction of change, since departures from the previous regulatory system, that is, one characterized by the definition of unrealistically strict limit values, may look like a lowering of regulatory stringency. In fact, however, in most cases the adoption of numerically laxer standards by the governments of CEE countries implies an improvement of the environmental policy arrangements, since the previous regulations were too strict to allow proper implementation.

Furthermore, the descriptive analysis revealed that many LA countries still lack basic environmental regulations such as air quality standards, limit values for PAH emissions into soil, and legal provisions concerning the commercial growing of GM maize. In this sense, it is important to stress that the problems of environmental degradation in emerging market democracies do not merely result from insufficient compliance with legislation as generally stated in the literature. Rather, they are also likely to be caused by the absence of formal regulations. Thus, the empirical evidence does not confirm the common impression that environmental standards are omnipresent yet not enforced in LA countries (see, e.g., McAllister 2008: 12).

The second question addressed in this section was whether there are significant differences in the regulatory approaches of CEE and LA countries. Except for the regulation of GM maize and SFM, the descriptive analyses revealed that the countries in CEE experienced more events of policy change than those in the LA. This is even more remarkable when one recalls that the legislation in place in the CEE countries before 1990 was not taken into consideration. Moreover, the average regulatory levels in CEE surpass the standards adopted by LA countries. In this context, it was also surprising to observe that the regulatory differences between both regions were sometimes not very marked. For instance, with respect to the regulation of air pollution, Brazil, Chile, Colombia, Costa Rica, Ecuador, El Salvador, and Peru adopted standards that are identical to those prescribed by the EU and the WHO. As a result, with regard to this policy item, these seven LA countries are more similar to the CEE countries than to the other LA countries.

However, the regulatory approaches vary not only across the regions, but also across the individual policy items. Table 5.8 gives an overview of those countries that were identified as particularly strict regulators. For the regulation of air, soil, and water pollution, the ranking is based on the mean stringency of the standards, taking into account all events of policy change. Concerning GM maize and SFM, the ranking is based on the timing of policy change, meaning that for these two items the table displays those countries that were particularly swift in adopting these two policies. The table highlights the fact that the rank of a country is likely to change when one looks at different policy items. Of the CEE countries, Poland is the only one that appears four times in the group of the strictest regulators, whereas Brazil is the LA country that is most often named in the table, that is, three times. The CEE countries that are never assigned to this top group are Latvia, Lithuania, and Romania. Likewise, Ecuador, Peru and the Central American countries are characterized by comparatively lax environmental protection standards. As concerns the remaining CEE and LA countries, they display a notable volatility concerning their appearance in the ranking.

To sum up, this section illustrated that the empirical realities do not allow for easy conclusions with regard to environmental policy change in CEE and LA. Policy change turned out to be characterized by both upward and downward changes. In addition, the setting of environmental protection standards in the CEE countries was initially still affected by the state-socialist regulatory approach. Furthermore, it is difficult to make general statements about the stringency of environmental policy in a country. As table 5.8 demonstrates, a country can belong to the group of strictest regulators for one policy item, but adopt comparatively lax regulations for the other ones. Therefore, employing a large number of policy items can be considered as a prerequisite for being able to make robust statements about the patterns and determinants of environmental policy change.

Table 5.8 Top-ranking countries

Rank	Water		Air		Soil		GM Maize		Forestry	
	CEE	LA	CEE	LA	CEE	LA	CEE	LA	CEE	LA
1	Estonia	Argentina	Ukraine	Colombia	Hungary	Argentina	Hungary	Paraguay	Poland	Venezuela
2	Ukraine	Venezuela	Poland	Chile	Bulgaria	Bolivia	Poland	Mexico	Slovakia	Nicaragua
3	Poland	Uruguay	Estonia	Brazil	Slovenia	Mexico	Bulgaria	Brazil	Slovenia	Brazil

Diffusion of Environmental Procuracies

Most empirical studies of policymaking in emerging market democracies emphasize that environmental degradation does not result from a lack of legislation but from an insufficient capacity or willingness to enforce the rules in place (see, e.g., Desai 1998; Holzinger and Knoepfel 2000; McAllister 2008; Buzogány 2009a). Certainly, these studies make an important point. As an example, plant-level inspections were extremely high in Mexico during the early 1990s when considerable international scrutiny was directed at the country in the context of the NAFTA debate. However, the enforcement efforts subsided once NAFTA entered into force (Mumme 1998). Even during the period when plant-level inspections were at their highest rate, inspectors visited only about 6 per cent of all establishments in the manufacturing sector (Gallagher 2002: 135). A similar observation was made for Bulgaria, where the government (temporarily) allowed enterprises to opt out of complying with more stringent air pollution regulations (Andonova 2004: 181). In this context, another major problem is represented by the existence of inappropriate institutions as pointed out by Karaczun (2005). He questions whether regulations aimed at a reduction of nitrate pollution of water by agriculture will be properly implemented in Poland, as there is insufficient institutional development.

Consequently, to evaluate environmental policy change in CEE and LA in a realistic manner, the issue of regulatory enforcement somehow has to be addressed. This study tackles it in a simplified way by analysing changes in the institutions in charge of regulatory enforcement. This means that it does not directly address the effectiveness of policy enforcement in the sense of whether the compliance with laws actually improves. Instead, the focus is on the governments' observable decisions to increase the costs of non-compliance through the creation of consequential enforcement institutions. In other words, the study examines whether "weak" administrative institutions are replaced by "strong" legal ones (McAllister 2008). Legal institutions can impose often severe criminal sanctions that are connected with social blame, which facilitates their serving as a deterrent preventing non-compliance with environmental protection standards (Bar 2004: 217). In this way, the involvement of prosecutors may reinforce otherwise weak environmental inspectorates and establish a more consequential enforcement regime (see, e.g., McAllister 2008; McAllister et al. 2010; Mueller 2010; for a discussion, see Blanc 2013).

Generally speaking, a broader public discussion on the importance of legal actions for improving compliance with environmental laws has just begun. In this context, some initiatives were launched in order to harmonize environmental prosecution at the European level. Directive 2008 / 99 / EC on the protection of the environment through criminal law, for instance, requires member states to apply criminal sanctions to breaches of any of a large number of EU directives and regulations. So far, however, the EU does not demand the establishment of environmental procuracies. Hence, the decision to establish an environmental procuracy or a specialized unit in charge of enforcing environmental law within the public prosecutor's office is one taken independently by national governments.

As already stated above, the literature has long suggested that CEE countries are not properly implementing their environmental regulations. In the meantime, these countries have invested significantly in increasing their institutional capacities to enforce environmental legislation. The Bulgarian government, for instance, which Andonova (2004) identified as struggling with proper regulatory enforcement, raised the sanctions for non-compliance and empowered the environmental inspectorate, which since 2004 can forward detected cases of environmental offences to the public prosecutor's office. Yet Bulgaria is not the only country that created environmental prosecution institutions. In fact, by the year 2004 all CEE countries had established such institutions.

The pioneering countries were the Czech Republic and Ukraine, which established specialized environmental-prosecutor departments within the public prosecutor's office in 1991. The Ukrainian case is particularly interesting, since the enforcement institution has significant authority to enforce environmental laws through the possibility of criminal prosecution (Parker and Smelik 2008: 411). This competency is based on the Law on the Protection of the Natural Environment, which previews administrative, criminal, civil, and disciplinary responsibility for violations of environmental law. Nevertheless, this institutional characteristic is often overlooked. For example, in its otherwise very comprehensive overview of the Ukrainian environmental protection arrangements, the United Nations Economic Commission for Europe (UNECE; 2007: 33–40) only examines the role of the ecological inspectorate, completely leaving aside the existing environmental prosecutor's department.

In 1992, the Slovak Criminal Act was amended and introduced new categories of criminal offences in relation to the environment (Huba 1997). As a consequence, a special environmental department was created within the prosecutor general's office. Hungary created an environmental procuracy in 1997 on the basis of substantive amendments made to Articles 280 and 281 of the Criminal Code (Bándi 2004: 132; see also Julesz 2010: 3). The Baltic States founded comparable institutions between 1997 and 1999. However, they do not possess encompassing environmental-prosecutor departments, but instead single prosecutors dealing with violations of environmental law. In light of the small size and the concentrated industrial activities in the Baltic States, this institutional design still seems to be appropriate. A similar system exists in Poland, where since 2002 some prosecutors address environmental issues when necessary. The reform of the Slovenian Penal Code in 2002 provided the basis for creating a Unit for Offences against the Environment, Space and Natural Amenities. In Romania, the National Environmental Guard set up in 2003 is in charge of investigating and prosecuting environmental offences (Ministry of Waters and Environmental Protection 2003).

As figure 5.2 shows, in many LA countries also independent environmental procuracies have been created or the public prosecutor's offices have been constitutionally charged with defending environmental interests. The first country to introduce such an environmental procuracy was Venezuela, which must be seen in the context of the enactment of the 1992 Penal Law of the Environment. The next ones to follow were the Central American states of Costa Rica (1993), Honduras (1993), El Salvador (1996), Guatemala (1996), Nicaragua (1996), and Panama (1998) (see Sbert 2004). In Brazil, the first prosecutorial activities were already carried out in the 1980s in the state of São Paulo. However, it was only with the enactment of the Brazilian Environmental Crimes Act in 1998 that an environmental procuracy was established at the federal level (Kellman 2002). In 1999 Paraguay established a specific Department for the Prosecution of Environmental Offences. Again, the broader context for institutionalizing legal actions against environmental offences was the new penal code. The Mexican General Directorate on Federal Environmental Crimes and Prosecution was created within the context of the reorganization of the Federal Attorney General for Environmental Protection in 2001 (Medina 2001). In the 2000s Ecuador (2001), Colombia (2003), Argentina (2006), and Peru (2007) established environmental procuracies.

Figure 5.2 Standardized diffusion patterns for environmental procuracies

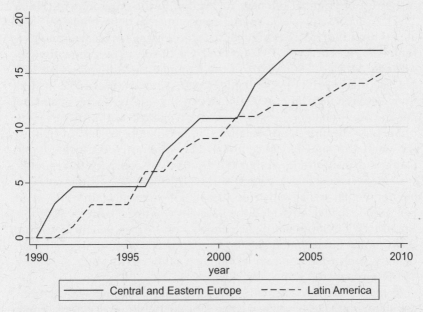

For a long time, enforcement in Chile relied on the coordination of various sectoral bodies endowed with inspection and prosecution authority, resulting in what the OECD (2005: 115) in its evaluation of the country's environmental performance called "not the most effective institutional arrangement to assure compliance." In reaction to this performance report and the country's desire to join the OECD, the Chilean government started a process of strengthening its environmental institutions. As a result, Law 20.417, adopted in January 2010, increased penalties and strengthened civil and criminal prosecution mechanisms for environmental violations as well as redesigning Chile's environmental enforcement institutions by creating the superintendence of the environment. This institution is in charge of executing and coordinating the surveillance of compliance with environmental regulations (Urrutia Riesco and Correa Achurra 2010: 69). In marked contrast to all other LA countries, Bolivia and Uruguay still lack environmental prosecution institutions.

As with SFM, the pattern of institutional change follows an S-shaped curve, which is typical for a diffusion process. The shape of the curve indicates that events of institutional change rise slowly at first, when relatively few governments establish legal institutions for enforcing environmental laws. Then, the curve takes off as more governments establish institutions endowed with the authority of prosecuting environmental offences. After a while, however, most governments will have established them and the diffusion curve begins to level off. This final stage of levelling off is observable for the CEE countries, as they all created enforcement institutions. Regarding the LA countries, by contrast, the curve at the end of the observation period is still quite steep, indicating that the diffusion process has not yet been completed. From this it can be concluded that at the aggregate level the governments of the CEE countries were swifter in strengthening their commitment to regulatory enforcement than those of the LA countries.

Conclusion

This chapter offered a first empirical consideration of this study's subject of interest, namely, changes in the governments' commitment to regulatory enforcement and strictness of environmental policy. To this end, it addressed the following three questions: Have environmental regulatory standards become stricter? Have the countries established environmental procuracies? Are there notable differences between the two regions? With respect to the first question, on average, the regulatory strictness increased over time in both regions regardless of the policy item under scrutiny. This development became most apparent with regard to the regulation of soil pollution and the adoption of the SFM principle. However, the empirical data on the regulation of water and air pollution as well as GM maize also showed that policy change is bidirectional, that is, it implies both a tightening and a relaxation of the regulatory level.

Most remarkable is the relaxation of the limit values for ozone concentrations, which in the CEE countries occurred immediately after they became accepted as EU members, that is, in the period from 2002 to 2004. One suggestive interpretation of this scenario is that the accession candidates simply responded to the incentives provided by the EU (see Andonova 2004: 25). To be sure, it would have been possible for all these states to preserve their more stringent national air protection standards, since the EU merely prescribes minimum standards that can be exceeded (see Holzinger and Knill 2008). Nevertheless, most CEE states decided to relax their ozone standards to bring them in line with the EU minimum standard. Hence, the CEE countries were unwilling to bear higher-than-necessary regulatory costs, indicating that they are indeed aware of competitive concerns when defining environmental policy.

A more general explanation of the downward adjustment in CEE refers to the regulatory legacies of the state-socialist system. In this sense, the relaxation of the overtly strict limit values in the course of system transformation might be seen as a learning process that motivated the setting of enforceable standards. Against this background, the relative persistence of the former approach to environmental regulation was one of the most surprising findings of this descriptive analysis. In this regard, Ukraine is certainly the CEE country that still predominantly relies on the old regulatory approach when setting environmental protection standards.

The reasoning about practicability considerations might also explain why Guatemala and Mexico reduced the strictness of their effluent standards. Various studies suggest that emerging market democracies tend to promulgate standards that are often copied from more advanced states and are therefore "overtly stringent and unrealistically suited to local conditions" (Oakley et al. 2000: 52). Based on the descriptive data presented in this chapter, one cannot explain what induces emerging market democracies to act in this way. Yet, it does not seem too daring to argue that the lowering of regulatory standards might indeed be associated with the objective of enhancing the enforceability of regulations in light of increasing environmental degradation.

The final section of this chapter demonstrated that a growing number of countries in both regions set up enforcement institutions with prosecutorial discretion. Two LA countries, however, have not displayed an enhanced commitment yet. While for Bolivia this finding is not overtly surprising, it is somehow puzzling for Uruguay, as this country is generally associated with an effective enforcement of environmental laws (see, e.g., Esty and Porter 2005; Porter, Schwab, and Lopez-Claros 2005: 612). More generally, the CEE countries were swifter than their LA counterparts in creating institutions endowed with the competence to prosecute environmental offences.

Turning to the final question, as concerns the regulation of water, air, and soil pollution, it can safely be stated that the CEE countries outperform the LA countries. The gap between them became in fact most visible with the regulation of soil contamination. Of the seventeen LA countries under scrutiny, only seven regulated soil pollution through contamination with PAHs. Less drastic is the situation for effluent standards, which are also rampant in LA countries, albeit defined at notably lower regulatory levels. Only with the regulation of GM maize was the share of LA countries adopting bans found to be higher than the share of CEE countries having relevant regulations in place. In this regard, however, it must also be noted that of the seven LA countries that introduced bans on the cultivation of GM maize, two revoked them again before the observation period ended. While some LA countries seem to become more critical of the growing of GM maize and GM crops in general, it is difficult to discern a uniform regulatory tendency for the region as a whole. In fact, countries such as Argentina and Chile represent influential supporters of GM crops, making it unlikely that the entire region will eventually be against their cultivation. The same ambivalence applies to the CEE countries, where both supporters and opponents of GM crops can be found. Finally, there is one policy item for which no significant differences could be detected across the regions, namely, sustainable forestry.

To conclude, the results presented in this chapter already drew attention to the different forms of policy and institutional change, thereby underscoring that these are demanding analytical concepts that do not allow for easy conclusions. However, the exploratory analysis provided a first picture only. Most notably, the analysis hitherto has neglected the impact of covariates, and has mostly focused on a descriptive cross-regional comparison. What is still missing is an analysis of why policy and institutional changes occur. Some suggestive explanations were given in the chapter, but these cannot substitute for a proper testing of hypotheses. How can the cross-country differences be explained? Which factors induce events of policy and institutional change? These questions will be addressed in the next chapter.

6 Economy, Politics, Institutions, or Demand? A Causal Analysis of Change

The descriptive empirical analysis conducted in chapter 5 demonstrated that in the last two decades most of the emerging market democracies under study noticeably strengthened their environmental policy arrangements. In this context, a central finding was that the CEE countries tend to outperform the LA countries in the strictness of their environmental policies. In addition, the CEE countries were shown to be generally more prone to policy change than their LA counterparts. One tentative explanation for this finding is that the CEE countries' accession to the EU triggered major environmental policy reforms. However, without a more systematic causal analysis, it cannot be said how influential EU accession has actually been for inducing policy change.

It is thus the objective of this chapter to empirically test the relevance of economic integration, domestic politics, and public demand along with the potential role of the EU for bringing about policy and institutional change. Which of these factors are the most important ones? Does their relevance vary across the policy items? Are enforcement decisions driven by the same factors that affect regulatory decisions? These three questions guide this chapter, which begins with some general clarifications concerning the empirical testing strategy. Subsequently, the findings for each of the six dependent variables are presented. These sections will show that the explanatory model yields many insights about the main drivers of change for five of the six dependent variables. It is, however, less suitable for pinpointing the causes for the regulation of GM maize. In light of this finding, this chapter will conclude that this policy item should be re-examined by using a more fine-grained research design.

Clarifications on the Empirical Testing Strategy

The empirical analyses to be carried out in this chapter are based on a regression framework consisting of six dependent variables and a linear combination of independent variables. Regarding the analysis of water, air, and soil pollution, the estimation models are specified in such a way that they explain the absolute levels of the dependent variables. This allows for taking into account both initial regulatory levels and changes to them. In contrast, the models treating the regulation of GM maize, SFM, and environmental prosecution units as dependent variables only measure the one-time occurrence of change. This different analytical lens results from the characteristics of the empirical data employed for assessing these policy items as discussed in chapters 4 and 5.

The dependent variables are linked to the independent variables through the generic estimation equations 6.1 and 6.2. In the first equation, "policy" stands for all five policy items and whether and how they are regulated in i countries in year t. "Institution" in the second equation indicates the assessment of enforcement commitment in terms of institutional change. The independent variables refer to the values for i countries in year t, reflecting the structure of pooled data. The notation $t-1$ indicates that the variables are lagged by one year to establish causality (see Lieberson 1987). Only the variables *EU accession* and *EU membership* are not lagged, as these variables already cover a long period of time and their joint use should adequately model different types of integration-related incentives for reforms.

$$
\begin{aligned}
\text{Policy}_{it} = \beta_0 + \textbf{FDI}_{it-1} + \textbf{Exports}_{it-1} + \text{Liberal government}_{it-1} \\
+ \text{Green government}_{it-1} + \text{Liberal president}_{it-1} + \text{NGOs}_{it-1} \\
+ \textbf{EU accession}_{it} + \textbf{EU membership}_{it} + \text{Income}_{it-1} \\
+ \text{Salience}_{it-1} + e
\end{aligned} \tag{6.1}
$$

$$
\begin{aligned}
\text{Institution}_{it} = \beta_0 + \textbf{FDI}_{it-1} + \textbf{Exports}_{it-1} + \text{Liberal government}_{it-1} \\
+ \text{Green government}_{it-1} + \text{Liberal president}_{it-1} \\
+ \text{INGOs}_{it-1} + \textbf{EU accession}_{it} + \textbf{EU membership}_{it} \\
+ \text{Income}_{it-1} + \text{Salience}_{it-1} + e
\end{aligned} \tag{6.2}
$$

In substantive terms, equation 6.1 states that the stringency of environmental policies is a linear function of the total inward FDI stock (*FDI*), the share of exports to industrialized countries (*Exports*), the partisan characteristics of the government and president (*Liberal government*,

Green government, and *Liberal president*), the cumulative number of environmental groups (*NGOs*), integration with the EU (*EU accession* and *EU membership*), *Income*, and the extent to which an environmental issue represents a public problem (*Salience*). The variable *Salience*, we may recall, is defined in a specific way for each of the five policy items and is accordingly also measured in different ways. Equation 6.2 follows the same logic; the only difference relates to the substitution of *INGOs* for *NGOs*. As explained in chapter 3, it is expected that the number of transnationally interlinked environmental groups matters for setting up an institution in charge of enforcement rather than the overall cumulative number of environmental groups.

The basic idea underlying the estimation equations is the following. The relationship between the variables shall be estimated several times to check the robustness of the findings. At the same time, though, the number of regressors shall be kept as low as possible to achieve parsimony. A parsimonious model is preferable for the present case, since with pooled data the actual number of cases is not as high as the number of observations might suggest (see, e.g., Kittel 1999; Kittel and Winner 2005). To accomplish this, the estimation equations consist of a "fixed" part and a "variable" part, of which the latter is printed in bold letters. The fixed part refers to those covariates that are included in all model specifications. The variable part contains those covariates that are somehow conceptually related to one another, which entails that they might absorb each other's effects. To avoid this, reduced models are fitted that contain only one of these variables at one time.

Another reason for applying this approach is given by potential problems of endogeneity. Endogenous variables have causal links with other variables in the model. For example, a country that is a member of the EU is also more likely to depend on exports to other EU members and to receive more investments from them. Although *EU accession* and *EU membership* refer to another theoretical construct, that is, international institutional integration, using these variables together with *Exports* and *FDI* might lead to wrong conclusions. Hence, computing multiple models within which some "critical" variables are sequentially included can be expected to limit these problems.

What are the implications of this proceeding for the testing of hypotheses? As a rule, a hypothesis is regarded as confirmed if the relevant variable produces a significant coefficient with the anticipated sign. More precisely, the coefficient has to be significant for at least one of the model specifications. Yet, if a coefficient is only significant in the full model, it is not regarded as a stable finding due to the problems discussed above. Consequently, the finding for the variable in question will not be interpreted as a confirmation of the hypothesis.

Explaining Changes in the Regulation of Organic Water Pollution

This study assesses changes in the strictness of water pollution regulations on the basis of transformed limit values for BOD in industrial waste-water emitted into continental water bodies. Limit values generally consist of only non-negative integers and represent an example of interval-scale measurement. Usually, such a scale of measurement allows for employing linear estimation models for pooled data (see, e.g., Beck and Katz 1995; Plümper, Troeger, and Manow 2005). As illustrated in appendix 2, the data at hand, however, display two characteristics that impede the use of such standard estimation models. First, about 27 per cent of all observed data points are zeros. Applying linear models to data that are marked by the excessive presence of zeros might lead to inconsistent estimators (Long 1997: 188–91).[1] Second, and related to the first, the data are considerably skewed and have a non-normal kurtosis.

Both problems of the data can be addressed by fitting a Tobit model, a specific estimation technique first proposed by James Tobin (1958). It is a regression-like model that works with a linear combination of explanatory variables, but allows them to be related to the "limited" dependent variable in a nonlinear way through a particular link function. More precisely, it takes into account the partly continuous and partly discrete distribution of the dependent variable. In this way, Tobit models utilize the entire empirical information and hence provide consistent estimates of the parameters. Another important feature of Tobit models is that they can be applied to the natural log of the dependent variable. This transformation ensures a more symmetrical distribution and rather normal kurtosis of the dependent variable, which can be expected to improve the performance of the estimation models (Cameron and Trivedi 2010: 545–9).

Table 6.1 presents the estimates of the random-effects Tobit model for lognormal data. To take into account that the data are clustered at the country level, the estimations are based on bootstrapped standard errors (Baum 2006: 266). To check the sensitivity of the estimation results, a total of five models were specified. Model 1 is the full model, including all covariates. Models 2 through 5 have a reduced number of those

Table 6.1 Random-effects Tobit model for the standards for biological oxygen demand

Covariates	Model 1 β(tobit) [MEs]	Model 2 β(tobit) [MEs]	Model 3 β(tobit) [MEs]	Model 4 β(tobit) [MEs]	Model 5 β(tobit) [MEs]
FDI	0.028 (0.005)*** [0.014 (0.003)***]	0.030 (0.005)*** [0.014 (0.003)***]	– –	– –	– –
Exports	−0.022 (0.008)*** [−0.011 (0.005)**]	– –	−0.011 (0.008) [−0.005 (0.003)]	– –	– –
Liberal government	0.159 (0.145) [0.083 (0.069)]	0.226 (0.152) [0.108 (0.069)]	0.354 (0.152)** [0.159 (0.073)**]	0.313 (0.149)** [0.140 (0.061)**]	0.357 (0.160)** [0.158 (0.063)**]
Green government	−0.348 (0.255) [−0.176 (0.119)]	−0.317 (0.274) [−0.148 (0.129)]	−0.094 (0.275) [−0.042 (0.120)]	−0.046 (0.247) [−0.021 (0.110)]	−0.075 (0.279) [−0.033 (0.127)]
Liberal president	−0.015 (0.157) [−0.008 (0.087)]	−0.092 (0.156) [−0.044 (0.076)]	−0.190 (0.153) [−0.085 (0.072)]	−0.179 (0.162) [−0.080 (0.080)]	−0.225 (0.178) [−0.099 (0.069)]
NGOs	0.348 (0.078)*** [0.181 (0.033)***]	0.508 (0.110)*** [0.242 (0.035)***]	0.577 (0.102)*** [0.259 (0.042)***]	0.516 (0.106)*** [0.231 (0.040)***]	0.587 (0.115)*** [0.260 (0.044)***]
EU accession	1.111 (0.301)*** [0.628 (0.210)***]	–	–	0.587 (0.216)*** [0.270 (0.121)**]	–
EU membership	0.816 (0.381)** [0.451 (0.264)*]	– –	– –	– –	0.422 (0.298) [0.191 (0.133)]
Income	−0.001 (0.004) [−0.001 (0.002)]	−0.002 (0.004) [−0.001 (0.002)]	0.014 (0.003)*** [0.006 (0.001)***]	0.016 (0.004)*** [0.007 (0.002)***]	0.008 (0.005) [0.004 (0.002)]
Water	−0.077 (0.022)*** [−0.040 (0.010)***]	−0.104 (0.018)*** [−0.050 (0.009)***]	−0.128 (0.020)*** [−0.058 (0.009)***]	−0.136 (0.020)*** [−0.061 (0.008)***]	−0.146 (0.023)*** [−0.065 (0.007)***]
Wald Chi2 (DF)	275.13 (10)***	191.04 (7)***	132.05 (7)***	120.00 (7)***	109.46 (7)***
Rho	0.85	0.91	0.94	0.94	0.94
Observations	560	560	560	560	560
Cases	28	28	28	28	28

Note: Dependent variable = logged BOD limit values; MEs = marginal effects; DF = degrees of freedom; estimation is based on 36 integration points; bootstrapped standard errors in parentheses; * significant at 10%; ** significant at 5%; *** significant at 1%.

regressors that are related to the impact of economic and institutional integration. Model 2 particularly tests the hypothesis on regulatory competition as it contains the variable *FDI*, whereas model 3 assesses the validity of the California effect by means of the variable *Exports*. The latter two models address the impact of *EU accession* and *EU membership*. The table reports the β-coefficients and the marginal effects of the truncated expected values measuring changes in the logged dependent variable regarding changes in the regressors among the subpopulation for which the dependent variable is different from zero.

The variables that are found to have a significant impact in accordance with the theoretical expectations are *NGOs*, *EU accession*, *Income*, and *Water*. To illustrate the interpretation of the Tobit coefficients, we rely on the effect of *NGOs* in model 5, as it represents the model with the greatest coefficient. If the dependent variable was not censored at zero, a one-unit increase in the per capita density of environmental groups (*NGOs*) would increase the logged strictness of effluent standards by 0.59 regulatory units. The corresponding marginal effect on the censored expected value suggests that for emerging market democracies that have relevant legislation in place (i.e., when the dependent variable is unequal to zero), a one-unit increase in *NGOs* raises the logged stringency of waste-water regulations by about 0.26 regulatory units.

Likewise, BOD limit values should become stricter if a country receives the status of an *EU accession* candidate and with rising *Income*, although the effect of the latter is only significant in models 3 and 4. The coefficient of the variable *EU membership* also displays a positive sign, but it is only significant in the full model and therefore its impact is not regarded as sufficiently stable. As concerns the access of emerging market democracies to freshwater resources (*Water*), the Tobit coefficients suggest a negative relationship. Hence, model 5 predicts that in countries having BOD limit values in place, improving access to freshwater reduces the logged stringency of the standards by 0.065 regulatory units. This finding is in line with the reasoning about the impact of environmental problem pressure. The better the access to freshwater resources, the lower is the incentive to protect water bodies from organic pollution, and conversely, the more likely becomes a reduction of regulatory standards.

Furthermore, the variables *FDI* and *Liberal government* display significant coefficients in at least two model specifications, but their signs contradict the causal relationships posited by the hypotheses. The positive sign of *FDI* indicates that increasing investment levels tend to have a positive effect on effluent standards. The finding for the variable *Liberal government* is equally interesting. Having an economically liberal party in government raises the logged strictness of effluent standards in emerging market democracies that have limit values in place by about 0.14 and 0.16 regulatory units, respectively. This finding is even more striking as the coefficients of the complementary variable, that is, *Green government*, are not significantly different from zero. One way of interpreting this finding is that economically liberal parties can become willing to support stricter effluent standards if they perceive them to be important for strengthening their country's economic competitiveness. This view matches well with the finding that the variable *FDI* has a positive impact on the tightening of effluent standards. Hence, under certain conditions political parties that are generally in favour of deregulation to foster economic growth can also become proponents of environmental protection standards. At the same time, however, this result underscores the empirical limitation of this study, as it assesses the environmental policy preferences of political parties on the basis of the static party-families approach. What this finding more generally shows is that even political parties that primarily focus on economic development do not automatically reject more demanding environmental protection standards.

Table 6.2 summarizes the main findings of the Tobit models and evaluates the hypotheses. Based on the estimation results, the hypotheses on the impact of *NGOs*, *EU accession*, *Income*, and *Water* can be confirmed. As already explained above, the effect of *EU membership* is deemed too unstable for one to compellingly argue that the corresponding hypothesis is confirmed. Similarly unstable is the finding for *Exports*, which produces a significant coefficient only in the full model.

Concerning the model fit, the significant statistics of the Wald test indicate that the models are specified correctly. The intra-cluster correlation coefficient *rho* further indicates that the principal source of variation in the data is due to differences across countries and not to time. Remarkably, between 85 and 94 per cent of the total variance can be attributed to the country-level variance component. If we recall the descriptive analysis of the data in chapter 5, this finding comes as no surprise, as it was already shown there that some countries modified their limit values for BOD concentrations only once during the observation period. However, such a large value of *rho* may entail that the quadrature approximation for calculating the random-effects model becomes inaccurate. Therefore, a sensitivity check of the quadrature

Table 6.2 Findings for the standards for biological oxygen demand

Mechanisms	Variables	Signs expected	Signs observed	Support for hypothesis
Economic integration				
Regulatory competition (H 1.1)	FDI	−	+	No
California effect (H 1.2)	Exports	+	0	No
Politics				
Party difference (H 2.1)	Green government	+	0	No
Party difference (H 2.2)	Liberal government	−	+	No
Party difference (H 2.3)	Liberal president	−	0	No
Lobbying (H 2.4)	NGOs	+	+	Yes
Institutional integration				
Learning (H 3.1)	Cooperation (EU accession)	+	+	Yes
Learning (H 3.1)	Cooperation (EU membership)	+	0	No
Public demand				
Functional response (H 4.1)	Income	+	+	Yes
Functional response (H 4.2)	Salience (Water)	−	−	Yes

Note: + = positive relationship; − = negative relationship; 0 = no stable effect.

approximation is needed (Stata Corporation 2005: 334). To this end, the model estimations are rerun using two different numbers of quadrature points. As appendix 3 shows, when the number of quadrature points are changed, the coefficients do not change by more than a relative difference of 0.01 per cent, indicating that the results can be confidently interpreted.

Explaining Changes in Air Quality Standards

Similarly to the previous policy item, the data for ozone limit values reveal distributional properties that do not allow for using standard estimation techniques for pooled data. Again, there is an excessive presence of zeros within the data, indicating the need for running a Tobit model. As the histogram in appendix 4 shows, there is not much variance in the observed limit values. This specific feature of the data was already highlighted by the descriptive analysis carried out in chapter 5. As the skewness and kurtosis of the dependent variables does not improve when one takes the natural log, for this analysis the untransformed dependent variable is used. Yet, in order to approach the normal distribution as much as possible, the Tobit model is fitted in such a way as to take into account the upper limit, that is, the zeros, as well as a lower limit, which is given by the far-right observations of the dependent variable with 22.22 regulatory units. As the Tobit model relies on normality, the imposition of two limits should deliver more accurate estimates (see Cameron and Trivedi 2010: 545).

Table 6.3 presents the random-effects Tobit models for ozone standards with two censoring points. In addition to the Tobit coefficients, the marginal effects of the truncated expected values are reported to facilitate the interpretation of the results. The main difference vis-à-vis the Tobit models fitted for BOD limit values is that in the present case issue salience is measured by the variable CO_2, which indicates the annual level of CO_2 emission per capita.

The first noteworthy observation is that the Tobit models produce a considerable number of significant coefficients, albeit only a few of them correspond with the theoretical reasoning of the hypotheses, namely, NGOs and EU accession. According to model 2, if the limit values were not censored at 0 and 22.22, then a one-unit increase in the number of environmental groups (NGOs) would increase the stringency of air quality standards by 1.8 regulatory units. Further, the marginal effects indicate that for emerging market democracies that have a regulation

Table 6.3 Random-effects Tobit model for ozone standards

Covariates	Model 1 β(tobit) [MEs]	Model 2 β(tobit) [MEs]	Model 3 β(tobit) [MEs]	Model 4 β(tobit) [MEs]	Model 5 β(tobit) [MEs]
FDI	0.090 (0.019)*** [0.038 (0.007)***]	0.069 (0.015)*** [0.029 (0.007)***]	– –	– –	– –
Exports	−0.050 (0.030) [−0.021 (0.013)]	– –	−0.045 (0.036) [−0.019 (0.012)]	– –	– –
Liberal government	−0.207 (0.593) [−0.087 (0.303)]	0.032 (0.720) [0.013 (0.288)]	0.411 (0.627) [0.171 (0.262)]	0.211 (0.643) [0.090 (0.264)]	0.329 (0.672) [0.138 (0.249)]
Green government	0.122 (1.048) [0.051 (0.428)]	0.187 (1.052) [0.078 (0.491)]	0.782 (1.223) [0.329 (0.510)]	0.928 (1.018) [0.403 (0.475)]	0.962 (0.984) [0.408 (0.520)]
Liberal president	1.040 (0.593)* [0.439 (0.268)]	0.295 (0.23) [0.124 (0.307)]	−0.173 (0.643) [−0.072 (0.277)]	0.022 (0.582) [0.010 (0.319)]	−0.021 (0.615) [−0.009 (0.277)]
NGOs	1.725 (0.296)*** [0.723 (0.133)***]	1.800 (0.240)*** [0.751 (0.105)***]	1.766 (0.237)*** [0.734 (0.113)***]	1.509 (0.259)*** [0.645 (0.105)***]	1.726 (0.302)*** [0.722 (0.121)***]
EU accession	0.704 (1.680) [0.299 (0.658)]	– –	– –	3.179 (0.913)*** [1.430 (0.550)***]	– –
EU membership	−5.888 (2.098)** [−2.272 (0.719)***]	– –	– –	– –	−5.075 (1.474)*** [−1.975 (0.506)***]
Income	−0.025 (0.021) [−0.010 (0.008)]	−0.086 (0.018)*** [−0.036 (0.007)***]	−0.045 (0.014)*** [−0.019 (0.006)***]	−0.034 (0.016)** [−0.015 (0.007)**]	0.011 (0.020) [0.004 (0.009)]
CO_2	−0.158 (0.060)** [−0.066 (0.021)***]	−0.132 (0.055)** [−0.055 (0.021)***]	−0.173 (0.056)*** [−0.072 (0.020)***]	−0.125 (0.057)** [−0.053 (0.020)**]	−0.192 (0.058)*** [−0.080 (0.019)***]
Wald Chi2	101.24	70.33	68.24	59.10	45.26
(DF)	(10)***	(7)***	(7)***	(7)***	(7)***
Rho	0.91	0.90	0.91	0.89	0.91
Observations	560	560	560	560	560
Cases	28	28	28	28	28

Note: Dependent variable = ozone limit values; MEs = marginal effects; DF = degrees of freedom; estimation is based on 72 integration points; bootstrapped standard errors in parentheses; * significant at 10%; ** significant at 5%; *** significant at 1%.

in place that is different from 22.22 regulatory units, a one-unit increase in *NGOs* increases the regulatory stringency by 0.75 units. Likewise, receiving the status of an *EU accession* candidate entails a tightening of the limit values. Although the effect of *EU accession* is constrained to model 4, the corresponding hypothesis can still be regarded as confirmed, since model 1 is likely to be less accurate due to the possibility of multicollinearity.

In marked contrast, the signs of the variables *FDI*, *EU membership*, and CO_2 contradict the predictions of the theoretical framework. In theory, higher CO_2 emission levels should entail a stronger demand for stricter air quality standards. The findings of the Tobit models, however, suggest that there is a negative relationship between pollutant emissions and ozone standards. Therefore, the reasoning about issue salience cannot be confirmed. In a similar vein, *FDI* is found to have a positive impact on the stringency of air quality standards. The same result was observed for BOD limit values: in both cases, more foreign investment appears to induce stricter environmental policy arrangements.

Most striking is the negative sign of the coefficients produced by the variable *EU membership*. Although this result completely contradicts the theoretical expectations, it is still not very surprising, as the descriptive analysis in chapter 5 already drew attention to the fact that the CEE countries lowered their ozone standards in the context of adopting the environmental acquis. Hence, our previous interpretation of this finding can be confirmed on the basis of the Tobit model: the CEE countries preferred adopting the laxer European ozone standards over keeping their stricter domestic standards. Considering that Europeanization research often suggests that the policy implications of *EU membership* are positive (see, e.g., Holzinger and Knill 2005, 2008), the finding for ozone standards represents an important qualification of this viewpoint.

Table 6.4 presents the main results of the analysis. In sum, only the hypotheses on the positive impact of *NGOs* and *EU accession* can be confirmed. Concerning the other variables that turned out to yield a significant effect on ozone standards, that is, *FDI*, *EU membership*, and CO_2, the directions of the observed causal relationships contradict the hypotheses. Moreover, the variables *Exports*, *Liberal government*, *Green government*, and *Liberal president* were not found to have any impact on the dependent variable.

Turning to the model fit, the Wald tests indicate that the estimation models are unlikely to suffer from omitted variable bias. Similarly to the limit values for BOD, the intra-cluster correlation coefficient *rho* indicates that between 88 and 91 per cent of the total variance originates

Table 6.4 Findings for ozone standards

Mechanisms	Variables	Signs expected	Signs observed	Support for hypothesis
Economic integration				
Regulatory competition (H 1.1)	FDI	−	+	No
California effect (H 1.2)	Exports	+	0	No
Politics				
Party difference (H 2.1)	Green government	+	0	No
Party difference (H 2.2)	Liberal government	−	0	No
Party difference (H 2.3)	Liberal president	−	0	No
Party difference (H 2.1)	Green government	+	0	No
Party difference (H 2.2)	Liberal government	−	0	No
Party difference (H 2.3)	Liberal president	−	0	No
Lobbying (H 2.4)	NGOs	+	+	Yes
Institutional integration				
Harmonization (H 3.2)	Compliance (EU accession)	+	+	Yes
Harmonization (H 3.2)	Compliance (EU membership)	+	−	No
Public demand				
Functional response (H 4.1)	Income	+	−	No
Functional response (H 4.1)	Salience CO_2	+	−	No

Note: + = positive relationship; − = negative relationship; 0 = no stable effect.

from the country-level variance component, which again calls for the performance of a sensitivity check of the quadrature approximation. The results of the test reported in appendix 5 reveal that the coefficients do not change by more than a relative difference of 0.01 per cent, which confirms that the estimation results are sound.

Explaining Changes in the Regulation of Soil Pollution

The measurement of soil pollution regulations is based on a count variable that reflects the number of limit values defined for the emission of PAHs into soil used for agricultural purposes. The count data at hand deviate from the standard structure, since they are characterized by an excessive presence of zeros (see appendix 6). There are two reasons for this observation. First, by the end of the observation period a considerable number of LA countries had no limit values for PAHs in place. Second, even the CEE and LA countries that defined soil pollution standards mainly introduced them towards the end of the observation period, causing the observation of many zeros. Due to the preponderance of zeros, regular count models would lead to inaccurate standard errors and incorrect test statistics. Another characteristic of the data is that it is overdispersed, that is, the variance is greater than the mean.[2] In light of this data structure, the most appropriate estimation technique is the zero-inflated negative binominal (ZINB) model.

This specific count model permits the exploration of two processes: first, it allows for exploring causes of the promulgation of relevant legislation, and second, it sheds light on the factors predicting the strictness of the adopted regulations. Hence, two regression equations are generated: a count part and a binary part. The count part contains coefficients for the countries belonging to the "not always zero" group, that is, countries that have introduced soil pollution regulations at some point in time. The coefficients can be interpreted just as the coefficients from regular negative binomial regressions. The binary part contains coefficients for changes in the odds of being in the "always zero" group (i.e., countries with no soil pollution regulations in place) compared with the "not always zero" group. The coefficients of the binary part can be interpreted in the same way as the coefficients of a logit model (Long and Freese 2006: 309).

Table 6.5 presents the ZINB models with robust standard errors to account for clustering at the country level and fixed effects for years. This estimation strategy is based on the approach adopted by Konisky and Woods (2010), who employ comparable data for analysing

Table 6.5 ZINB estimation for the standards for polycyclic aromatic hydrocarbons

Covariates	Model 1		Model 2		Model 3		Model 4		Model 5	
	exp β(count)	exp β(binary)	exp β(count)	exp β(binary)	exp β(count)	exp β(binary)	exp β(count)	exp β(binary)	exp β(count)	exp β(binary)
FDI	1.009**	0.991	1.010***	0.988	–	–	–	–	–	–
	(0.005)	(0.009)	(0.003)	(0.009)						
Exports	0.996	1.004	–	–	1.008**	1.006	–	–	–	–
	(0.003)	(0.009)			(0.004)	(0.008)				
Liberal government	0.908	1.145	0.940	1.176	0.994	1.173	1.037	1.091	1.059	1.241
	(0.085)	(0.403)	(0.081)	(0.384)	(0.096)	(0.375)	(0.088)	(0.358)	(0.101)	(0.437)
Green government	0.999	1.008	1.014	1.013	0.952	0.968	1.006	1.007	1.013	1.116
	(0.067)	(0.462)	(0.083)	(0.384)	(0.107)	(0.367)	(0.107)	(0.369)	(0.105)	(0.517)
Liberal president	1.114	1.247	0.942	1.170	0.906	1.140	0.994	1.338	0.893	1.096
	(0.187)	(0.445)	(0.116)	(0.398)	(0.140)	(0.387)	(0.176)	(0.468)	(0.127)	(0.375)
NGOs	1.000	1.031	1.007	1.032	1.016*	1.024	1.008	1.011	1.008	1.035
	(0.007)	(0.034)	(0.006)	(0.030)	(0.009)	(0.029)	(0.008)	(0.029)	(0.007)	(0.032)
EU accession	2.267***	1.506	–	–	–	–	1.832***	2.276*	–	–
	(0.326)	(0.722)					(0.269)	(0.980)		
EU membership	1.345*	0.125*	–	–	–	–	–	–	1.230*	0.091**
	(0.228)	(0.137)							(0.146)	(0.103)
Income	1.001	0.972***	1.002*	0.970***	1.001	0.969***	1.002*	0.968***	1.001	0.973***
	(0.002)	(0.004)	(0.001)	(0.003)	(0.001)	(0.004)	(0.001)	(0.004)	(0.001)	(0.004)
Land	1.018	0.006***	1.219	0.004***	2.008***	0.005***	1.511**	0.003***	1.295	0.006***
	(0.291)	(0.005)	(0.215)	(0.003)	(0.499)	(0.004)	(0.308)	(0.003)	(0.259)	(0.005)
Wald Chi2 (DF)	11672.55 (30)***		9590.32 (27)***		10126.24 (27)***		8302.97 (27)***		7912.07 (27)***	
Vuong	7.90***		7.41***		7.11***		7.50***		7.29***	
Observations	560		560		560		560		560	
Cases	28		28		28		28		28	

Note: Dependent variable = PAH limit values; DF = degrees of freedom; all models contain year fixed effects (not reported); constant not reported; robust standard errors in parentheses; * significant at 10%; ** significant at 5%; *** significant at 1%.

environmental enforcement in the United States. For a more straight-forward interpretation of the estimation results, the table reports the exponentiated coefficients. Due to the two parts of the ZINB model, both count and binary β-coefficients are reported.

In the count part, the variables *FDI*, *Exports*, *EU accession*, and *EU membership* as well as *Income* and *Land* have a significant impact on the strictness of PAH standards. As models 1 and 2 show, in those emerging market democracies having relevant regulations in place, a one-unit increase in *FDI* increases the expected stringency of the soil pollution standards by a factor of 0.009 and 0.010, respectively. The same positive impact can be attributed to the variable *Exports*. Further, as models 1 and 4 show, receiving the status of an *EU accession* candidate increases the expected stringency of PAH standards by a factor of 2.27 and 1.83, respectively. Likewise, models 1 and 5 show that being granted *EU membership* raises the expected stringency of PAH standards by a factor of 1.35 and 1.23, respectively. The impact of *Income* is less stable, but in models 2 and 4 the coefficient of the variable displays the antici-pated positive sign. Similarly, in models 3 and 4 the coefficient of the variable *Land* is significant and positive. Hence, among those countries having regulations in place, the more arable land areas they have, the stricter the regulations should be. The variable *NGOs* also displays the expected sign, but its effect is only significant in model 3 and weak, thus lending no support to the hypothesis on the role of environmental groups.

Turning to the binary part, the variables that yield significant effects are *EU accession*, *EU membership*, *Income*, and *Land*. As models 1 and 4 show, *EU membership* reduces the odds of not regulating soil pollu-tion by a factor of 0.13 and 0.10, respectively. In this part of the ZINB model, the *Income* variable yields a very stable effect. An increase in *Income* decreases the odds of not regulating soil pollution by a factor of 0.97. Likewise, the variable *Land* decreases the odds of not having any relevant legislation in place. Only the finding for *EU accession* is counterintuitive. The coefficients suggest that becoming an *EU acces-sion* candidate increases the odds of not promulgating PAH standards by a factor of 2.28. To be sure, soil pollution standards for PAHS are not regulated at the European level and there is hence no explicit pres-sure for adopting them. Nevertheless, the existence of such a strong negative stimulus for policy change is indeed puzzling. One possible explanation for this finding relates to the considerable amount of other kinds of environmental regulations that the CEE countries had to adopt

Table 6.6 Findings for the standards for polycyclic aromatic hydrocarbons

Mechanisms	Variables	Signs expected	Signs observed	Support for hypothesis
Economic integration				
Regulatory competition (H 1.1)	FDI	–	+	No
California effect (H 1.2)	Exports	+	+	Yes
Politics				
Party difference (H 2.1)	Green government	+	0	No
Party difference (H 2.2)	Liberal government	–	0	No
Party difference (H 2.3)	Liberal president	–	0	No
Lobbying (H 2.4)	NGOs	+	0	No
Institutional integration				
Learning (H 3.1)	Cooperation (EU accession)	–	+ / –	No
Learning (H 3.1)	Cooperation (EU membership)	+	+	Yes
Public demand				
Functional response (H 4.1)	Income	+	+	Yes
Functional response (H 4.2)	Salience (Land)	+	+	Yes

Note: + = positive relationship; – = negative relationship; 0 = no stable effect.

during the accession period. As soil pollution standards are not part of the environmental acquis, it is conceivable that the CEE countries first exclusively focused on their adoption obligations and postponed the regulation of other issues, including soil pollution, to a later point in time. This would also explain why the variable *EU membership* indeed shows the expected positive sign.

As table 6.6 shows, the findings of the ZINB support the hypothesized positive impact of trade relationships with industrialized countries (*Exports*). In addition, they support the expected positive relationship between *EU membership*, *Income* levels, and the variable *Land*. Regarding the implications of *EU accession* for policy change, the binary coefficients revealed a negative relationship that clearly contradicts the hypothesis. At the same time, however, the count coefficients indicated that *EU accession* candidates tend to have stricter limit values for PAH emissions in place. However, as the primary interest lies in explaining the likelihood that policy change occurs, the binary coefficients must be seen as more relevant, and these lend no support to *EU accession*. As a result, the hypothesis on the impact of *EU accession* is not regarded as supported by the empirical evidence.

The Wald statistics indicate a good fit of the ZINB models. To make sure that the application of a zero inflation indeed represents the most appropriate estimation strategy, for each model a Vuong test was computed. This test compares the zero-inflated model with an ordinary negative binomial model. The significant test statistics confirm that the zero-inflated models perform better than ordinary negative binomial models.

Explaining Changes in the Regulation of Genetically Modified Maize

Event history analysis represents the most appropriate estimation technique for determining the factors that induce governments to restrict the commercial cultivation of GM maize. One can generally choose between parametric and semi-parametric event history models. The main advantage of event history models over other estimation techniques for binary outcomes such as Logit or Probit regressions is that they allow for directly modelling the time dependency exhibited in the data. The modelling of time dependency is accomplished by specifying a distribution function for the "failure" time, that is, the time that passes until a certain event occurs, which can be conceived to be increasing, decreasing, or constant over time.

Table 6.7 Comparison of event history models for genetically modified maize

Model	DF	AIC	BIC
Cox (semi-parametric)	9	63.57	101.43
Exponential	11	50.03	96.30
Weibull	12	50.37	100.85
Gompertz	12	50.65	101.14
Lognormal	12	48.57	99.05
Loglogistic	12	48.74	99.22

Note: N = 496; DF = degrees of freedom; AIC = Akaike Information Criterion; BIC = Bayesian Information Criterion.

Event history models that are based on such a particular distribution function are known as parametric models. Under the condition that the shape of the hazard rate (i.e., the probability that an event occurs in a given time period) of the parametric model is specified correctly, it may provide very precise estimates of covariate parameters. Incorrectly parameterized, however, the conclusions drawn from the event history model can be flatly wrong. Consequently, in cases where there is no compelling theoretical reason for expecting a specific shape of the hazard rate, one should rather opt for the semi-parametric Cox proportional hazards (Box-Steffensmeier and Jones 2004: 21). The Cox model is less concerned with the specific form of time dependency, but focuses on the relationship between the dependent variable and the covariates of theoretical interest.

Although it is generally expected that a growing number of countries will restrict the cultivation of GM maize, the description of the dependent variable in chapter 5 highlighted that only ten out of the twenty-eight countries under scrutiny have formally adopted relevant legislation. Such a small number of events makes it difficult to argue that the hazard rate is increasing over time. Thus, to avoid the risk of running and interpreting a parametric model that is incorrect, table 6.7 displays two values that allow for reliably comparing and ranking competing event history models based on their model fit reflected in Akaike's (1974) Information Criterion (AIC) and Bayesian Information Criterion (BIC) (Schwarz 1978). As a rule, the model with the lowest AIC and BIC values corresponds to the one with the best model fit. The values are computed for various parametric models as well as the semi-parametric Cox model.

In the present case, the AIC and BIC values deviate from each other, which is unusual and may be interpreted as confirmation of the

Table 6.8 Log-normal model for the regulation of genetically modified maize

Covariates	Model 1 exp(β)	Model 2 exp(β)	Model 3 exp(β)	Model 4 exp(β)	Model 5 exp(β)
FDI	0.995 (0.015)	0.984 (0.019)	–	–	–
Exports	1.000 (0.014)	–	0.999 (0.012)	–	–
Liberal government	0.573 (0.246)	0.545 (0.290)	0.664 (0.270)	0.553 (0.226)	0.647 (0.262)
Green government	0.593 (0.623)	0.298 (0.256)	0.300 (0.228)	0.270 (0.212)*	0.560 (0.425)
Liberal president	2.702 (1.335)**	2.018 (0.985)	1.648 (0.621)	1.921 (0.696)*	2.423 (1.082)**
NGOs	1.824 (0.500)**	1.658 (0.516)	1.430 (0.278)*	1.391 (0.239)*	1.785 (0.438)**
EU accession	19.409 (11.895)***	–	–	68.682 (73.334)***	–
EU membership	0.049 (0.073)**	–	–	–	0.047 (0.059)**
Income	1.011 (0.009)	0.998 (0.007)	0.998 (0.006)	0.997 (0.006)	1.010 (0.008)
Insecticides	0.967 (0.014)**	0.971 (0.016)*	0.978 (0.012)*	0.980 (0.011)*	0.968 (0.012)***
Wald Chi2 (DF)	49.06 (10)***	7.54 (7)	10.18 (7)	53.75 (7)***	13.87 (7)*
Reduction LL	12.35	9.52	9.01	9.94	12.76
Sigma	0.77	0.83	0.72	0.72	0.74
Observations	496	496	496	496	496
Cases	28	28	28	28	28

Note: Dependent variable = (partial / temporal) ban of GM maize; Reduction LL = (log pseudo-likelihood null) – (log pseudo-likelihood model); DF = degrees of freedom; robust standard errors in parentheses; * significant at 10%; ** significant at 5%; *** significant at 1%.

peculiarity of the data structure. According to the AIC values, the model best suited for the analysis is the Log-normal model, that is, a distribution that allows for non-monotonic hazard rates. The Exponential model, in contrast, displays the lowest BIC value, indicating that this model should be preferred over other parameterizations. In short, the comparison of the different modelling strategies by means of the model fit does not help much in determining how to proceed. Consequently, to minimize the risk of incorrect parameterization, it seems reasonable to estimate both a log-normal and an exponential model and to check whether they yield the same insights.

Table 6.8 presents the estimation results of the Log-normal model computed with robust standard errors to account for clustering at the country level. Before interpreting the coefficients, it should be noted that the Wald tests of models 2 and 3 are insignificant, indicating that the models most likely leave out decisive factors. Remarkably, these are the models that do not include variables related to *EU accession* or *membership*. Moreover, it should be noted that model 5 is only significant at the 10 per cent level. The table further reports the extent to which the log pseudo-likelihood was reduced by including covariates as compared to the null model. The higher the values for the reduction attained in the log pseudo-likelihood, the better the fit of the models. In this regard, models 1 and 5 clearly perform better than the other three models. However, the shape parameter *sigma* is insignificant in all models, which again raises concerns about the correct specification of the functional form.

The Log-normal model is an accelerated failure-time model, which has important implications for the interpretation of the coefficients. If the exponentiated coefficient is greater than 1, then time is decelerated and the event of interest would be expected to occur later. If the exponentiated coefficient is smaller than 1, then time is accelerated and the event of interest would be expected to occur sooner. If the exponentiated coefficient equals 1, time passes at its "normal" rate (see Cleves et al. 2008: 232).

The models produce significant coefficients for *Liberal president*, *NGOs*, *EU accession* and *membership*, and *Insecticides*. The coefficients for *Liberal president* and *EU accession* imply that these factors are responsible for significantly slowing down time until a more restrictive approach to GM maize is adopted, which supports the reasoning of the corresponding hypotheses. While the effect of *EU accession* is entirely plausible, as the CEE countries in fact had to liberalize the cultivation of MON810 maize in order to adopt the acquis communautaire, the coefficient of the variable *EU membership* does not match with the empirical reality. One cannot convincingly argue that being a member of the EU significantly accelerates the imposition of a cultivation ban. On the contrary, the European Commission at various instances underscored its disapproval of member states restricting the cultivation of GM maize (see, e.g., Pollack and Shaffer 2009: 255–61).

However, the finding for *EU membership* is not the only puzzling observation. It is surprising that environmental groups (*NGOs*) are found to slow down the restrictions imposed on the cultivation of MON810 maize. In both regions there are growing numbers of environmental groups that are exclusively dedicated to drawing attention to the harmful effects of GM crops on human health and the environment (see, e.g., Bernauer and Caduff 2006; Poitras 2008). Against this background, it is very counterintuitive that larger numbers of *NGOs* would help to preserve laissez-faire GMO regulations. Similarly, the estimation findings suggest that the consumption of *Insecticides* accelerates the restrictions on GM maize, which is equally puzzling. To be sure, high consumption rates of *Insecticides* imply that countries are confronted with difficulties in achieving satisfactory levels of agricultural production. As MON810 is an insect-resistant type of maize and would therefore improve agricultural productivity without using high levels of *Insecticides*, it is more compelling to hypothesize that countries with high consumption levels are less likely to restrict its cultivation.

Table 6.9 presents the re-estimated models based on the exponential parameterization. Using the exponential distribution has clearly improved the fit of the five models as indicated by the Wald tests. The estimation findings remain the same for *Liberal president*, *NGOs*, *EU accession* and *membership*, and *Insecticides*. Accordingly, *EU membership* and the consumption of large amounts of *Insecticides* would again accelerate policy change, whereas the incumbency of a *Liberal president*, high numbers of *NGOs*, as well as the status of an *EU accession* candidate are likely to significantly slow down the partial or temporary banning of GM maize. However, it should be noted that the effect of *Liberal president* is now restricted to models 1 and 5 and generally weaker. In this context, another variation refers to the significant coefficient produced by *FDI* in model 2, which is yet not stable and therefore not interpreted as a rejection of hypothesis H1.1. Another important observation refers to the gigantic coefficients produced by the variable *EU accession*, which again indicates estimation problems based on the specific characteristics of the data.

Table 6.10 reports the observed signs of the variables that were found to be significant in both event history models. In summary, the estimation results only lend support to the hypotheses on the impact of the variables *Liberal president* and *EU accession*. As concerns the findings for *NGOs*, *EU membership*, and *Insecticides*, these clearly contradict the reasoning underlying the hypotheses. No stable findings could be achieved for *FDI*, *Exports*, *Green government*, and *Liberal government*.

Despite the fact that the two event history models allow for confirming two hypotheses, there are several hints that the theoretical considerations guiding this study may not be very well suited for explaining changes in the regulation of GM maize. Most important, these refer to

Table 6.9 Exponential event history model for the regulation of genetically modified maize

Covariates	Model 1 exp(β)	Model 2 exp(β)	Model 3 exp(β)	Model 4 exp(β)	Model 5 exp(β)
FDI	0.985 (0.014)	0.972 (0.013)**	–	–	–
Exports	0.995 (0.027)	–	0.991 (0.020)	–	–
Liberal government	0.454 (0.308)	0.399 (0.296)	0.506 (0.353)	0.415 (0.279)	0.512 (0.331)
Green government	0.910 (0.944)	0.328 (0.271)	0.173 (0.179)*	0.178 (0.194)	0.559 (0.303)
Liberal president	4.926 (4.361)*	3.485 (3.126)	3.258 (2.785)	4.015 (3.535)	4.951 (4.342)*
NGOs	1.884 (0.414)***	1.600 (0.298)**	1.585 (0.264)***	1.490 (0.227)***	1.927 (0.402)***
EU accession	1357350 (1114650)***	–	–	24056024 (17836583)***	–
EU membership	0.033 (0.037)***	–	–	–	0.018 (0.014)***
Income	1.009 (0.008)	0.997 (0.008)	0.994 (0.008)	0.992 (0.009)	1.009 (0.009)
Insecticides	0.971 (0.009)***	0.976 (0.009)***	0.975 (0.008)***	0.977 (0.009)***	0.967 (0.009)***
Wald Chi2 (DF)	1204.29 (10)***	19.44(7)***	12.78(7)*	981.49(7)***	46.08(7)***
Reduction LL	10.11	6.30	4.86	5.82	9.57
Observations	496	496	496	496	496
Cases	28	28	28	28	28

Note: Dependent variable = (partial / temporal) ban GM maize; Reduction LL = (log pseudo-likelihood null) − (log pseudo-likelihood model); DF = degrees of freedom; robust standard errors in parentheses; the interpretation of the coefficients is reversed, with coefficients smaller than 1 indicating a positive relationship and vice versa; * significant at 10%; ** significant at 5%; *** significant at 1%.

Table 6.10 Findings for the regulation of genetically modified maize

Mechanisms	Variables	Signs expected	Signs observed	Support for hypothesis
Economic integration				
Regulatory competition (H 1.1)	FDI	–	0	No
California effect (H 1.2)	Exports	+	0	No
Politics				
Party difference (H 2.1)	Green government	+	0	No
Party difference (H 2.2)	Liberal government	–	0	No
Party difference (H 2.3)	Liberal president	–	–	Yes
Lobbying (H 2.4)	NGOs	+	–	No
Institutional integration				
Harmonization* (H 3.2)	Compliance (EU accession)	–	–	Yes
Harmonization* (H 3.2)	Compliance (EU membership)	–	+	No
Public demand				
Functional Response (H 4.1)	Income	+	0	No
Functional Response* (H 4.2)	Salience (Insecticides)*	–	+	No

* The sign deviates from the theoretical expectations for the other policy items.
Note: + = positive relationship; – = negative relationship; 0 = no stable effect.

the problems revealed by inspecting the fit of the models displayed in table 6.8, the unrealistically large coefficient of *EU accession* in table 6.9, and the deviating results of the comparison of the models by means of AIC and BIC reported in table 6.7. A good deal of the insufficient performance of the explanatory model can certainly be attributed to the low number of cases in which policy change actually occurred. Yet, this does not exclude the possibility that this policy item might be affected by factors different from those taken into account by the explanatory model. An additional indicator for possible model miss-specification is that refitted models with inverse-Gaussian frailties, which are generally used to check unobserved heterogeneity, could not be computed. Instead of doing detailed model diagnostics in order to identify ways of marginally improving the estimation findings, a more promising approach seems to be provided by re-analysing this particular policy item by employing a more refined research design.

Explaining the Adoption of Sustainable Forest Management

Event history analysis again provides the best method for assessing the factors that induced the government of CEE and LA countries to adopt SFM. In contrast to the previous policy item, however, the characteristics of the data make the selection of a parametric model straightforward. Chapter 5 revealed that the adoption of SFM followed an S-shaped diffusion curve, indicating that the adoption rose quite slowly at first, but then became steeper as an increasing number of governments decided to adopt it. After a while, when most governments had adopted SFM, the diffusion curve began to level off. Therefore, a parametric model that takes into account this time dependency should produce particularly good estimation results. This reasoning is supported by the AIC and BIC values presented by table 6.11. Both values are lowest for the parametric Weibull model, which will accordingly be employed for the analysis.

Table 6.12 exhibits the estimation results of the Weibull models with robust standard errors. In contrast to the analysis of GM maize, the Weibull model is specified as a parametric proportional hazards model, which entails a different interpretation of the coefficients. The coefficients are exponentiated, which means that a value larger than 1 indicates a positive relationship (i.e., that the odds for the occurrence of an event increase) and a value smaller than 1 a negative one (i.e., that the odds for the occurrence of an event decrease). Before discussing the results, it should be noted that the variables usually measuring the

Table 6.11 Comparison of event history models for sustainable forest management

Model	DF	AIC	BIC
Cox (semi-parametric)	9	142.73	171.76
Exponential	10	77.85	110.11
Weibull	11	51.83	87.31
Gompertz	11	53.69	89.17
Lognormal	11	61.55	97.03
Loglogistic	11	59.49	94.98

Note: N = 186; DF = degrees of freedom; AIC = Akaike Information Criterion; BIC = Bayesian Information Criterion.

Table 6.12 Results of the Weibull model for sustainable forest management

Covariates	Model 1 exp(β)	Model 2 exp(β)	Model 3 exp(β)	Model 4 exp(β)
FDI	0.95 (0.02)***	0.95 (0.02)***	–	–
Exports	1.00 (0.01)	–	1.00 (0.01)	–
Liberal government	0.72 (0.24)	0.71 (0.23)	0.91 (0.36)	0.85 (0.31)
Green government	1.12 (0.51)	1.07 (0.37)	1.32 (0.61)	1.03 (0.58)
Liberal president	0.67 (0.41)	0.67 (0.34)	0.69 (0.33)	0.74 (0.37)
NGOs	0.97 (0.03)	0.97 (0.02)	0.98 (0.02)	0.96 (0.03)
EU application	1.01 (0.64)	–	–	1.58 (0.89)
Income	1.01 (0.01)	1.01 (0.01)	1.00 (0.01)	1.00 (0.01)
Forest	1.05 (0.02)**	1.05 (0.02)**	1.04 (0.02)**	1.04 (0.02)**
Wald Chi2 (DF)	23.51 (9)***	19.97 (7)***	21.95 (7)***	25.76 (7)***
Reduction LL	16.61	16.52	12.44	12.58
p	3.17***	2.36***	2.34***	3.21***
Observations	186	186	186	186
Cases	27	27	27	27

Note: Dependent variable = adoption SFM; Reduction LL = (log pseudo-likelihood null) – (log pseudo-likelihood model); DF = degrees of freedom; robust standard errors in parentheses; * significant at 10%; ** significant at 5%; *** significant at 1%.

impact of the institutional integration, that is, *EU accession* and *EU membership*, turned out to cause collinearity problems in light of the specific data structure. They thus had to be substituted with the variable *EU application*, which starts measuring the impact of the EU with the date of the CEE countries' application for membership. While this measurement still mirrors the theoretical construct of interest, namely, international institutional integration, the drawback is that the separate effects of candidacy and membership status can no longer be discerned.

Another particularity of the model refers to the number of country clusters – 27 instead of 28. This stems from the fact that Venezuela incorporated the SFM principle into its forest legislation before 1990. As event history analysis drops observations of the dependent variables once they are coded as 1 (i.e., event occurrence), all observations for the case of Venezuela were dropped right at the beginning of the estimation process.

The statistics of the Wald test reported at the bottom of the table indicate that the models were most probably specified with the correct number of covariates. Further, for each model specification the Weibull parameter p is significant and positive, which means that the hazard rate is monotonically increasing with time. In spite of the very good model fit and the considerable reduction in the log pseudo-likelihood, the estimation findings for SFM reveal that only two factors induced governments of emerging market democracies to adopt the SFM principle. In this context, the most central finding is that the variable *Forest* increases the likelihood of sustainable forestry. Accordingly, governments of countries with large areas of forests are more likely to adopt this principle in response to the issue's salience. Yet, theoretically more interesting is the variable *FDI*, as it points to the existence of a negative relationship. The coefficients reported for models 1 and 2 indicate that a one-unit increase in investment levels reduces the likelihood of adopting SFM by 5 per cent, which – for the first time – supports the hypothesis on regulatory competition. This finding underlines the fact that economic considerations indeed matter for explaining changes in forest-related legislation (see, e.g., Cashore, Auld, and Newsom 2003: 237–8; Nijnik and Oskam 2004: 116). At the same time, it challenges the view that emerging market democracies are willing to strengthen SFM in order to attract investments (see, e.g., Laaksonen-Craig 2004: 368). What the governments are rather likely to do is to postpone reforms of forest policy if this ascertains higher *FDI* levels.

Remarkably, none of the variables related to domestic politics is found to affect the governments' decision to adopt SFM. This observation is more surprising for the variable *NGOs* than for the other factors, as with the other policy items the impact of environmental groups was quite stable, with the important exception of the analysis of GM maize, of course. As concerns the insignificant effect of the EU, this finding could have been anticipated on the basis of the relatively similar adoption curves for the CEE and LA countries (see figure 5.1). Table 6.13 gives an overview of the main findings of the Weibull model for SFM.

Table 6.13 Findings for sustainable forest management

Mechanisms	Variables	Signs expected	Signs observed	Support for hypothesis
Economic integration				
Regulatory competition (H 1.1)	FDI	–	–	Yes
California effect (H 1.2)	Exports	+	0	No
Politics				
Party difference (H 2.1)	Green government	+	0	No
Party difference (H 2.2)	Liberal government	–	0	No
Party difference (H 2.3)	Liberal president	–	0	No
Lobbying (H 2.4)	NGOs	+	0	No
International integration				
Learning (H 3.1)	Cooperation (EU accession)	+	0	No
Learning (H 3.1)	Cooperation (EU membership)	+	0	No
Public demand				
Functional response (H 4.1)	Income	+	0	No
Functional response (H 4.2)	Salience (Forest)	+	+	Yes

Note: + = positive relationship; – = negative relationship; 0 = no stable effect.

While the model fit and the overall performance of the models are good, it is still useful to check whether unobserved heterogeneity may be a source of model misspecification. To this end, the full Weibull model was refitted with inverse-Gaussian frailties. Heterogeneity is particularly likely to occur if relevant covariates are left out because they are immeasurable, unobservable, or simply not taken into consideration by the theoretical model. The statistics of the likelihood-ratio test allow for rejecting the null hypothesis that the data are heterogeneous (Cleves et al. 2008: 312–13).[3] The findings of the Weibull models can hence be regarded as valid.

Explaining the Creation of Environmental Procuracies

Similarly to the two previous items, the establishment of environmental procuracies is a binary variable. Hence, in order to learn more about the reasons why governments of emerging market democracies decide to establish such an institution, the use of parametric event history analysis again represents the best methodological choice. Table 6.14 presents the AIC and BIC values for the semi-parametric Cox model as well as a variety of parametric models. Both values suggest that a model based on the Gompertz distribution represents the most appropriate parameterization for the data at hand. The Gompertz distribution treats the hazard rate as an exponential function of the duration time. It can be monotonically increasing, decreasing, or flat (Box-Steffensmeier and Jones 2004: 38).

Table 6.15 exhibits the estimation results of the fitted Gompertz models with robust standard errors. Again, the variables *EU accession* and *EU membership* proved incompatible with the data structure and were therefore replaced by *EU application*. The Wald test yields a very good model fit for each specification of the estimation models. The shape parameter of the Gompertz model *gamma* is significant and positive, indicating that the hazard function increases with time. The number of observations is now larger than with the event history models for SFM, but lower than in the case of GM maize. Essentially, this means that the diffusion process of environmental procuracies was not as swift as in the case of SFM, but in contrast to GM maize the majority of the countries under study still established them at some point in time during the observation period (see also figure 5.2).

The table yields three major insights about the incidence of institutional change. The variables *INGOs* and *Energy* have a positive impact on the likelihood of creating an environmental procuracy. Thus, a

Table 6.14 Comparison of event history models for environmental procuracies

Model	DF	AIC	BIC
Cox (semi-parametric)	9	141.11	173.39
Exponential	10	84.10	119.97
Weibull	11	74.10	113.56
Gompertz	11	70.87	110.33
Lognormal	11	77.31	116.77
Loglogistic	11	78.62	118.08

Note: N = 267; DF = degrees of freedom; AIC = Akaike Information Criterion; BIC = Bayesian Information Criterion.

Table 6.15 Results of the Gompertz model for environmental procuracies

Covariates	Model 1 exp(β)	Model 2 exp(β)	Model 3 exp(β)	Model 4 exp(β)
FDI	0.97 (0.02)*	0.97 (0.02)	–	–
Exports	1.04 (0.02)**	–	1.04 (0.02)**	–
Liberal government	1.03 (0.61)	1.04 (0.61)	1.01 (0.59)	1.01 (0.57)
Green government	2.83 (2.86)	1.47 (1.30)	2.48 (2.49)	1.34 (1.04)
Liberal president	1.37 (1.12)	0.92 (0.61)	1.41 (1.10)	1.05 (0.69)
INGOs	1.11 (0.04)***	1.10 (0.03)***	1.07 (0.03)***	1.08 (0.03)***
EU accession	0.84 (0.44)	–	–	1.35 (0.63)
Income	1.00 (0.00)	1.00 (0.00)	1.00 (0.00)	1.00 (0.00)
Energy	1.02 (0.01)**	1.01 (0.00)***	1.02 (0.01)***	1.01 (0.01)*
Wald Chi2 (DF)	31.72 (9)***	29.10 (7)***	21.96 (7)***	20.46 (7)***
Reduction LL	11.82	8.84	10.85	7.89
Gamma	0.27***	0.18***	0.21***	0.13***
Observations	267	267	267	267
Cases	28	28	28	28

Note: Dependent variable = adoption prosecution unit; Reduction LL = (log pseudo-likelihood null) – (log pseudo-likelihood model); DF = degrees of freedom; robust standard errors in parentheses; * significant at 10%; ** significant at 5%; *** significant at 1%.

one-unit increase in the number of transnationally interlinked environmental groups (*INGOs*) increases the odds that the government of an emerging market democracy will establish an environmental procuracy by about 10 per cent (see models 1 and 2). Appendix 7 presents the estimation results of the same estimation models fitted with *NGOs* instead of *INGOs*. While the effects of the other covariates remain the same, the estimation results find no significant effect of the numerical strength of environmental groups (*NGOs*). Therefore, it can be safely stated that

Table 6.16 Findings for environmental procuracies

Mechanisms	Variables	Signs expected	Signs observed	Support for hypothesis
Economic integration				
Regulatory competition (H 1.1)	FDI	–	0	No
California effect (H 1.2)	Exports	+	+	Yes
Politics				
Party difference (H 2.1)	Green government	+	0	No
Party difference (H 2.2)	Liberal government	–	0	No
Party difference (H 2.3)	Liberal president	–	0	No
Lobbying (H 2.4)	NGOs	+	+	Yes
Institutional integration				
Learning (H 3.1)	Cooperation (EU accession)	+	0	No
Learning (H 3.1)	Cooperation (EU membership)	+	0	No
Public demand				
Functional response (H 4.1)	Income	+	0	No
Functional response (H 4.2)	Salience (Energy)	+	+	Yes

Note: + = positive relationship; – = negative relationship; 0 = no stable effect.

issues related to the enforcement of environmental policies crucially depend on the presence of environmental groups that are involved in processes of transnational communication.

In a similar vein, the salience of environmental degradation measured by per capita energy consumption (*Energy*) is found to induce the governments of CEE and LA countries to establish environmental prosecution units. More precisely, as models 1 through 4 show, a one-unit increase in energy consumption entails an increase in the odds of institutional change by 1 or 2 per cent, respectively. This effect of issue salience is intuitive, since increasing environmental degradation lowers the standard of living, which, in turn, puts pressure on the political actors to effectively lower pollution levels if they are not to endanger their re-election.

The positive sign of the coefficient of the variable *Exports* suggests that a one-unit increase in a country's exports to industrialized countries entails an increase in the chances of establishing an environmental procuracy by about 4 per cent. This positive relationship concurs with the hypothesis on the California effect. Furthermore, the variable *FDI* displays a negative sign, but the coefficient is only weakly significant in the full model and thus the related hypothesis cannot be regarded as confirmed.

Table 6.16 summarizes the main findings of the four Gompertz models and evaluates to what extent they confirm the hypotheses put forward in chapter 3. The table highlights the fact that trade relationships with industrialized countries as well as transnationally linked environmental groups and problem pressure are the most important drivers of the establishment of an environmental prosecution unit.

To assess whether unobserved heterogeneity represents a source of model miss-specification, model 1 is refitted with inverse-Gaussian frailties. The statistics of the likelihood-ratio test allows for rejecting the null hypothesis that the data are heterogeneous.[4]

Discussion of the Findings

The empirical analyses performed in this chapter produced many insights regarding the determinants of policy and institutional change. The main findings of the quantitative analysis are summarized in table 6.17. Most important, the explanatory power of the theoretical model put forward in chapter 3 was found to vary considerably across the individual items. The theoretical model performed best for explaining changes in the stringency of waste-water and soil pollution standards. It also provided some valuable insights into the factors affecting a government's decision to set up an environmental procuracy. The explanatory model performed moderately well for pinpointing the causes of changes in the regulation of air quality standards and the adoption of the SFM principle. While with both policy items the fit of the estimation models was very good, only two hypotheses could be confirmed on the basis of the empirical evidence.

In marked contrast, the analysis of the regulation of GM maize revealed some counterintuitive relationships. For example, the estimation findings in both event history models underlined a negative relationship between the number of environmental groups and the likelihood of restricting the cultivation of GM maize. Two reasons for the insufficient explanatory power of the theoretical model in this particular case seem plausible. First, it is conceivable that measurement problems affect the dependent variable, the independent variables, or perhaps even both. Second, the poor performance of the explanatory model might be attributed to the omission of important explanatory factors and therefore insufficient theorizing. Since the regulation

Table 6.17 Overview of the support for the explanatory model

Variables	Support for hypothesis					
	Water	Air*	Soil	GMOs*	Forest	Procuracy
Economic integration						
FDI (H 1.1)	–	–	–	–	✓	–
Exports (H 1.2)	–	–	✓	–	–	✓
Politics						
Green government (H 2.1)	–	–	–	–	–	–
Liberal government (H 2.2)	–	–	–	–	–	–
Liberal president (H 2.3)	–	–	–	✓	–	–
(I)NGOs (H 2.4)	✓	✓	–	–	–	✓
Institutional integration						
EU accession (H 3.1 / 3.2) Cooperation / compliance	✓	✓	–	✓	–	–
EU membership (H 3.1 / 3.2) Cooperation / compliance	–	–	✓	–	–	–
Public demand						
Income (H 4.1)	✓	–	✓	–	–	–
Salience (H 4.2)	✓	–	✓	–	✓	✓

* Policy items associated with international harmonization instead of cooperation.

of GM maize represents a "deviant case," a more refined analysis of this particular item seems indispensable for a better understanding of the determinants of policy change. Therefore, it will be re-examined in chapter 7 by means of an in-depth analysis. Such a complementary qualitative analysis is useful for learning about alternative explanations and performing an additional evaluation of the theoretical model (see Lieberman 2005).With respect to economic integration, this chapter showed that there is only limited evidence supporting the hypothesis on regulatory competition (H 1.1). Only the analysis of the SFM provided support for the expectation that the variable *FDI* lowers the likelihood of policy adoption. Concerning the regulation of water, air, and soil pollution, *FDI* was even found to significantly stimulate a tightening of standards. From this it follows that the hypothesis on regulatory competition cannot be confirmed, which also corresponds to the findings of other empirical studies (see, e.g., Drezner 2007: 15; Holzinger, Knill, and Arts 2008; Holzinger, Knill, and Sommerer 2008, 2011). Even more ambivalent are the findings regarding the effect of the share of exports to industrialized countries. Only in the cases of PAH standards and environmental prosecution units was the hypothesis on the California effect (H 1.2) found to hold true. However, by combining this result with the mostly positive sign of the variable *FDI*, it is not too daring to conclude, there is evidence in support of a positive impact effect of trade and investment liberalization. Again; this finding is in line with the main insights provided by the literature (see, e.g., Prakash and Potoski 2006; Perkins and Neumayer 2011).

Compared to economic integration, the empirical evidence about the impact of the partisan composition of the government is very straight-forward to interpret. The estimation findings revealed that neither a government composed of economically liberal (H 2.1) nor green parties (H 2.2) yield a significant impact on environmental policy change. To be sure, the Tobit models for waste-water regulations even showed that a government featuring an economically liberal party has a positive impact on the setting of BOD limit values. By contrast, with the analysis of the regulation of GM maize a president belonging to an economically liberal party was indeed found to significantly lower the likelihood of imposing a ban. Overall, however, there is very limited support for the expected effects of party difference. Hence, hypotheses 2.1 and 2.2 can be safely rejected, while for hypothesis 2.3 there is limited support.

Much clearer are the results for hypothesis 2.4 on the role of environmental groups. The analyses of water and air pollution as well as environmental procuracies demonstrated the importance of environmental groups for bringing about change. Considering the generally very good performance of the theoretical model for explaining changes in the regulation of soil pollution, it is surprising that environmental groups were not found to matter. One tentative explanation for this observation is that in CEE and LA soil pollution does not represent a priority field of action to environmental groups, which often focus on topics such as natural resources, biodiversity conservation and preservation, environmental health, or environmental justice (see, e.g., Carmin 2010).

Another important finding relates to the impact of institutional integration. As a rule, while both hypotheses 3.1 and 3.2 can be confirmed, the impact of the EU was generally more pronounced and led to the predicted results during the accession stage rather than with membership. This makes perfect sense as policy change was mainly triggered by the requirement of adopting the environmental acquis before becoming accepted as a full member. That being said, the dominance of accession effects over membership effects signals that the external incentives to which the CEE accession candidates reacted during the negotiations may vanish once they are granted membership (see, e.g., Cirtautas and Schimmelfennig 2010). Instead, in the membership period domestic politics should become more important for environmental policymaking in these countries. The finding for ozone standards lends support to this view. Many CEE governments switched from "over-compliance" with the relevant EU directives to regular compliance, which entailed a lowering of standards.

The final category of explanatory factors is represented by public demand. In this context, the variable *Income* was found to only yield a positive effect on policymaking with water and soil pollution standards. Thus, there is support for hypothesis 4.2, but the empirical evidence is not overtly strong. By contrast, the estimation results for four items highlighted the relevance of issue salience, indicating that environmental policymaking in emerging market democracies is, among other things, a functional response to environmental problems. This is a noteworthy finding, since it shows that policymaking and public demand are interrelated, even or especially when countries are undergoing major political and economic changes. Hence, it is perhaps this responsiveness of political actors that represents a major characteristic of policymaking in transition countries, since this signals a break with their autocratic past (see, e.g., Duquette 1999).

When one compares the findings for policy change with those for institutional change, it becomes apparent that they follow the same logic. The main difference relates to the importance of transnationally linked environmental groups and the clear existence of a California effect, which was otherwise only observed for the regulation of soil pollution standards. In addition, pressures emerging from environmental degradation were found to matter for institutional change. In fact, the relevance of problem pressure is quite intuitive, since increasing environmental degradation lowers the standard of living, which in turn puts pressure on political actors to actually reduce pollution levels in order to avoid endangering their re-election. By and large, however, enforcement decisions are guided by no other considerations than policy decisions.

Conclusion

This chapter empirically tested the relevance of economic integration, domestic politics, international institutional integration, and public demand for environmental policy arrangements. In doing so, it addressed the following three questions: Which of these factors are the most important ones? Does their relevance vary across policy items? Are enforcement decisions driven by the same factors that affect regulatory decisions? The factors that were found to matter most are issue salience, institutional. integration, and environmental groups. Investment levels also turned out to matter, but contrary to the theoretical expectations, as they stimulate the adoption of more stringent environmental protection standards rather than laxer ones. The estimation results only allow for clearly rejecting the importance of two variables, namely, the participation of either an economically liberal or a green party in government.

The predictive power of the explanatory framework turned out to vary across the six items, with the best estimation results attained for the regulation of water and soil pollution. The item that could be explained least by this study's explanatory framework is the regulation of GM maize. Many of the estimation findings were puzzling and the diagnostics of the models highlighted that there are some methodological problems. As a result, the regulation of GM maize will be re-examined in the next chapter by means of a case-study design. More generally, however, the variation in the findings for the individual policy areas has important implications for the state of research, as this basically means that there is not one universal explanation for environmental policy change. Rather, empirical studies should seek to base their analysis on a wide range of items, as only such a proceeding may eventually allow for drawing generalizable conclusions.

The final category of findings relates to the creation of environmental prosecution units, which can be explained well on the basis of the theoretical model. The only difference was the fact that it is the strength, not of all environmental groups that matters in this case, but that of environmental groups that are actively involved in processes of transnational communication. Moreover, the estimation model provided support for the California effect. Accordingly, emerging market democracies are likely to improve their environmental image if they are mainly trading with industrialized countries.

7 Case Studies on Changing Regulation of Genetically Modified Maize

The quantitative analysis carried out in the preceding chapter has shown that the theoretical model guiding this study possesses a limited explanatory power in the case of the regulation of GM maize. Consequently, this chapter re-examines the patterns and determinants of policy change in this particular case by means of a different methodological approach, namely, by conducting case studies. Since by 2010 only a few countries had restricted the commercial cultivation of GM maize, the in-depth studies primarily focus on these cases. To make sure that the empirical findings are not subject to a bias stemming from the selection of the dependent variable (see Geddes 2003: chapter 3), the case studies on countries in which policy change occurred are complemented by failed efforts to institute cultivation restrictions. The complementary qualitative analysis is guided by the following two research questions: Which factors are responsible for policy change in the case of GM maize? Why did the quantitative analysis fail to produce compelling insights?

The chapter proceeds as follows: the next section discusses potential problems regarding the measurement of the variables and provides some reflections on possible conceptual and analytical inaccuracies in view of the specific characteristics of GM maize. These considerations are followed by the in-depth analysis of policy change in the CEE countries, which comprises Bulgaria, Hungary, Poland, Romania, and Ukraine. Subsequently, the empirical focus is shifted to LA, starting with Mexico and Paraguay as the first two countries that prohibited the cultivation of GM maize. The chapter continues with the analysis of Bolivia, Ecuador, and Venezuela as the three countries that adopted an anti-GMO stance on the occasion of the ascension to office of left-wing presidents or governments. The case of Peru as the most recent country to impose a (temporary) cultivation ban is addressed separately in the next section. Moreover, Brazil and El Salvador are analysed as the two countries that made a U-turn in their biosafety policies. Finally, the main findings of the case studies are discussed and some concluding remarks are presented.

Potential Measurement and Conceptual Issues

It is conceivable that inaccurate measurement or conceptualization are responsible for the partly puzzling findings for GM maize. In terms of measurement, potential problems can be related to both the dependent variable and the independent variables. Concerning the measurement of the dependent variable, the main source of incorrect measurement refers to the moratoriums, that is, decisions meaning a delay or suspension of an activity, which were adopted by some governments to temporarily ban the commercial cultivation of MON810 maize. Since moratoriums are meant to be temporary limiting measures, it is challenging to compare them with regulations or bans. Of course, the latter can also be revoked in the course of time, but there are usually no temporal limits inherent in them. Moreover, a moratorium can also be interpreted as a strategic action in order to postpone a "real" policy decision and the associated political conflicts.

Further to this, while the effect of moratoriums may be identical to that of regulations and bans, in some political systems like Brazil's, they are not adopted by elected officials but result from court rulings. This is an important point, as judges may base their decisions on considerations different from those of politicians, especially since the former are not likely to display vote-seeking behaviour. As a result, the theoretical model's assumptions presented in chapter 3 may be violated since it is not exclusively the behaviour of political actors that leads to policy change, but also the actions taken by judges.

Another aspect related to the measurement of the dependent variable concerns Brazil and El Salvador, that is, the cases in which a cultivation ban was instituted at first, but then revoked. In the quantitative analysis, however, only the adoption of the restricting measures was taken into account, since event history analysis drops the observations after the event of interest occurred. The estimation of a model with repeated events did not provide an alternative either due to the generally low number of policy changes. Thus, the estimation findings might have been influenced by the failure to use the entire empirical information available for Brazil and El Salvador. To be sure, however, there are more cases for which the measurement of the dependent variable can be regarded as imperfect. For example, in Romania and Ukraine some actors tried to institute legal restrictions on the commercial cultivation of MON810, but these efforts were unsuccessful. Then, the Latvian case is difficult to assess, since local governments are only authorized to institute cultivation bases. Even more critical is the empirical assessment of the regulatory situation in Venezuela, since President Chávez publicly announced a cultivation ban, but never started a legislative process to prohibit GM maize through binding law.

This leads us to the more general observation that in many of the countries where legislation is in place, the actual status of GM maize is still unclear, even when one leaves unconsidered the issue of illegal growing. For instance, while the cultivation of GM maize is still officially prohibited in Mexico, since 2002 the secretary of agriculture has awarded permits for its commercial growing in northern areas of the country (Pechlaner and Otero 2008: 364). It goes without saying that observations like these complicate the accurate assessment of policy change with regard to GM maize.

Potential measurement issues may also affect the independent variables. When applying quantitative methods, it is important to gather data for all units of analysis, which often entails the use of proxies rather than direct measurement of the theoretical constructs of interest. The main reason for adopting this procedure is related to restrictions in data availability. In the present study, proxies had to be employed for many independent variables. For example, the per capita number of environmental groups is an admittedly imperfect way of assessing pro-environment lobbying. Nevertheless, this measurement still represents one of the best available approximations. Similarly, only focusing on green and economically liberal parties is a serious empirical limitation. However, there are no better proxies available for both regions and the full length of the observation period. Despite possible inaccuracies regarding the measurement of the independent variables, the analyses of all other specifications of the dependent variable generated plausible findings, indicating that the operationalization generally works well. Yet this does not exclude the possibility that the measurement of the independent variables is less appropriate for explaining the regulation of GM maize.

The particular features of GM maize may require a different operationalization of the key independent variables. Since biotech crops are not only perceived to affect the environment but also public health, it is likely that consumer protection groups and farmers' associations are as important as environmental groups for the lobbying process. However, the variable *NGOs* does not take other types of interest groups into account. Concerning partisanship, it is conceivable that the "left turn" of LA politics – also labelled the "pink tide" – and the growing anti-capitalist and anti-American stances of the political parties in power may be relevant for the regulation of GM maize. However, these policy dimensions were not taken into consideration when coding the political parties in CEE and LA.

Besides measurement problems, there are also some potential conceptual issues, emerging from the particular type of policy change analysed, that is, the imposition of bans. This book generally treats all types of policy change in the same manner. Some theoretical work, however, argues that certain types of policy change are more feasible than others (see, e.g., Hall 1993; Sabatier and Jenkins-Smith 1999; Sabatier and Weible 2007; Baumgartner and Jones 2009). With this in mind, it could be argued that a ban represents an instance of major policy change. Consequently, it may well be the case that policy change consisting of a ban must meet more demanding conditions in order to be attained than other types of policy change.

Another reason why the theoretical model put forward in chapter 6 could be inappropriate is that the regulation of GM maize represents a field not only of environmental policy, but also of consumer protection and agriculture policies. With regard to consumer protection policies, the potential health risks of GM maize are at the centre of attention. From the perspective of agriculture policy, GM maize is mainly discussed as a means of ensuring lower-priced and better-quality food (Anderson 2006: 125). The aspect regarding food supply is expected to be of lesser importance to European countries due to their higher average income and food supply levels, but it is likely to matter to some of the poorer LA countries. Moreover, maize in particular represents the most essential food product in many LA countries, and a shortage in supply can easily lead to social unrest (Otero and Pechlaner 2008: 44–7).

From this it also follows that the number of relevant political actors may be greater in the case of GM maize, as it cuts across policy fields, which would bring along a higher likelihood of diverging or even conflicting views on the most preferable regulatory approach. As a consequence, the veto player theory presented in chapter 2 might be of more relevance for this policy item than for the others. Put differently, the regulation of GM maize might be susceptible to specific kinds of influences and hence require the elaboration of a distinct theoretical model.

Finally, it must be emphasized that there is considerable pressure stemming from the United States and the WTO to liberalize the cultivation of GM crops (see, e.g., Pollack and Shaffer 2009: chapter 6; Winham 2009). In fact, the approval of MON810 maize for cultivation in the EU member states can be regarded as the consequence of these pressures. Since it is the European Commission that is involved in international negotiations and hence politically responsible for any decision taken regarding the cultivation of GM crops, she must be informed by each member state that orders a suspension of the growing of MON810 maize. The European Commission can challenge the national safeguard bans and has in fact done so in most cases, which represents another impediment for member states for undertaking such a step (see, e.g., Pollack and Shaffer 2009, 2010). From this it follows that all CEE states but Ukraine (as it is not an EU member state) should be confronted with higher political costs related to the imposition of a cultivation ban than their LA counterparts.

Regulation of Genetically Modfied Maize in Central and Eastern Europe

There are few issues over which the member states of the EU are as divided as the case of GMOs. On the one side, there are known supporters of biotechnology such as Estonia, Finland, the Netherlands, Sweden, and the United Kingdom, who would like to approve more GM crops for commercial cultivation (see Sabalza et al. 2011: 315). On the other side, there are a growing number of countries that either banned or tried to ban MON810 maize. According to the website of the Seventh European Conference of GMO-Free Regions, there are cultivation bans in place in Austria, France, Germany, Greece, Italy, Luxembourg, and Switzerland.[1] This group of GMO opponents is complemented by Bulgaria, Hungary, and Poland. This section discusses the causes of policy change in these three CEE countries and sheds light on the failed efforts to ban the commercial cultivation of MON810 maize in Romania and Ukraine.

Determinants of Policy Change in Bulgaria, Hungary, and Poland

Of the three CEE countries that instituted a ban on the commercial cultivation of MON810 maize, the case of Bulgaria is certainly the most surprising one, since in the past the country was known as GMO-friendly. MON810 maize was already approved for commercial cultivation there in 2000 (James 2002: 104). Shortly thereafter, however, Bulgarian citizens started to become uncomfortable with the liberal regulations surrounding cultivation, which culminated in a rejection of GMOs by 97 per cent of the Bulgarian population as a poll of the Bulgarian National Centre for Public Opinion carried out in March 2010 revealed (Novinite 2010). It was the growing public resistance that forced the ruling party, Citizens for European Development of Bulgaria, to propose legislation prohibiting the growing of GM crops.

Citizens for European Development of Bulgaria is centre-right, pro-European, and generally associated with business-friendly policies. Therefore, the party's original plan was to introduce a licensing system that would have restricted but not fully banned the growing of GM crops. However, the ongoing protests from NGOs, farmers, and citizens induced the party to abandon its initial plan and to propose an encompassing five-year-ban (Reuters 2010). The legislative proposal was also welcomed by the other Bulgarian political parties. Hence, in March 2010 the Bulgarian parliament passed amendments to the GMO Act which in practice meant that all GM crops were banned from the country. One hundred and forty-four Members of Parliament in the hall voted in favour of this suggestion, only one voted against it, and three abstained (Nikolova 2010). The five-year ban of March 2010 was transformed into a temporally unrestricted ban in February 2011 (Novinite 2011a). The adoption of the ban was motivated by reference to the likelihood of insects developing resistance to the toxin that MON810 maize contains, and to the possibility that the toxin may be damaging for the soil (Novinite 2011b).

Similarly to the case of Bulgaria, it looked unlikely that the Polish government would develop an anti-GMO stance. In its "National Environmental Policy for 2003–2006 and 2010 Outlook", the Polish Council of Ministers (2002: 33) recognized that the growing of GM crops meant an economic chance for Poland and that the major political task would be to overcome the public's mistrust. In March 2005, however, the government announced that it would place a ban on seventeen of the thirty-one varieties of MON810 maize allowed for cultivation in the EU. The bill was pushed through mainly by the then ruling conservative Law and Justice Party. This step was motivated by the recognition of the risk of a crossing of GM maize varieties with native ones. This new perception of the risk related to biotechnology was the result of intense lobbying by numerous NGOs such as the International Coalition to Protect the Polish Countryside.[2] Another reason that surely facilitated the ban is that Polish maize does not need to be treated with large amounts of insecticides (Brookes 2008: 160). In the opposite case, the imposition of a ban would have been more controversial, as MON810 maize can potentially replace the use of insecticides.

The lobbying in the Polish case occurred in the form of inside advocacy through personal contacts with policymakers, which were used to provide them with relevant information. In contrast to Bulgaria, mostly environmental groups were involved in lobbying, whereas, for example, farmers' associations did not participate in this process. This may also be the reason why there has been an ongoing debate – fuelled by the Polish Association of Maize Producers – about whether the restrictive law on agricultural biotechnology should be relaxed. Although some agriculture groups were originally against GM crops, many of them have changed their minds in the meantime and now support biotechnology due to increasing food imports (Figurska 2010). Nonetheless, in 2012 the Polish government even extended the ban, which is widely attributed to protests by anti-GMO groups and beekeepers (Digital Journal 2012).

Clearly less surprising was the banning of GM maize in Hungary in 2005, as the Socialist Party elected into government in 2002 had expressed its sceptical stance on GM crops for many years. The maintenance of the ban by successive governments is even more remarkable when one considers that the European Commission challenged it. The ban could remain in place, since the overwhelming majority of the other member states supported the Hungarian approach and voted against the European Commission (Pollack and Shaffer 2010: 352).

The groups supporting GMOs were small, consisting of biotech companies and some research institutes allied with this industry. However, all but one farmers' organization was strongly opposed to the growth of GM crops, since this would have negatively affected their GM-free reputation, which has given them a profitable market niche (Budapest Sun 2005). To understand this broad rejection of GM crops, it is important to note that Hungarian farmers have a comparative advantage in producing and exporting maize and maize seeds to other European countries. The release of GM maize would have exposed seed producers to the risk of contamination and may have meant a loss of important foreign markets. Already in the late 1990s , the Hungarian farmers allied themselves with the environmental lobby and pushed parliament to restrict the growth of GMOs (Harper 2003: 4). This is an important observation in light of the research literature, since it is often argued there that only groups representing small or organic farmers tend to support anti-GMO movements (see Ansell, Maxwell, and Sicurelli 2006: 101). Indeed, in the Hungarian case, almost all farmers' associations – including the ones representing the large producers – opposed the legalization of MON810 maize.

Another factor that facilitated the banning of MON810 maize can be seen in the composition of the Reporting Committee on Biotechnology Activities, which prepares decisions and gives opinion on new biotechnology products or field trials of new plant varieties. The committee consists of seventeen representatives, of whom six are NGO members. Their numerical strength gives the NGO members the power to block more liberal regulations. Moreover, industry representatives are excluded from the committee, which has impeded the introduction of GM maize in Hungary (Demont et al. 2008: 465).

To sum up, the case studies demonstrate that anti-GMO groups and the ruling political parties' responsiveness to public demand were decisive in making the cultivation bans in Bulgaria, Hungary, and Poland possible. In addition, they show that anti-GMO groups not only matter for triggering policy change by raising public awareness and mobilizing the masses, but also by providing information to policymakers and therewith stimulating processes of policy learning as was the case in Poland. This supports some of the theoretical approaches to policy change presented in chapter 2, namely, the advocacy coalition framework, the theories of policy-oriented learning, and the policy-subsystem adjustment model. Moreover, the Hungarian case study illuminated the role of the economic importance of maize production for policy change, as it was this factor that induced powerful farmers' associations to support the ban of GM maize.

Reasons for Failed Policy Change in Romania and Ukraine

Romania's lands were heavily cultivated with GM crops before the country joined the EU in 2007. In 1998, different varieties of GM potatoes, maize, and soy were grown, of which the latter represented the most extensive culture. In order to meet the provisions of the acquis communautaire, the Romanian government had to ban GM soy and other GM crops that are not allowed to be grown in the EU. Since then, Romanian farmers who previously profited from soy production have been lobbying hard to reintroduce this GM variety. The League of Agricultural

Producers of Romania, for instance, has sent an open letter urging the government to permit GMOs. Moreover, numerous Romanian agricultural academics declared themselves in favour of GMOs, emphasizing the GMOs' role for benefiting for lowering food prices (Diplomat 2011).

Against this background, the announcement of the then environment minister Attila Korodi in March 2008 to institute a ban on the cultivation of MON810 maize indeed came as a surprise. To increase the chances of effectively implementing the ban, however, Korodi had to gain the support of two more actors. First, he needed to receive an opinion from the Romanian Biosafety Commission, and second, he had to ensure the support of the minister of agriculture. The biosafety commission is a scientific body with a consultative role in assessing GMO notifications in Romania. To receive its approval for the legislative proposal, the environment minister ordered that a new biosafety commission should be formed, as the members of the previous one were known to have strong ties with the biotech lobby. Upon the environment minister's announcement instituting a cultivation ban, the designated president of the biosafety commission made strong statements against the safety of MON810 maize. However, once the new commission was formed, the situation changed profoundly. The president and eleven of the twelve members of the biosafety commission had completely changed their minds about the potential risks of MON810 maize. Thus, the biosafety commission approved the cultivation of GM maize instead of proposing a ban (Paun 2011: 7).

While the biosafety commission's approval of GM maize threatened the realization of the cultivation ban, the prospect of policy change became further reduced by the refusal of Agriculture Minister Dacian Cioloş to support the ban (Pelc 2009: 38). The reason for Cioloş's lack of support would seem to be based on personal considerations about defending his position within the cabinet, as Prime Minister Popescu-Tăriceanu (2004–8) also began dismissing the idea of a cultivation ban (see Paun 2011). In 2010, another effort to ban MON810 was undertaken by the new environment minister, László Borbély. Again, the ban was circumvented by the agriculture minister, Valeriu Tabără, who is known for his favourable stance on GM crops.[3]

The failed efforts to ban MON810 in Romania underscore the relevance of the reasoning presented above that this policy item is different from the others, as it brings together a larger number of relevant actors due to its inter-sectoral character. This is reflected in the fact that two ministers had to collaborate to realize a cultivation ban. The agriculture minister, however, has to take into account other considerations than those related to the environment. In terms of GM crops, it is mostly the farmers organizations' views that must be respected, and they have been in favour of biotechnology in Romania. Another important observation in this regard is that the profound changes in the position of the biosafety commission were most probably the result of lobbying by the agrochemical industry (see Paun 2011). The impact of the pro-GMO lobby distinguishes this case from the previous ones, since in those policy change was predominantly triggered by anti-GMO groups.

Another example of a failed trial to ban GM crops is provided by Ukraine. This case, however, is clearly different from the Romanian one, since it was not the government that took the initiative, but two deputies in the Ukrainian parliament. Draft law 5286, "On Prohibition of Using Genetically Modified Organisms in Ukraine," was submitted in October 2009 by a deputy of the Party of Regions. Draft law 5286-1, "On Proclamation of Ukraine as a Territory Free from Genetically Modified Organisms," was registered in November 2011 by a deputy of the Communist Party.[4] On the website of the Ukrainian parliament the status of both draft laws is defined as "rejected and withdrawn from consideration."[5]

Both proposals aimed at an absolute prohibition of GMO product usage and dissemination in the territory of Ukraine. Despite their ambitious goals, the proposals were brought into the legislative process without the consent of the majority factions or the government, and thus must be seen as isolated actions. They were turned down due to a lack of political support. To be sure, there seems to be neither a clear political nor public demand for restricting or even banning the growth of GM crops. According to Blume (2000: 18), the Ukrainian public generally has a predominantly positive stance on GMOs. Public concerns rather centre on the introduction of mandatory labelling for all products containing GMOs. As there is no well-defined public demand for banning GM crops, Ukrainian policymakers seem to be walking "a road that may turn either 'pro GMO' or 'against GMO'" (Dubinyuk 2010: 7).

Regulation of Genetically Modfied Maize in Latin America

Concerning GM crops, LA is divided between countries such as Argentina that are globally known to strongly support biotechnology and countries such as Peru that oppose them (see Newell 2009: 28). It is difficult to say whether, on average, the region has become more pro- or anti-GMOs in the last two decades, since both upward and downward changes regarding the regulation of GM maize – and GM crops in general – can be observed. In other words, a number of LA countries imposed a cultivation ban on MON810 maize towards the end of the observation period, but at the same time Brazil and El Salvador liberalized their regulatory approach, and there are additional cases in which this might happen in near future. What can, however, be said is that the causes underlying policy change in LA are manifold.

Paraguay and Mexico: The Relevance of the Social and Cultural Value of Maize

Paraguay is one of the world's biggest exporters of soybeans and grew GM soybean varieties unofficially for several years until the government approved their use in 2004 (Traxler 2006: 58; James 2009: 127). In comparison to the other countries of the South Cone, Paraguay can be seen as a laggard in adopting biotechnology. In marked contrast to its neighbouring countries Argentina and Chile, Paraguay signed and ratified the Cartagena Protocol, which indicates that the country is generally aware of the potential risks of the release of GMOs into the environment. More specifically, since 1993 the commercial cultivation of GM maize has been prohibited on the grounds of the Environmental Impact Assessment Law. The adoption of this law was a response to the Rio Declaration on Environment and Development of 1992 and represents one of the first efforts undertaken by President Juan Carlos Wasmosy (1993–8) of the conservative Colorado Party to strengthen the country's environmental policy.

The stimulus for the introduction of obligatory environmental-impact assessments can be seen in the transnational communication processes that took place in the context of the Rio Earth Summit. The inclusion of a cultivation ban for GM maize into this law, however, mostly stems from cultural and social considerations. Maize is central to the Paraguayan diet and there are various native maize types that have been produced by indigenous communities (Latinamerican Press 2011). Therefore, the cultivation ban is primarily the result of the recognition of the specific cultural value of maize by the Paraguayan policymakers and was not caused by grassroots activities or other types of anti-GMO lobbying.

There are, however, hints that the restrictive approach to GM maize might be abandoned soon. In October 2010, the minister of agriculture, Enzo Cardozo Jiménez, signed a resolution allowing field trials for several GM maize varieties. This resolution yields a drastic shift in the country's previous regulatory approach, as it removed the requirement for environmental licences for field trials (Yankelevich 2010: 2). Furthermore, in January 2011 the Paraguayan Institute of Agriculture Technology, which was established by President Fernando Lugo of the left-wing Patriotic Alliance for Change, authorized field experiments with MON810 maize (Latinamerican Press 2011). The reason for this gradual weakening of the government's restrictive policy is the considerable increase of investments into the country by the Monsanto Company (Reuters 2011). Officially, however, the commercial cultivation of MON810 maize is still prohibited.

Turning to the Mexican case, it must immediately be stressed that the country's accession to NAFTA has played a crucial role in its approach to biotechnology (Falkner and Gupta 2009: 120). It was while preparing the country's accession to NAFTA that the government of Mexico permitted field testing of GM crops in the late 1980s. Right from the start of the field trials there have been controversies over the GM varieties due to the cultural and social relevance of maize, which is even more pronounced than in Paraguay (Antal 2007). As the country is widely regarded as the "biological center of origin of maize (and center of genetic diversity)" (Jansen and Roquas 2008: 101), there have been intense debates about the potential gene flow from GM maize to native varieties. Notwithstanding the importance of anti-GMO groups such as Greenpeace Mexico and the National Union of Autonomous Regional Peasant Organizations (Poitras 2008), it was not only lobbying that led to the imposition of a moratorium on the release of GM maize in 1998. The decision was taken by the members of the Directorate of Plant Health, which were presented with scientific evidence which they found convincing enough to conclude that the country would not benefit from growing GM maize and that there was the risk of genetic contamination of native varieties (Fitting 2008: 139–40). After this, however, a number of decisions were taken that seem to prepare the liberalization of policies on the commercial growth of GM maize.

In 2004 the moratorium was lifted for experimental trials by the administration of President Vicente Fox (2000–6) of the centre-right National Action Party (Falkner and Gupta 2009: 124). In 2009 the administration of Felipe Calderón approved twenty-one experimental field trials of GM maize. The trials were approved following the passage of the biosafety law in 2005 and additional related legal acts. However, as in Paraguay, the commercial cultivation of GM maize is still illegal in Mexico.

The main motivation for allowing field trials can be seen in new insights regarding the potential for increasing maize production. The Mexican government seeks to produce enough crops so that the country does not have to rely on imports. The 2007 "tortilla crisis" showed that this goal has not yet been achieved. The doubling of the price for tortillas, which mainly consist of maize flour, prompted about 70,000 people to take to the streets (Epoch Times 2008). At the same time, a well-organized anti-GMO lobby exists, consisting of environmental groups, farmers, and indigenous organizations, which form the Network for the Defence of Maize (Salgado Ramírez 2009: 99). This network serves as a watchdog and seeks to prevent a further relaxation of Mexican regulations. It is very well-informed and has carried out considerable work in publicizing the issue in the Mexican media (Antal 2007: 26). Therefore, it is difficult to predict how the Mexican regulatory approach to GM maize will look in future.

The analysis of policy change in Paraguay and Mexico supports the view that maize possesses some characteristics that clearly distinguish this policy item from the others. Most importantly, the prohibition of a commercial cultivation of GM maize was the result of a top-down decision-making process based on social and cultural considerations. Remarkably, the value attached to native species also corresponds to the main determinant of policy change in Hungary. At the same time, however, the still restrictive policies could be relaxed in the near future. One reason is that the Monsanto Company is investing considerably in the development of biotechnology in Paraguay. Concerning Mexico, the skyrocketing maize prices induced the government to adopt a more liberal stance on GM maize by allowing field trials. Another issue with respect to the Mexican case is that NAFTA helped to undermine the country's previous regulatory approach. As a consequence of NAFTA, Mexico has to import maize from Canada and the United States that often corresponds to GM varieties (Fitting 2006). As a result, a genetic contamination of native maize varieties has already been registered (see Jansen and Roquas 2008: 100–2).[6] However, once contamination has occurred, it becomes relatively easy for proponents of biotechnology to push for a more liberal regulatory framework. Therefore, it can be stated that GM maize imports from its northern neighbours have made it more complicated for the Mexican government to effectively keep up the cultivation ban.

Bolivia, Ecuador, and Venezuela: The Pink Tide
and Its Consequences for Policy Change

The presidents of Bolivia, Ecuador, and Venezuela personalize the left turn in LA politics. They are broadly perceived as left-wing, nationalist, populist, and determined to launch projects aimed at profound social change (Conaghan and de la Torre 2008: 270). The administrations of the Ecuadorian president, Rafael Correa, and the Bolivian president, Evo Morales, in particular, have embraced environmental issues motivated by their mostly indigenous political base (Rénique 2009: 22). Similarly, President Chávez of Venezuela has demonstrated his willingness to address environmental issues if these correspond to his overall political goals. Hence, the adoption of an anti-GMO stance of these three presidents must be seen against their political-ideological background.

The country with the most restrictive elements in its biotechnology policy is Bolivia. The new Bolivian constitution of 2009 imposes a ban on the growth of any types of GM crops. In addition, in June 2010, President Morales decreed a five-year transition period in which to eliminate GM crops from the entire national territory. Policy change can be regarded as a direct result of the new partisan composition of the Bolivian government. The ruling party, Movement for Socialism, emphasizes the promotion of social and cultural inclusion of the indigenous people, state intervention, and redistribution of revenue from natural resources such as gas and oil reserves.

Concerning environmental issues, the party draws on indigenous philosophies. Moreover, the party is in favour of traditional forms of agriculture, supporting small-scale enterprises that empower individual farmers to grow enough crops to sustain their families (see, e.g., Rénique 2009; Petras and Veltmeyer 2010). With the election of Evo Morales, who himself is a former coca farmer belonging to the indigenous Aymara group, the agriculture policy that previously favoured landowners and agriculture companies was altered in such a way as to support subsistence farmers producing for local markets. This new approach towards agriculture policy stands in marked contrast with a production structure that would emerge with the growth of GM crops (see Otero and Pechlaner 2008: 50–2). Most important, with virtually all GM crops, farmers must purchase new seed annually from the biotech company with which they collaborate, which increases their economic dependence.

Beyond the shifts in Bolivian agriculture policy, President Morales also demonstrated on various occasions his political commitment to environmental protection. Probably the best known statement he has made was at the Seventh Session of the United Nations Permanent Forum on Indigenous Issues in 2008, when he presented his "Ten Commandments to Save the Planet, Humanity, and Life." More specifically, at the 2010 World People's Conference on Climate Change, President Morales declared his personal reservations about GM food. He suspects these products to have a negative impact on human health, which makes the restrictive regulatory approach to GM crops even more plausible (El País 2010; for a discussion see, e.g., Aguirre and Cooper 2010).

The Ecuadorian case parallels the Bolivian one to the extent that President Correa has also attempted to appeal to indigenous communities and various social movements, especially by using an anti-neoliberal rhetoric (see Close 2010: 123–4). Again, the main motivation of the Correa administration for declaring Ecuador a zone free from GM seeds and crops can be seen in the president's ideological background. Rafael Correa is the leader of the socialist movement Alliance for a Proud and Sovereign Fatherland, which is comparable to the Bolivian Movement for Socialism. At various instances, President Correa has stated his desire to curtail neoliberal policies and implement social and economic strategies that would benefit the majority of the Ecuadorian people (Becker 2011: 47). In this context, the enactment of a new constitution represented his foremost political objective. During the drafting of the new constitution, various civil society organizations – mostly farmers, indigenous groups, environmentalists, and consumer groups – managed to influence the sections addressing the issue of GM crops (see Gudynas 2009). Compared to Bolivia, however, the Ecuadorian approach appears less stringent, since exemptions from the cultivation ban are possible if these are in the interest of "national security."

Venezuelan President Chávez's announcement to ban GMOs in Venezuela in April 2003 also corresponds to his political ideology, that is, Bolivarianism, which is mostly based on social reforms, participatory democracy, and the nationalization of key industries. Moreover, Bolivarianism emphasizes a food system free of corporate control, neoliberal economic policies, and unfair trade rules (Parker 2008; Schiavoni and Camacaro 2009: 2). In this context, it should be noted that "agricultural biotechnology is a US-dominated project and the USA has considerable influence on the global stage" (Pechlaner and Otero 2008: 353; see also Pollack and Shaffer 2009: chapter 6; Winham 2009). This is another important characteristic of GM crops that collides with the ideological world view of the Venezuelan president.

Shortly after being elected in 1998, President Chávez staged a referendum on a constituent assembly and elections for the assembly. In this way, he was able to enact a new constitution that endowed the executive with greater powers and allowed for presidential re-election (Conaghan and de la Torre 2008: 269–70). As a result, Venezuela has increasingly adopted features of a presidential system (Wiarda and Kline 2007: 220; Close 2010). Therefore, public policy is predominantly determined by the preferences of the president, which also became apparent in the case of GM crops.

During the process of negotiating a contract with the Monsanto Company, President Chávez changed his mind when the international peasants' organization Via Campesina approached him to argue that legalizing GM crops would contradict the interests and needs of the country's farmers (El Correo de la Diaspora Latinoaméricaine 2004). According to Bravo (2009: 68), the president explained his intention to ban GM crops by stressing that he would not be willing to accept that the Venezuelan people could be poisoned by food products, while agrochemical multinational companies benefited from increasing profits.

Even though the president's ideological predisposition and the lobbying activities of Via Campesina suggest a plausible picture of policy change, this particular case is puzzling, since the cultivation ban has not been incorporated into a legal act (Altieri 2009: 11; Bravo 2009: 68–9). Therefore, the actual status of GM crops in the country is very difficult to assess. On the one side, there is evidence that the Monsanto Company is still operating in the country, which it would not be doing if the ban was effective. On the other side, the overview of the commercial production of GM crops provided by James (2009) suggests that no such activities are taking place in Venezuela. This latter point suggests that the coding of the data based on legal acts might have been inaccurate, as apparently no GM maize is grown in Venezuela. However, the de facto absence of GM maize still does not justify basing the entire coding procedure on this criterion, since this can quickly lead to arbitrary measurement. Consequently, despite the difficulties in properly assessing the Venezuelan case, it must still be seen as reasonable to rely on legal acts for coding the data.

Party Politics and Trade Relations with the EU: The Case of Peru

For many years, Peru has maintained a strict stance on the cultivation and importation of GMOs, but it was only in November 2011 that this became formalized by means of a ten-year moratorium on cultivation and importation. However, before this step was taken, it looked as if the country would liberalize its biosafety policy. After many years of intense political debate that mostly centred around the opposing positions of the Ministry of Agriculture and the newly created Ministry of the Environment (see Montoro Zamora 2009: 44), in April 2011 the outgoing president, Alan García, signed the Biosafety Regulation, which would have meant the liberalization of research, production, and trade of GMOs. Congress – which is composed of many members opposing GMOs – responded immediately to this step and passed the moratorium brought into the legislative process by the Ministry of Environment.

In July 2011, President García of the centre-left American Popular Revolutionary Alliance refused to sign the legislative act instituting a moratorium. He stated that by imposing a moratorium the country would violate the responsibilities emerging from its WTO membership and that it might have harmful effects on research on biotech crops. The moratorium draft was thus sent back to Congress with comments on why this action was not in the country's best interest (Nolte 2011: 2). In other words, the president used his veto power to impede policy change.[7] The adoption of the moratorium only became possible with the ascension into office of the new left-wing president, Ollanta Humala, who is closely affiliated with other Pink Tide leaders in Latin America and ideologically particularly close to Bolivia's President Morales. Similarly to Morales, Humala opposes GMOs and was willing to sign the moratorium that had failed earlier.

In addition to the change in government, there is another reason that explains the adoption of the moratorium, namely, Peru's efforts to be added to the EU's list of preferred organic food suppliers. The president of the Agrarian Commission, José León, has explained that prohibiting GMOs is important for preserving the country's biodiversity, which is vital for ensuring that it can further develop its position as a producer of food products (El Comercio 2011). The process of accreditation is reaching its final stage, and as soon as the country is added to the list it will make it easier for Peruvian producers to export organic food to the EU market. Consequently, the present case can be associated with the logic of the California effect, since despite the legal status of MON810 maize, the EU can be seen as a market that generally opposes GMOs (see, e.g., Skogstad 2006; Pollack and Shaffer 2009, 2010). Therefore, it is rational step for the Peruvian government to impose a general ban on GMOs in order to ensure access to the European market.

Brazil and El Salvador: Explaining the U-Turn in Biosafety Policy

Biosafety policy in Brazil and El Salvador is characterized by an initial tightening of regulations that subsequently became relaxed. The occurrence of both kinds of policy change, that is, a tightening followed by a relaxation, turns these two countries into interesting cases for better understanding the specific characteristics of biosafety policy.

The centre-right coalition of President Fernando Cardoso (1995–2002) took the first major step towards regulating the release of GMOs into the environment by passing the Brazilian biosafety law in 1995. This law authorized the executive branch to form a new regulatory institution, the National Biosafety Technical Commission, consisting of specialists, government officials, and some private-sector representatives to oversee and regulate any aspect of GMOs. The government subsequently developed a consensus policy characterized by three key aspects. First, it permitted and regulated GMO-related research. Second, the policy allowed the sale of commercial products containing GMOs, given that these were properly labelled. Third, the commercial production of GM crops was prohibited (Jepson, Brannstrom, and Stancato de Souza 2008: 221).

This consensus policy, however, became challenged when in 1998 the Monsanto Company requested permission from the Brazilian government to commercialize its GM soybeans. In reaction to the National Biosafety Technical Commission's acceptance of Monsanto's request, a coalition of NGOs spearheaded by the Brazilian Institute for Consumer Defence filed suit in federal court. Other groups opposing GM crops were environmental groups such as Greenpeace Brazil, farmers' associations, trade unions, academics, the Movement of Landless Rural Workers, and the democratic-socialist Workers' Party (Jansen and Roquas 2008: 99).

The consensus policy of the Cardoso administration definitely ended with the ascension to power of the administration of President Luiz

Inácio Lula da Silva (2003–11). During the 2002 presidential campaign, the Workers' Party's candidate Lula declared that he was against the release of GMOs (Pelaez 2009: 63), but once in power he took a number of decisions that effectively led to the legalization of GM crops. Most important, well-known supporters of biotechnology were appointed key ministers involved in biosafety policy, such as the former agriculture minister, Roberto Rodrigues (Scoones 2008: 324).

Then, two issues urged the Lula administration to develop biosafety legislation, which brought about the regulatory U-turn. First, in 2002 China, as the main importer of Brazilian soybeans, imposed the legal requirement that GM crops had to be labelled. This requirement became quite complicated to fulfil since, on the one hand, the government knew that GM soybeans were grown illegally. On the other hand, declaring that Brazilian soybeans exports did contain GM varieties would have meant admitting that the government approved of this illegal act. The second issue was that farmers who illegally grew GM soybeans in the state of Rio Grande do Sul were to harvest them in the first month of 2003. The idea of destroying the illegally planted GM soybeans could have had unfavourable political consequences for the government, as it was attempting to implement a nationwide program to eradicate hunger (Jepson, Brannstrom, and Stancato de Souza 2008: 234–5).

As a result, the government allowed the cultivation of GM crops by applying an ad hoc legal means, "known as a 'conduct adjustment,' under which farmers who had broken the law would be forgiven for the 2003 harvest, as long as they promised not to plant GMOs again" (Pelaez 2009: 64). Moreover, a National Biosafety Council was set up with the task of drafting major reforms in biosafety legislation. It took two years of intense partisan disputes to have the new law approved by Brazilian congress. In its current form, the law of 2005 approves of commercially planting GM crops and gives considerable power to the National Biosafety Technical Commission to authorize the commercial release of GMOs, subordinating the registration and control agencies of the health, agriculture, and environment ministries to its decisions. While some draft versions contained more restrictive elements, it was the mobilization of pro-GMO groups in the Brazilian senate that determined the law's final content.

Pro- and anti-GMO lobbying is certainly the most important explanation of policy change in Brazil. What make this case quite unique are the opposing stances of legislature, executive, and judiciary on the issue of GM crops. The strong role played by the judiciary is particularly unusual and highlights the fact that policy change may be brought about by more actors than previously expected. This lends support to the perspective of veto player theory, which emphasizes the role of the courts in policy change. Further, it was the imposition of stricter regulatory requirements by Brazil's main trading partner China that generated the need to reform legislation. Ironically, however, this event did not lead to a tightening of Brazilian standards, but to a liberalization of its biosafety policy.

Another case in which policy change first implied a tightening of GMO regulations and then the adoption of a notably more liberal regime is represented by El Salvador. Until the year 2000, GM crops were not important for the Salvadoran government as the country did not produce any. It was on the occasion of signing the Cartagena Protocol that the government adopted the planting seed law in 2001, of which article 30 stated that it was prohibited to import, conduct research on, produce, or commercialize GM seeds (Campos 2009: 88). This article was added to the law in response to criticism by environmental groups, and hence represents another successful case of anti-GMO lobbying (Gutiérrez 2002: 244; Ibarra Turcios et al. 2004: 40). However, in 2008, the Salvadoran parliament decided to reform the law and to abolish the article.

The main reason for abolishing the restrictions on the cultivation of GM crops stems from the country's structural dependence on the importation of food products. The ban of GM crops entailed rising food costs and culminated in a food crisis in the spring of 2008 (Inter Press Service 2008). About 70 per cent of Salvadoran households are net consumers of so-called sensitive agricultural commodities, and are thus susceptible to short-term net declines in welfare due to increases in basic food prices (World Bank 2008: 28). It was the emerging social unrest that induced the Salvadoran government to abolish article 30 of the planting seed law. Another stimulus for giving up the restrictive position on GM crops was lobbying by the private sector (Herrera 2008: 5). With the abolition of article 30 of the planting seed law, the country can now cultivate biotech crops within its own territory and is less dependent on crop imports from the United States. In fact, since May 2009 GM maize has been grown for experimental purposes (Campos 2009: 88).

To sum up, the first instance of policy change in El Salvador can be attributed to the involvement of environmental groups as well as a certain enthusiasm stemming from the negotiation of the Cartagena

Protocol. However, when confronted with serious constraints in ensuring food supply, the Salvadoran government considered its policy and decided to liberalize the commercial planting of GM crops.

Tying the Case Studies Together: Implications for the Theoretical Model

The previous sections presented various explanations for the causes of changes in the regulation of GM maize, of which partisanship, lobbying, and the existence of native varieties turned out to be the most important. Starting with partisanship, resistance against GM crops in Bolivia, Ecuador, Peru, and Venezuela can be attributed to the leftist ideologies of their administrations and their generally negative stance on neoliberal globalization. These governments primarily reject GM crops since they would increase farmers' dependence on agrochemical multinationals such as the Monsanto Company and therewith displace traditional forms of agriculture based on the principles of self-sufficiency and production for local markets.

Of these four countries, however, the presidents of Bolivia and Peru adopted the most restrictive approach towards GM crops, whereas the Ecuadorian legislation leaves the door somewhat open for the approval of GMOs. The Venezuelan case is the most puzzling one since, despite President Chávez's rhetoric, no legally binding ban has been instituted. In marked contrast, the left turn of Brazilian politics led to a temporary legalization of the cultivation of GM crops in 2003 due to a "political and economic emergency" (Pelaez 2009: 65). The temporary legalization was followed by a permanent one in 2005 when pro-GMO groups managed to convince the Brazilian senate of the positive aspects of biotechnology. Concerning the CEE countries, the impact of political-ideological factors was very limited, if not to say absent. This finding is intuitive, as in this region no comparable left-wing, anti-globalization parties exist.

The in-depth studies further underscored the relevance of lobbying for policy change. Remarkably, the opponents of GM crops made use of various lobbying tactics, namely, inside, outside, and grassroots advocacy. The Polish ban, for instance, can be attributed to inside advocacy, as anti-GMO groups established personal contacts with policymakers and supplied them with information. In this way, the government adopted a different view on GMOs and proposed more restrictive legislation. Likewise, in Ecuador and El Salvador anti-GMO groups were directly involved in the drafting of legislation. Moreover, the anti-GMO stance of Peru's congress is perceived to be the result of the anti-GMO lobbying (Nolte 2011: 2). Outside advocacy – that is, informing the public about the potential risks of GMOs – was, for example, practised in Romania. Grassroots advocacy through mass mobilization was the lobbying tactic particularly observed in Brazil and Bulgaria, although only in Bulgaria it could bring about a permanent ban. The role of societal mobilization corresponds to policy-subsystem approaches such as the punctuated equilibrium model (Baumgartner and Jones 2009) or the subsystem-adjustment model (Howlett and Ramesh 2002). The main reasoning of these models is that the anti-GMO groups "expanded the policy subsystem and altered the range of ideas present within it" (Cashore and Howlett 2006: 144; see also Hoberg 2003). This provides a complementary view on the effectiveness of NGOs for policy change.

The final category of explanatory factors corresponds to the cultural, economic, and social importance attached to domestic maize varieties. Hungary, for instance, is a major maize and maize seed producer in Europe and therefore the government is strongly interested in having legislation in place that safeguards the Hungarian producers' GMO-free status, as this gives them a comparative advantage vis-à-vis other producers. Similarly, the Polish government decided to institute restrictions on MON810 maize to protect native species from GM varieties. Even more marked is the cultural and social significance of native varieties in Mexico and Paraguay, which induced the governments to establish a special protection regime.

What do these findings imply for the theoretical model underlying this study? First of all, the more fine-grained analysis helped to get the empirical picture straight regarding the role of lobbying and issue salience. As shown above, lobbying by both anti- and pro-GMO groups was decisive for the (non-)occurrence of policy change. It has become clear that it was the operationalization of this variable that led to puzzling results. As the measurement of the variable used for the quantitative analysis only took into account environmental groups and excluded other anti-GMO groups, for instance, farmers' associations, indigenous organizations, and consumer groups, it underestimated the overall lobbying potential. Therefore, a great deal of the poor performance of the statistical analysis can be explained on grounds of this measurement problem.

The same holds true for issue salience. To recall, the quantitative analysis employed the consumption of pesticides as a proxy for issue salience. The in-depth studies, however, underlined that it is rather the agricultural aspect of this policy item than the environmental one that matters for policy change. Most important, considerations about food security and the threat of social conflicts, for instance, induced the Salvadoran government to re-liberalize the cultivation of GM crops.

Concerning economic integration, it must be stated that there is limited evidence only for the California effect, which was found to be somehow effective in the case of policy change in Peru. To recall, the country applied for being added to the EU's list of preferential third countries supplying organic food. However, in this context it should also be noted that Argentina as one of the main supporters of GM crops already benefits from this status, which has not induced the country to adopt a more restrictive regulatory approach. This suggests that the California effect is primarily likely to be effective if there are favourable domestic factors as there were in the Peruvian case with the ascension to power of President Humala, who opposes GMOs for ideological reasons.

More generally, the limited evidence for the California effect is quite plausible, since in the case of GM maize the United States – often the main trading partner of the LA countries (see Gallagher, K.P. 2008) – supports their liberalization (see Drezner 2007). Consequently, in this specific case the United States cannot trigger a regulatory upward ratcheting. Further to this, there are hints that investments by the Monsanto Company could matter for changes in the regulation of GM maize. This was suggested by the Paraguayan case, where observers expect the revocation of the official cultivation ban for GM maize in near future because of increased investments. However, the empirical evidence presented here is too weak to convincingly argue that regulatory competition is effective.

All in all, the case studies support the role of lobbying, political parties, and issue salience. They provide limited support for the theoretical model's reasoning regarding the California effect. Yet there are at least four variables that need to be added to the theoretical model to make it suitable for explaining changes in the regulation of GM maize. The first variable refers to the role of leftist governments in LA. The second variable concerns the relevance of maize for a country's culture. The third variable involves a country's status as an exporter of maize and maize seeds. Finally, the countries' situation regarding food security should make a difference in their regulatory approach to GM maize. Despite these theoretical shortcomings, the issue that is dominant and indeed causes the conceptual problems is the nature of the dependent variable. The case studies did not provide evidence that it is the magnitude of policy change that matters or the fact that some countries use moratoriums instead of legislation to (temporarily) end the growing of MON810 maize. Rather, they highlighted the fact that the agricultural aspects of this policy item indeed turn it into a specific case.

Conclusion

It was the objective of this chapter to address the following two research questions: Which factors facilitate the imposition of a cultivation ban? Why did the quantitative analysis fail to produce plausible answers? The in-depth analyses showed that there are three main factors inducing governments in emerging market democracies to adopt more restrictive biosafety legislation. First, governments with a strong anti-globalization stance such as the left-wing administrations of Bolivia, Ecuador, Peru, and Venezuela are likely to institute a growing ban. What is, however, arguably even more important is lobbying by anti-GMO groups, which represents the second facilitating factor. Third, countries possessing native maize varieties or exporting maize seeds are likely to protect this resource by means of a growing ban for GM varieties. These findings are quite different from what the results of the quantitative analysis suggested.

While the poor performance of the statistical model can be attributed to the inappropriate operationalization of the independent variables, the core problem must be seen in the characteristics and measurement of the dependent variable. Most important, GM maize is not exclusively an environmental policy issue. The case studies demonstrated that the agricultural aspects of this policy item dominate over the environmental ones. This represents an important finding and calls for a broader scholarly debate about whether inter-sectoral policy items should be addressed by specific theoretical models or whether they can be accommodated within existing ones. The results of this study rather suggest that specific theoretical models are needed, but this might only hold true for the case of GM maize. Thus, more systematic research on the causes of changes in inter-sectoral policies can be regarded as a valuable complement to the literature.

8 Stability and Change in Emerging Market Democracies: Concluding Remarks

The central objective of this book was to examine policy and institutional change in the field of environmental policy in the emerging market democracies of Central and Eastern Europe and Latin America. To this end, it described in detail changes in the regulation of air, soil, and water pollution and sketched the adoption of restrictions on the commercial cultivation of GM maize and the SFM principle in the period between 1990 and 2010. In a next step, the study illustrated the diffusion of institutions possessing the competence to prosecute environmental offences. In this way, the book sought to address the concerns frequently expressed in the literature that improvements in environmental quality in emerging market democracies are hampered by the governments' insufficient commitment to regulatory enforcement (see, e.g., Porter 1999; Gallagher 2002, 2004; Konisky 2007; Knill, Tosun, and Heichel 2008; Bechtel and Tosun 2009). To explain the empirically observed patterns of policy and institutional change, the book focused on the impact of economic integration, domestic politics, integration with international institutions, and responsiveness to public demand. To uncover the causal relationships in the most rigorous way, it employed a quantitative research design, which was complemented by a qualitative analysis of the regulation of GM maize.

This concluding chapter presents the key insights gained from studying policy and institutional change in the context of system transformation in CEE and LA. It is organized into three parts. The first part summarizes the main findings in order to answer the research questions posed at the beginning of this study. Subsequently, the chapter discusses the study's theoretical and empirical limitations. The final section points the way towards the most promising avenues for further research that build on the empirical data provided by this study.

Responding to the Research Questions

The introductory chapter posed three central research questions addressing the patterns and causes of policy and institutional change in the field of environmental policy in emerging market economies: How have the consequences of dual system transformation affected environmental policy arrangements? Have CEE and LA countries developed similar environmental policy patterns? How have the consequences of dual system transformation influenced the governments' commitment to enforce the set rules? It is the objective of this section to answer these questions on the grounds of the comprehensive empirical data analysed in the book.

Consequences of Political and Economic Transformation

The first and foremost goal of this book was to illustrate how political and economic transformation affects environmental policymaking in CEE and LA. To facilitate the empirical testing of the impact of this dual system transformation, chapter 3 elaborated a theoretical framework that concentrated on four dimensions of system transformation: economic integration with international markets, the existence of a polity characterized by party competition and the participation of civil society actors, integration with the EU, and responsiveness to public demand.

The theoretical approaches related to economic integration led to the formulation of two hypotheses. The first hypothesis on regulatory competition anticipated that in order to maximize FDI inflows, the governments of CEE and LA countries would be inclined to preserve their regulatory status quo or even lower existing environmental protection arrangements. The second hypothesis followed David Vogel's (1995, 1997) argument about the California effect. This hypothesis posited that larger shares of exports to high-regulating economies might raise domestic regulatory stringency in emerging market democracies in response to the risk of being expelled from attractive markets (see also Hoberg 1991, 2002; Prakash and Potoski 2006, 2007; Perkins and Neumayer 2012). The quantitative analysis provided only limited support for the effectiveness of regulatory competition. The only exception was the analysis of SFM, which indeed confirmed the expectation that

FDI reduces the odds of adopting this particular forest management principle. This finding challenges arguments in the literature that posit a positive relationship between FDI and SFM (see, e.g., Laaksonen-Craig 2004). The analyses of changes in the regulation of air, soil, and water pollution, however, actually revealed that increasing FDI levels stimulate a tightening of environmental protection standards. Consequently, for most policy items analysed, competition for FDI does not provide an incentive for the governments in CEE and LA to preserve lax environmental regulations (see also, e.g., Sorsa 1994; Hoberg 2001; Prakash and Potoski 2007; Holzinger, Knill, and Sommerer 2008, 2011). From this it follows that inward FDI can help to strengthen environmental protection standards in emerging market democracies.

More ambivalent, however, are the findings for the hypothesized effect of exports to high-regulating economies. A stable California effect was only observed for quality standards. Furthermore, the in-depth study of the regulation of GM maize revealed that the direction of trade can indeed matter, but with outcomes that vary depending on the characteristics of the form of economic dependence. In the case of Mexico, for instance, intensified trade with Canada and the United States – which both support GMOs (see Skogstad 2006; Pechlaner and Otero 2008) – are about to bring down the cultivation restrictions imposed on GM maize in 1998. The opposite outcome was observed for Peru, which imposed a ten-year moratorium on the cultivation of any kind of GMOs in 2011. This step was partly motivated by the country's wish to be included in the EU's preferred list of organic-food-supplying countries. While in the EU the cultivation of MON810 is legal, many other types of GMOs are not and therefore it is a reasonable strategy for Peruvian policymakers to impose a ban on all GMOs, including GM maize, to be on the safe side. Remarkably, this finding demonstrates that there is no automatism about the upward ratcheting of environmental protection standards in competing countries (Vogel 1997: 561). Rather, the occurrence of a California effect is contingent on the respective regulatory arrangements of the main high-regulating trading partner of an emerging market democracy (see also Drezner 2007). Thus, low-regulating countries that seek to supply the European market will be more cautious about legalizing the cultivation of GM maize or GMOs in general than those aiming to enter the North American market.

The second dimension of the theoretical framework stressed the implications of party competition and the participation of environmental groups in formulating policies. The hypotheses on partisanship expected that the entering into office of a government including an economically liberal party or a president with such a partisan background would entail either policy inertia or downward policy change. By the same token, upward policy change was anticipated if a green party joined the government. The empirical evidence on the impact of governments' partisan composition was generally very limited. The quantitative analyses for the different policy items revealed that neither the partisan composition of the government nor the party affiliation of the president yield a significant impact on environmental policy change. An important exception is represented by the regulation of GM maize, since the quantitative analysis supported the reasoning that a president of an economically liberal party is unlikely to institute a cultivation ban. Similarly, the complementary in-depth analysis of this policy item underscored the fact that the governments of Bolivia, Ecuador, and Peru adopted more restrictive regulations with respect to GM maize due to their specific ideological backgrounds, which combine leftist views with a marked anti-globalization or even anti-American position and indigenous philosophies (see, e.g., Close 2010). Apart from the case of the regulation of GM maize, however, there is no support for the expected effects of partisanship.

Notably more compelling were the findings concerning the role of environmental groups for triggering upward policy change. In fact, the strength of environmental groups turned out to be one of the most robust determinants of change in the regulation of air and water pollution as well as the adoption of a cultivation ban for GM maize. With regard to the latter policy item, it was the qualitative analysis that illustrated the importance of environmental NGOs and other anti-GMO groups for the adoption of a more restrictive policy, as they managed to expand the conflict over the issue (see Baumgartner and Jones 2009: chapter 5). Speaking in the words of Baumgartner and Leech (2001), GMOs represent a "bandwagon" issue, that is, they are subject to a large proportion of societal and political mobilization (see also Halpin 2011). While existing studies already highlighted the fact that the influence of NGOs was pervasive for West European countries (see, e.g., Bernauer and Meins 2003; Ansell, Maxwell, and Sicurelli 2006; Skogstad 2011), the present study contributes to this body of literature by underscoring their relevance for policy change in CEE and LA.

The third dimension of the theoretical framework related to the importance of integration with international institutions vested with the power of setting legally binding rules for the design of environmental policies. In this regard, the focus was exclusively on the

CEE countries and the EU, since comparable international institutional arrangements are absent in LA. To be sure, Mercosur was initially quite ambitious about creating environmental institutions and achieving a certain degree of policy coordination, but the weak environmental components of Mercosur were downgraded in the course of time (Hochstetler 2003). As a result, no environmental-policy-related impetus can be expected from Mercosur membership. Similarly, NAFTA possesses environmental protection components, but these are also less concerned with coordinating or harmonizing policies (see Stevis and Mumme 2000). While NAFTA was actually highly influential for strengthening Mexican environmental policy (see, e.g., Blair 2003; Diez 2006), this did not happen because of international cooperation or harmonization, but rather as a consequence of the country's strong dependence on trade with the United States and the uncertainty of the realization of this project (see, e.g., Mumme 1998; Knill, Tosun, and Heichel 2008; Bechtel and Tosun 2009). Hence, NAFTA's potential for triggering environmental policy change in Mexico corresponds rather to the causal mechanism underlying the California effect hypothesis than that of institutional integration.

The impact of the EU was clearly manifested in the data. In this regard, it is important to stress that the policy-shaping influence of the EU was primarily effective during the accession stage rather than the period of full membership. This makes perfect sense, as policy change was mainly triggered by the requirement of adopting the environmental acquis (see Schimmelfennig and Sedelmeier 2004; Knill, Tosun, and Heichel 2008; Cirtautas and Schimmelfennig 2010). Although international cooperation and harmonization by means of EU membership were found to generally yield a positive impact on environmental policy change, the study also demonstrated that these mechanisms can hinder the governments of the CEE countries from unilaterally adopting policy arrangements that they prefer over the European provisions. This became most apparent in the case of GM maize. Principally, the member states are free to prohibit the cultivation of MON810 maize if they can convincingly argue that it poses a risk to public health or the environment. The European Commission, however, can challenge the national safeguard bans and has done so in most of the cases where a member state instituted a cultivation ban. In this regard, the European Commission was, for instance, very eager to waive the national ban in Hungary, which was only circumvented by the other member states (Pollack and Shaffer 2010: 352). This suggests that in comparison to the LA countries, the

CEE countries (except for Ukraine, as it is not an EU member state) were confronted with higher political costs related to the imposition of a cultivation ban. To date, only few studies have drawn attention to these implications of policy harmonization at the European level for environmental protection standards.

The final category of explanatory factors was represented by public demand. In the theoretical framework, public demand is associated with increasing income levels and the salience of environmental degradation. Overall, the empirical evidence supporting the anticipated positive impact of raising income was not very strong. In marked contrast, issue salience turned out to be the most robust predictor of policy change in emerging market democracies. This is a noteworthy finding, since it shows that policymaking and public demand are interrelated, even or especially when countries are undergoing major political and economic changes. This result supports the reasoning that an increasing responsiveness to public demand is a direct consequence of the transformation process. Accordingly, the stronger the degree of democratization, the greater the likelihood that policymaking is driven by functionalist considerations (see Assetto, Hajba, and Mumme 2003; John 2003: 484–5). Another conclusion to be drawn from this finding concerns the usefulness of item-specific indicators for assessing the extent of environmental problem pressure and issue salience. In this context, it should be noted that the present study is one of only a few that employ different indicators for assessing the salience of a specific environmental issue. Yet the good performance of this variable across the different estimation models suggests that it could be equally profitable for other empirical studies to employ more precise indicators of degradation problems and salience of environmental issues.

Overall, the establishment of a democratic polity and market-economic structures strengthened the environmental policy arrangements in the countries examined in this study. However, once the compound variable "environmental policy" is disaggregated in order to make it measurable, the empirical picture becomes more nuanced and complicates the drawing of clear-cut conclusions. The case of Chile is a good example for illustrating how much variation there can be within one and the same country across the five policy areas. The data revealed that Chile possesses relatively strict standards for air and water pollution, but it has not defined limit values for soil contamination and the commercial growing of GM maize is hardly subject to legal restrictions. Furthermore, it took the Chilean government a very long time to adopt SFM. This differential performance of the Chilean regulatory approach across the different policy items makes it difficult to judge the overall progress regarding environmental policy.

More generally, chapter 5 showed that there are only a few countries that display a similarly strict regulatory approach to all policy items. Brazil and Poland are the countries that could be identified as the most constant "strict" regulators, which means that they were ranked in the top group for three and four policy items, respectively. Regarding all the other countries of the sample, there was even more variation in their regulatory approaches across the policy items. Therefore, it came as no surprise that the explanatory factors found to be decisive for environmental policy change in CEE and LA varied equally from one policy item to another, as highlighted in chapter 6.

Comparative Assessment of Regulatory Patterns

The empirical analysis revealed that in both regions the average regulatory strictness increased over time. This judgment of the policy developments includes the first-time adoption of environmental protection standards as well as changes in the stringency of existing ones. Although there is a tendency towards upward policy change, this does not mean that policy change occurred frequently. In fact, one of the most important findings of the descriptive analysis in chapter 5 was that environmental policies turned out to be relatively stable over time and often only changed once during the entire observation period. Therefore, the general empirical picture is rather one of policy stability with occasional events of change than one characterized by policy dynamics. When one puts this finding into perspective with the policy-analytical literature, it even means a qualification of those views that stress the occurrence of incremental changes as the rule regarding policy dynamics (see, e.g., Lindblom 1959; Baumgartner and Jones 2009).

Here, the similarities between the two regions end. There are in fact three main differences between the regulatory patterns of the emerging market democracies of CEE and LA. First, even though policy change generally took place only sporadically, it was more often observed in the CEE countries. This holds particularly true for the regulation of air and soil pollution. With regard to limit values for ozone concentrations in ambient air, all CEE countries with the exception of Ukraine modified their regulations at least twice, whereas Ecuador is the only LA country that reformed its standards more than once. Likewise, all CEE countries adopted standards limiting the contamination of soil, whereas in LA only eight countries have taken this step. The regulation of GM maize represents an exception, since with this policy item the LA countries displayed a marginally higher propensity to undertake reforms than the emerging market democracies of CEE. In this context, however, it should be noted that in both regions restrictions on the commercial cultivation of GM maize were defined by only a few countries.

Another key difference relates to the direction of policy change. Concerning the regulation of water pollution and air quality standards, more instances of downward policy change were identified for the CEE than the LA countries. This finding can in part be explained by the regulatory legacies of the state-socialist systems in CEE. In this sense, the relaxation of the overtly strict limit values in the course of system transformation might be seen as a learning process that motivated the setting of enforceable standards (see Oakley et al. 2000). From this it follows that not only differences in the direction of policy change, but also the existence of regulatory legacies related to the previous state-socialist regime distinguish the CEE countries' regulatory patterns from those of the LA countries. In other words, with regard to the regulation of air and water pollution there is a crucial difference between the regions in terms of the initial policy levels, which also has important implications for the interpretation of the direction of change. Again, this observation underscores how demanding the accurate measurement of policy change is.

The final difference concerns the average strictness of environmental protection standards. For the regulation of air, soil, and water pollution it can safely be stated that the CEE countries outperform the LA countries. The gap between them became in fact most visible with the regulation of soil contamination. Less drastic is the situation for effluent standards; they exist in all LA countries, but are defined at notably lower regulatory levels. Regarding GM maize, it is difficult to determine whether the regulations in place in CEE are more stringent than the ones adopted by the LA countries. Indeed, as explained in chapter 7, there are countries in both regions for which the actual regulatory situation of GM maize is difficult to judge. As concerns SFM, no statements can be made regarding substantive difference between the two regions, as the measurement approach only enabled the observation of the timing of the adoption of this principle. In this regard, however, it can be clearly stated that policy adoption occurred faster in CEE than in LA.

Determinants of Governments' Commitment to Regulatory Enforcement

When studying environmental policymaking in emerging market democracies, focusing on policy setting might only produce an incomplete picture, since environmental protection standards are often not properly enforced (Desai 1998; Holzinger and Knoepfel 2000; Andonova 2004; Knill, Tosun, and Heichel 2008; McAllister, van Rooij, and Kagan 2010). Departing from the work of McAllister (2008) and Mueller (2010), this study concentrated on the establishment of organizational units in charge of prosecuting non-compliance with environmental protection standards to explore how the governments' commitment to regulatory enforcement changed over time. The data displayed some interesting differences in terms of the creation of environmental procuracies in CEE and LA.

First, the CEE countries were notably swifter in creating environmental procuracies. While Bulgaria was the last CEE country to create such an organization in 2004, it took Chile until 2010 to set up the Superintendence of the Environment. Second, not all LA countries had created environmental procuracies by the end of the observation period. To date, no environmental prosecution institutions exist in Bolivia and Uruguay. Accordingly, despite the simplicity of the measurement of governmental enforcement commitment, cross-country variation regarding the existence and the timing of the establishment of environmental procuracies was observed. This finding suggests that an institutionalist approach to the study of regulatory enforcement bears the potential of facilitating cumulative knowledge through cross-country comparisons.

Which factors affect a government's decision to set up an organizational unit endowed with the competence of prosecuting environmental offenders? The event history analysis revealed that there are three causes of changes in a government's commitment to enforce environmental regulations. First, the strength of environmental groups that are members of the IUCN and therewith actively participate in processes of transnational communication was found to be a crucial determinant of institutional change. Remarkably, an alternative model fitted with the general indicator of environmental group strength performed notably poorer. Therefore, the theoretical considerations presented in chapter 3 regarding the importance of transnational communication and the fact that environmental groups belonging to the IUCN are richer in resources and better organized was supported by the empirical analysis. The strong impact of transnationally interlinked NGOs on the governments' enforcement commitment is a crucial finding, as it underscores the importance of international collaboration between civil society actors (see, e.g., Ayres 1998; Hogenboom 1998).

The second cause of institutional change is the salience of environmental degradation as measured by energy consumption. Again, this finding is entirely plausible, since increasingly visible environmental problems require the government to address them. Based on this observation, one could argue that symbolic policymaking, which predominantly consists of setting environmental protection standards without enforcing them, is only a feasible option as long as degradation remains below a critical level. The more general implication of this reasoning would be that in functioning democracies symbolic policymaking can only be seen as a short- or medium-term strategy, since with intensifying degradation policymakers will be held responsible for their inaction in terms of enforcement.

The third major driver of institutional change involves the share of an emerging market democracy's exports to a high-regulating economy. The more important the trade with such economies, the greater are the chances that the government will display an increased commitment to regulatory enforcement. This finding challenges existing studies arguing that regulatory competition occurs at the level of policy enforcement (see, e.g., Porter 1999; Gallagher 2002, 2004; Konisky 2007; Knill, Tosun, and Heichel 2008). Instead, emerging market democracies seem to be well aware of the fact that they are under scrutiny. Consequently, they signal their commitment to prosecute non-compliance with environmental legislation. This observation underlines once again that economic integration, on average, tends towards more positive implications for environmental policymaking in emerging market democracies than negative ones.

Conceptual and Empirical Limitations of the Study

The main strengths of this book include a systematic investigation of the multiple forms of environmental policy change, a broad empirical basis with respect to the country sample and policy items under consideration, the use of both quantitative and qualitative techniques of analysis, and the inclusion of considerations about regulatory enforcement. From this perspective, the findings presented in this book can be seen as an important complement to existing studies of governmental behaviour regarding environmental protection and sustainable development in emerging market democracies. There are, however, a number of conceptual, theoretical, and empirical issues that lie outside this study's purview, of which the most important ones shall be addressed in this section.

Regarding the concept of policy change, this study has adopted a rather simple approach. Most importantly, it did not differentiate between instances of major and minor policy change (see, e.g., Baumgartner and Jones 2009). With the regulation of air, soil, and water pollution, the analysis treated the first-time adoption of regulations in exactly the same manner as modifications to existing ones. Similarly, no specific theoretical expectations were formulated or tested for the different kinds of policy and change. This decision was based on the consideration that classifying different types of change is problematic and strongly depends on the eyes of the beholder (see Knill and Lenschow 2001; Howlett and Cashore 2009). Nevertheless, this does not preclude the possibility that a more nuanced definition of the dependent variable and a more differentiated theoretical approach may lead to an even better understanding of environmental policy change in emerging market democracies.

To measure events of change there is no alternative to disaggregating different elements of a policy (Howlett and Cashore 2009: 37). Since limit values are a widely used environmental policy instrument, this study relied on them to adequately trace policy dynamics (see also Holzinger, Knill, and Arts 2008; Holzinger, Knill, and Sommerer 2008, 2011; Knill, Schulze, and Tosun 2012). This approach enabled a relatively precise measurement of the changes in the stringency of environmental protection standards. At the same time, however, the narrow empirical focus can be regarded as the main reason why only few events of change could be observed over time. The narrower the empirical focus, the less likely is the observation of multiple events of change over time. Yet a broadening of the empirical information taken into consideration lowers the comparability of the data gathered for the individual units of analysis. Moreover, the approach adopted here enabled the assessment of the size and direction of the moves away from the status quo. Nevertheless, the limitation remains that on the basis of the data used for this study, it is difficult to say whether the relative stability observed for the policy items selected represents the rule or rather an exception.

In theoretical terms, the analysis neglected two important points. First, the explanatory framework established a rather simple, additive relationship between the variables. In so doing, it did not take into consideration that effects might operate simultaneously and .produce results that are non-additive in nature. The lack of attention paid to such interaction effects may have prevented the exploration of more complex causal relationships between the variables.

Second, the quantitative part did not include variables that directly account for transformation processes or progress in transformation such as the degree of democratization. Rather, the theoretical model aimed at explaining policy and institutional change by employing a set of classical policy-analytical factors and testing their relevance for emerging market democracies. Hence, despite the numerous empirical insights provided by the theoretical model, it must be stressed that the study does not allow for drawing any specific conclusions regarding the impact of the transformation processes per se.

Furthermore, there are empirical limitations to the study. Environmental policy covers many different areas and involves a large number of policy instruments (see, e.g., Sterner 2002; Holzinger, Knill, and Arts 2008; Holzinger, Knill, and Sommerer 2008, 2011; Knill, Schulze, and Tosun 2012), which complicates the general assessment of changes in the entire policy field. For reasons of measurement, this study relied on a limited number of environmental policy items. Even though they were selected in accordance with theoretical considerations and with regard to their relevance in CEE and LA, five environmental policy items are a small sample from which to draw conclusive findings.

Likewise, the measurement of enforcement commitment through the establishment of an organizational unit in charge of prosecuting environmental offences represents a rather crude measurement. There is no question that the establishment of an environmental prosecution institution represents a costly decision to make for the governments of emerging market democracies and therefore indicates their willingness to improve regulatory enforcement (see, e.g., McAllister 2008; Abbot 2009; McAllister, van Rooij, and Kagan 2010). However, the operationalization employed by this study leaves out the administrative aspects of policy enforcement, which certainly represent an important empirical limitation (see Abbot 2009; Blank 2013; Gray and Shimshack 2011). Moreover, the measurement does not take into account changes in the capacities of the prosecution institutions over time, such as changes in personnel and budget. Finally, no judgment was possible as to whether the prosecution units are either strong or weak institutions, and how effective they actually are for motivating the regulatees to comply with environmental protection standards (see Levitsky and Murillo 2005).

The measurement of enforcement commitment, however, must be seen in conjunction with severe problems of data availability. Gathering reliable information on enforcement institutions in the emerging market democracies of CEE and LA is a tedious task (see, e.g., Palacios and Chávez 2005; Ehrke 2010). Another problem encountered by this study was that there exist hardly any comparative studies of environmental law enforcement, which could have served as a point of reference with respect to measurement (see McAllister, van Rooij, and Kagan 2010: 2). That being said, the measurement approach adopted by this study represents the best possible approximation of the governments' enforcement commitment in emerging market democracies.

Concerning the measurement of the independent variables, the most important limitation involves the assessment of the political parties' role for policy and institutional change. The lack of longitudinal data on the environmental policy positions of political parties in LA and the difficulties in disaggregating the individual parties' shares of votes in CEE led to the adoption of an admittedly crude measurement of possible party effects. This approach entailed that only explicitly economically liberal and green parties were taken into account, as only for them relatively clear theoretical expectations could be stated. However, the qualitative analysis of GM maize demonstrated that at least with regard to this policy item, the ascension of left-wing parties into office indeed mattered. This finding of the in-depth analysis suggests that the actual impact of political parties and their respective environmental policy preferences may have been underestimated throughout the study.

In summary, it must be stated that both the theoretical model and the empirical evidence in their present forms are still incomplete. The main source of this incompleteness is, without question, a lack of data availability. Often better data were available, but they were only provided for one of the two regions, which effectively impeded the comparative analysis. This problem mostly affected the measurement of the role of political parties, but it was equally an issue with other variables such as the proxies used for assessing the salience of the various forms of environmental problems. Hence, even though more accurate data were principally available, they could not be employed for the analysis as the data sources for the CEE countries and the LA countries did not match. The problems encountered by this study, however, do not preclude the possibility that a better empirical analysis is possible. Thus, it will depend on future research to show whether the results presented in this book will find or lose empirical support.

Looking Ahead: Future Research Avenues

There are three ways in which this study offers a starting point for future research. The first one involves the extension of the database in order to increase the number of observations and therewith to further increase the confidence in the findings. Another option for future studies is given by the use of different analytical concepts for the dependent and independent variables. Finally, it may be rewarding to compare the patterns of environmental policy and institutional change detected for the emerging market democracies in CEE and LA with those for advanced democracies. This section considers these three possible research avenues in turn.

Broadening the empirical database is the most straightforward, yet also the most challenging way of improving the insights provided by the present study. An expansion of the empirical basis may refer to the observation period, the country sample, or the policy items. For extending the temporal dimension, it is advisable to use more current data and to check whether the findings still hold true. In this regard, data for those cases in which by 2010 no regulations or enforcement institutions were in place could alter the conclusions drawn from this empirical analysis substantially. Including more measurement points is comparatively easy to achieve, since international organizations regularly update the data they offer for research purposes. Moreover, access to newer legal acts is easier than to older ones. Therefore, a temporal update of the database can be regarded as the most practicable extension of this study.

More difficult to realize is the expansion of the number of countries under scrutiny. Researchers seeking to add new countries to the sample will need good language skills and local contact people who possess a certain degree of expertise in the area of environmental policy. If these conditions are met, the inclusion of more CEE countries would be desirable in order to achieve identical sizes for the country subsamples. The countries of the Western Balkans would be particularly suitable for an extended analysis, since many of them are at earlier stages of system transformation and therefore quite similar to some LA – or more precisely Central American – countries. In addition, since in some of these countries virtually no environmental protection standards existed until recently, they would be less prone to an inaccurate measurement of policy change than countries with regulatory legacies. Likewise, the extension of this study to the Commonwealth of Independent States as well as to Turkey might yield many additional insights.

Another way of broadening the empirical scope is represented by the inclusion of more policy items. Essentially, this could be achieved in two ways. First, one can identify interesting policy items for other areas of environmental protection, such as waste management, protected areas, or marine ecosystems, and add these to the already existing ones. The second strategy entails increasing the number of policy items by broadening the regulatory coverage of those areas already addressed by this study. For example, in addition to soil contamination by PAHs, a replication study could include other pollutants, such as pesticides or various heavy metals. Similarly, the number of policy items could be increased by addressing a wider range of environmental policy instruments (see, e.g., Sterner 2002; Holzinger, Knill, and Arts 2008; Holzinger, Knill, and Sommerer 2008, 2011; Knill, Schulze, and Tosun 2012). This study has, for instance, not paid attention to participation and information rights or market-based instruments such as pollution taxes. Extending the study to this latter instrument type would be particularly rewarding since several CEE countries used such market-based instruments during state socialism. Today, with the transformation process being almost completed in most CEE countries, these instruments are hardly used. Against this backdrop, future research could explain why these instruments became gradually replaced by command-and-control regulation. Another interesting observation in this regard is that in LA, market-based instruments have been used to a notably lesser extent, which again calls for a systematic analysis.

Alternatively, the empirical information provided in chapter 5 could be coded in a different way in order to see if the findings still hold true. For example, the data could be re-coded in a way to differentiate between the first-time adoption of a policy and modifications to existing ones. Such a replication strategy is easy to implement and may yield additional interesting insights.

Turning to the measurement of the independent variables, future research might consider replicating this study with more accurate data on the political parties' environmental policy stances (see, e.g., Knill, Debus, and Heichel 2010; Schulze 2013). In fact, the Comparative Manifesto Project is currently performing content analyses of party manifestos in LA countries. The resulting data would represent an ideal source for completing the empirical information used by this study. The central drawback, however, is that the extended data set of the Comparative Manifesto Project can only be expected to be available by 2015. Moreover, the use of a more detailed measurement of the policy-shaping powers of NGOs would advance this study. In this context, it would be rewarding to think of ways to measure the environmental groups' resource availability, mobilization potential, organizational values, and degree of institutionalized participation in policymaking (see, e.g., Botcheva 1996; Fagan 2004; Bernhagen 2007, 2008; Macdonald 2007; Carmin 2010; Fagan and Carmin 2011).

However, the most crucial task for future analyses is to improve the comparative measurement of regulatory enforcement. This study conceived of enforcement commitment in terms of creating a consequential institution. McAllister, van Rooij, and Kagan (2010: 9) generally acknowledge the possibility of empirically assessing regulatory enforcement by focusing on institutions. However, they caution that studies of regulatory enforcement in emerging market democracies warrant particular attention to institutional change. In this regard, a more fine-grained assessment of the institutions' characteristics would be desirable in order to judge whether the enforcement institutions are weak or strong. In a second step, the effectiveness of the enforcement institutions could be explored by combining new data with already existing information on environmental quality. In this way, a veritably comprehensive assessment of enforcement issues in emerging market democracies could become attainable.

Finally, future research may want to make comparative statements about the observed patterns of policy change. On the basis of this study, no statements can be made about whether there exists a particular pattern of environmental policy change for emerging market democracies due to absent reference values for advanced democracies. Therefore, a particularly promising way of further developing this study would be to compare the present findings with those for advanced democracies. This would allow for evaluating whether emerging market democracies are characterized by specific patterns of environmental policy change. Further to this, a systematic comparison would be helpful for constructing a general expected value for the likelihood of environmental policy reforms in the presence of democratic structures and a market economy.

Appendices

Appendix 1: Summary statistics of independent variables

Variables	Transformations	Mean	SD	Min	Max
Economic integration					
FDI		26.47	23.03	0.15	192.75
Exports	Multiplied by 100	58.33	17.51	6.60	95.08
Politics					
Liberal government		0.47	0.50	0	1
Green government		0.08	0.27	0	1
Liberal president		0.31	0.46	0	1
NGOs	Divided by population; multiplied by 1.000.000	3.47	4.37	0.10	20.89
INGOs	Divided by population; multiplied by 1.000.000	5.95	7.47	0	34.14
Institutionalintegration					
EU accession		0.21	0.41	0	1
EU application		0.27	0.45	0	1
EU membership		0.10	0.31	0	1
Public demand					
Income	Divided by 100	89.26	47.16	17.43	271.97
Water	Divided by 1.000	26.78	23.3	1.27	89.10
CO_2	Multiplied by 10	41.65	35.19	4.88	163.05
Land	Multiplied by 100	32.30	20.62	4.07	83.63
Insecticides	Multiplied by 100.000	16.18	25.53	0.00	181.03
Forest		39.53	16.38	5.26	72.71
Energy		74.29	49.21	8.54	211.39

N = 588; SD = Standard deviation; Min = Minimum value; Max = Maximum value.

Appendix 2: Histogram and kernel density plot of the dependent variable "standards for biological oxygen demand"

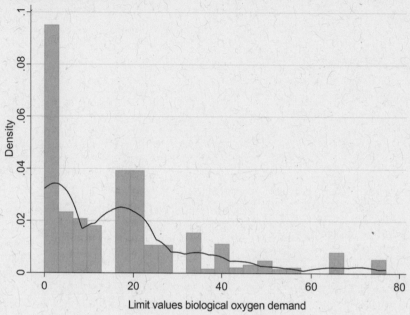

Appendix 3: Results of the quadrature check for the dependent variable "standards for biological oxygen demand"

	Fitted quadrature 42 points	Comparison quadrature 56 points	Relative difference in per cent
Log likelihood	−773.62092	−773.62089	−0.00
FDI	.02772732	.02772721	−0.00
Exports	−.02158252	−.02158236	−0.00
Liberal government	.15948628	.15948492	−0.00
Green government	−.34772821	−.34772477	−0.00
Liberal president	−.01482901	−.01482696	−0.01
NGOs	.34769618	.34769993	0.00
EU accession	1.1113589	1.1113569	−0.00
EU membership	.81600354	.81600676	0.00
Income	−.00148676	−.00148684	0.01
Water	−.07749205	−.07749345	0.00
Constant	3.0498123	3.0498059	−0.00
Sigma u	2.5747586	2.5748017	0.00
Sigma e	1.0760925	1.0760915	−0.00

Appendix 4: Histogram and kernel density plot of the dependent variable "ozone standards"

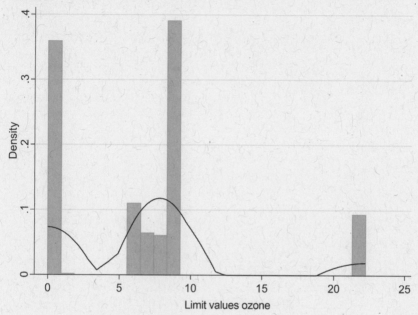

Appendix 5: Results of the quadrature check for the dependent variable "ozone standards"

	Fitted quadrature 72 points	Comparison quadrature 96 points	Relative difference in per cent
Log likelihood	−1159.4256	−1159.4256	0.00
FDI	.08960991	.08960987	−0.00
Exports	−.04957391	−.04957372	−0.00
Liberal government	−.20695951	−.20695986	0.00
Green government	.12200869	.12201606	0.01
Liberal president	1.0400176	1.0400155	−0.00
NGOs	1.7248091	1.7248119	0.00
EU accession	.7044016	.70441905	0.00
EU membership	−5.8878814	−5.8878692	−0.00
Income	−.02455755	−.0245576	0.00
CO_2	−.15800707	−.15800492	−0.00
Constant	7.5648212	7.5643548	−0.01
Sigma u	15.022508	15.022491	−0.00
Sigma e	4.5974133	4.5974153	0.00

Appendix 6: Histogram and kernel density plot of the dependent variable "standards for polycyclic aromatic hydrocarbons"

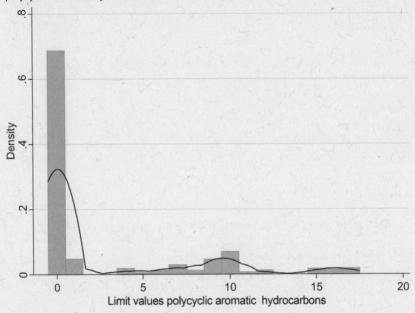

Appendix 7: Gompertz models for the dependent variable "environmental procuracies" with NGOs

Covariates	Model 1 exp(β)	Model 2 exp(β)	Model 3 exp(β)	Model 4 exp(β)
FDI	0.99 (0.01)	0.99 (0.01)	–	–
Exports	1.04 (0.02)**	–	1.04 (0.02)**	–
Liberal government	1.06 (0.57)	0.97 (0.51)	0.96 (0.51)	0.97 (0.53)
Green government	1.93 (1.78)	1.03 (0.84)	1.72 (1.60)	1.01 (0.76)
Liberal president	1.52 (1.24)	1.11 (0.71)	1.61 (1.26)	1.14 (0.76)
INGOs	1.02 (0.05)	1.00 (0.05)	1.01 (0.05)	0.99 (0.05)
EU accession	0.69 (0.35)	–	–	1.17 (0.47)
Income	1.00 (0.00)	1.00 (0.00)	1.00 (0.00)	1.00 (0.00)
Energy	1.02(0.01)**	1.01 (0.01)*	1.02 (0.01)**	1.01 (0.01)*
Wald Chi2 (DF)	19.79(9)**	15.28 (7)**	19.63 (7)***	13.54 (7)*
Reduction LL	8.89	5.71	8.53	5.52
Gamma	0.22***	0.15***	0.19***	0.13***
Observations	267	267	267	267
Cases	28	28	28	28

Note: Dependent variable = adoption prosecution unit; Reduction LL = (log pseudo-likelihood null) – (log pseudo-likelihood model); DF = degrees of freedom; robust standard errors in parentheses; * significant at 10%; ** significant at 5%; *** significant at 1%.

Notes

Chapter 1

1 For a more complete understanding of the main characteristics of economic integration, see Baldwin and Venables (1995), Jovanović (2006, 2011), and Krugman and Obstfeld (2010).
2 For an example of a study that takes into account paradigmatic change, see Cashore and Howlett (2006).

Chapter 3

1 The primary goal of a government, or more generally political parties, is to win as many votes as possible. From a general perspective, the latter increases the chances of a party winning or remaining in control over governmental offices and therewith implementing their policy goals as promised during the election campaign (Downs 1957). Therefore, following Strøm and Müller (1999), political parties are always vote-, office-, and policy-seeking.
2 Some empirical studies on Western Europe show that left-libertarian parties are also equally supportive of strict environmental standards (see, e.g., Neumayer 2003, 2004). Empirical studies on CEE and LA are absent and hence there is no sufficient basis to formulate expectations with regard to the impact of left-libertarian parties on environmental policy change.
3 Here the assumption is made that there is no difference between single-party governments and coalition governments. As recent studies on coalition agreements and portfolio allocation in coalition governments show, green parties win control over the environmental ministry when becoming a member of a coalition government. Generally, this results in more progressive environmental regulations. Conversely, the government

position moves right when economically liberal parties enter a coalition government (see, e.g., Debus 2008).

4 Generally, a semi-presidential system is characterized by the existence of a popularly elected fixed-term president alongside a prime minister and cabinet who are responsible to parliament.

5 For a general overview of democratic participation in CEE, see Bernhagen and Marsh (2007).

Chapter 4

1 The data were taken from the following website: www.freedomhouse.org (retrieved on 10 March 2011).

2 Some of the CEE countries were even founded after 1990. However, the fact that national data are available for these countries as of 1990 still made it possible to choose this year as the common starting point for all observation.

3 The reports were taken from the following website: www.iclg.co.uk (retrieved on 20 March 2011).

4 Detailed information about the coding of the partisan composition of governments as well as the party affiliation of the president is provided in a codebook available on the author's website at www.mzes.uni-mannheim.de.

Chapter 5

1 An alternative approach would be to focus on predefined industry-specific limit values and compare those to the universal ones. However, industry-specific limit values vary strongly depending on whether one looks at an industry that produces plenty of organic water pollution, e.g., food processing, or at an industry that produces hardly or even no organic water pollution, e.g., the electronic sector (see OECD 1999: 70). Depending on which industry-specific limit values are chosen, they could be judged as either too strict or too lenient relative to the BOD limit values in countries relying on universal effluent standards.

2 The limit values do not refer to the amount of dissolved oxygen consumed in five (i.e., BOD_5) but seven days (i.e., BOD_7). Therefore, they were transformed by using the following formula given by Lithuanian Regulation D1-236/2006: $BOD_5 = BOD_7 / 1.15$.

3 To transform the 1-hour or 24-hour averages into 8-hour averages the following formulas were employed: 8-hour average = 1-hour average / 1.5 and 8-hour average = 1.5 × 24-hour average.

4 In 2006, the EU Commission made a proposal for a framework directive that sets out common principles for protecting soils across the member states. To date, however, this proposal has not been adopted. Therefore, there is no European reference value for strict soil protection standards.

Chapter 6

1 Wooldridge (2006: 595) refers to a variable for which a non-trivial fraction of the population is zero, but which is otherwise roughly continuously distributed over positive values, as a "corner solution response."
2 The existence of overdispersion was tested on the basis of a likelihood ratio test. For the full model, it produced the following test statistic: $G^2 = 1055.31$, $p < 0.01$.
3 The Likelihood-ratio test of theta = 0 produced the following statistic: chibar2(01) = 0.00 Prob > = chibar2 = 1.00.
4 The Likelihood-ratio test of theta = 0 produced the following statistic: chibar2(01) = 0.15 Prob > = chibar2 = 0.35.

Chapter 7

1 Retrieved on 10 May 2011 from http://www.gmo-free-regions.org/gmo-free-regions.html
2 Retrieved on 19 May 2011 from http://www.icppc.pl/eng/.
3 Retrieved on 22 May 2011 from http://www.infomg.ro/web/en/Home/News/3/1654.
4 Retrieved on 19 May 2011 from http://chamber.ua/wg/gmo/?print=1
5 See http://w1.c1.rada.gov.ua/pls/zweb_n/webproc4_1?pf3511=36422 and http://w1.c1.rada.gov.ua/pls/zweb_n/webproc4_1?id=&pf3511=36455.
6 In 2001, the scientists David Quist and Ignacio Chapela published an article in *Nature* magazine in which they report the discovery of modified genes in native maize varieties in the Mexican state of Oaxaca. This finding compromised the Mexican government's credibility, since it revealed its inability to effectively implement its own policy of prohibiting the growing of GM maize (Antal 2007: 18).
7 In Peru, the president has veto power and possesses the ability to attach amendatory observations, which provides him/her with a valuable tool for shaping legislation. A simple majority may accept the amendatory observations introduced by the executive, and if no vote is taken the status quo prevails. The override threshold is greater than 50 per cent of members of the legislature (Tsebelis and Alemán 2005: 405).

References

Abbot, C. 2009. *Enforcing Pollution Control Regulation: Strengthening Sanctions and Improving Deterrence.* Oxford: Hart Publishing.

Aguilar, S. 2002. "Environmental Non-Governmental Organizations in Argentina." *Review of European Community & International Environmental Law* 11 (2): 225–34. http://dx.doi.org/10.1111/1467-9388.t01-1-00319.

Aguirre, J.C., and E.S. Cooper. 2010. "Evo Morales, Climate Change, and the Paradoxes of a Social-Movement Presidency." *Latin American Perspectives* 37 (4): 238–44. http://dx.doi.org/10.1177/0094582X10376362.

Akaike, H. 1974. "A New Look at the Statistical Model Identification." *IEEE Transactions on Automatic Control* 19 (6): 716–23. http://dx.doi.org/10.1109/TAC.1974.1100705.

Albaek, E., C. Green-Pedersen, and L.B. Nielsen. 2007. "Making Tobacco Consumption a Political Issue in the United States and Denmark: The Dynamics of Issue Expansion in Comparative Perspective." *Journal of Comparative Policy Analysis* 9 (1): 1–20. http://dx.doi.org/10.1080/13876980601145581.

Albrecht, C. 1998. "Environmental Policy in the Czech Republic and Slovakia." In *Ecological Policy and Politics in Developing Countries: Economic Growth, Democracy, and Environment,* ed. U. Desai, 267–94. Albany: State University of New York Press.

Albright, E.A. 2011. "Policy Change and Learning in Response to Extreme Flood Events in Hungary: An Advocacy Coalition Approach." *Policy Studies Journal: The Journal of the Policy Studies Organization* 39 (3): 485–511. http://dx.doi.org/10.1111/j.1541-0072.2011.00418.x.

Alcántara, M.S., and F. Freidenberg, eds. 2001a. *Partidos políticos de América Latina: Centroamerica, Mexico y República Dominicana.* Salamanca: Ediciones Universidad de Salamanca.

Alcántara, M.S., and F. Freidenberg, eds. 2001b. *Partidos políticos de América Latina: Países Andinos*. Salamanca: Ediciones Universidad de Salamanca.

Altieri, M. 2009. "Reflexiones sobre el estado de la agricultura a base de transgénicos y agrocombustiles en América Latina." In *América Latina: La transgénesis de un continente. Visión Crítica de una Expansión Descontrolada*, ed. M.I. Manzur, G. Catacora, M.I. Cárcamo, E. Bravo, and M. Altieri, 6–13. Berkeley: SOCLA and Heinrich Böll Foundation.

Anderson, K. 2006. "Interactions between Trade Policies and GM Food Regulations." In *Regulating Agricultural Biotechnology: Economics and Policy*, ed. R.E. Just, J.M. Alston, and D. Zilberman, 125–43. New York: Springer. http://dx.doi.org/10.1007/978-0-387-36953-2_7.

Anderson, L., M. Lewis-Beck, and M. Stegmaier. 2003. "Post-socialist Democratization: A Comparative Political Economy Model of the Vote for Hungary and Nicaragua." *Electoral Studies* 22 (3): 469–84. http://dx.doi.org/10.1016/S0261-3794(02)00009-4.

Andonova, L.B. 2004. *Transnational Politics of the Environment: The European Union and Environmental Policy in Central and Eastern Europe*. Cambridge, MA: MIT Press.

Andonova, L.B., E.D. Mansfield, and H.V. Milner. 2007. "International Trade and Environmental Policy in the Postcommunist World." *Comparative Political Studies* 40 (7): 782–807. http://dx.doi.org/10.1177/0010414006293215.

Angel, D.P., H.S. Brown, R. Broszkiewicz, and S. Wronski. 2000. "The Environmental Legislations of Privatized Industry in Poland." *Environment and Planning C: Government & Policy* 18 (5): 575–92. http://dx.doi.org/10.1068/c9807j.

Ansell, C., R. Maxwell, and D. Sicurelli. 2006. "Protesting Food: NGOs and Political Mobilization in Europe." In *What's the Beef? The Contested Governance of European Food Safety*, ed. C. Ansell and D. Vogel, 97–122. Cambridge, MA: MIT Press.

Antal, E. 2007. "Between Global Regimes and Local Demands: The Regulation." In *Maize and Biosecurity in Mexico: Debate and Practice*, ed. E. Antal, L. Baker, and G. Verschoor, 11–32. Amsterdam: Centre for Latin American Studies and Documentation.

Armingeon, K., and R. Careja. 2007. *Comparative Data Set for 28 Post-Communist Countries, 1989–2007*. Berne: Institute of Political Science, University of Berne.

Assetto, V.J., E. Hajba, and S.P. Mumme. 2003. "Democratization, Decentralization, and Local Environmental Policy Capacity: Hungary and Mexico." *Social Science Journal* 40 (2): 249–68. http://dx.doi.org/10.1016/S0362-3319(03)00007-7.

Atlas, M. 2007. "Enforcement Principles and Environmental Agencies: Principal–Agent Relationships in a Delegated Environmental Program." *Law & Society Review* 41 (4): 939–80. http://dx.doi. org/10.1111/j.1540-5893.2007.00330.x.

Aubourg, R.W., D.H. Good, and K. Krutilla. 2008. "Debt, Democratization, and Development in Latin America: How Policy Can Affect Global Warming." *Journal of Policy Analysis and Management* 27 (1): 7–19. http:// dx.doi.org/10.1002/pam.20304.

Ayres, J.M. 1998. *Defying Conventional Wisdom: Political Movements and Popular Contention against North American Free Trade.* Toronto: University of Toronto Press.

Bailey, J.E. 1993. "Free Trade and the Environment: Can NAFTA Reconcile the Irreconcilable?" *American Journal of International Law and Policy* 8 (4): 839–53.

Baldwin, R.E., and A.J. Venables. 1995. "Regional Economic Integration." In *Handbook of International Economics*, vol. 3, ed. G.M. Grossman and K. Rogoff, 1597–1644. Amsterdam: Elsevier.

Bándi, G. 2004. "Liability and Sanctions: Criminal Liability in Hungary." In *Environmental Crime in Europe*, ed. F. Comte and L. Krämer, 129–44. Groningen: Europa Law Publishing.

Bar, M. 2004. "Criminal Sanctions for Environmental Offences in the Acceding Countries: Example of Poland." In *Environmental Crime in Europe*, ed. F. Comte and L. Krämer, 217–29. Groningen: Europa Law Publishing.

Baum, C.F. 2006. *An Introduction to Modern Econometrics Using Stata.* College Station, TX: Stata Press.

Baumgartner, F.R. 2006. "Punctuated Equilibrium Theory and Environmental Policy." In *Punctuated Equilibrium and the Dynamics of U.S. Environmental Policy*, ed. R. Repetto, 24–46. New Haven: Yale University Press.

Baumgartner, F.R., J.M. Berry, M. Hojnacki, D.C. Kimball, and B.L. Leech. 2009. *Lobbying and Policy Change: Who Wins, Who Loses, and Why?* Chicago: University of Chicago Press.

Baumgartner, F.R., and B.D. Jones. 2009. *Agendas and Instability in American Politics.* Chicago: University of Chicago Press.

Baumgartner, F.R., and B.L. Leech. 2001. "Interest Niches and Policy Bandwagons: Patterns of Interest Group Involvement in National Politics." *Journal of Politics* 63 (4): 1191–1213.

Bechtel, M., and J. Tosun. 2009. "Changing Economic Openness for Environmental Policy Convergence: When Can Bilateral Trade Agreements Induce Convergence of Environment Regulation?" *International Studies Quarterly* 53 (4): 931–53. http://dx.doi.org/10.1111/j.1468-2478.2009.00563.x.

Beck, N., and J.N. Katz. 1995. "What to Do (and Not to Do) with Time-Series Cross-Section Data." *American Political Science Review* 89 (3): 634–47. http://dx.doi.org/10.2307/2082979.

Becker, G.S. 1968. "Crime and Punishment: An Economic Approach." *Journal of Political Economy* 76 (2): 169–217. http://dx.doi.org/10.1086/259394.

Becker, M. 2011. "Correa, Indigenous Movements, and the Writing of a New Constitution in Ecuador." *Latin American Perspectives* 38 (1): 47–62. http://dx.doi.org/10.1177/0094582X10384209.

Bennett, C.J. 1991. "What Is Policy Convergence and What Causes It?" *British Journal of Political Science* 21 (2): 215–33. http://dx.doi.org/10.1017/S0007123400006116.

Bennett, C.J., and M. Howlett. 1992. "The Lessons of Learning: Reconciling Theories of Policy Learning and Policy Change." *Policy Sciences* 25 (3): 275–94. http://dx.doi.org/10.1007/BF00138786.

Bernauer, T., and L. Caduff. 2006. "Food Safety and the Structure of the European Food Industry." In *What's the Beef? The Contested Governance of European Food Safety*, ed. C. Ansell and D. Vogel, 81–95. Cambridge, MA: MIT Press.

Bernauer, T., and V. Koubi. 2009. "Effects of Political Institutions on Air Quality." *Ecological Economics* 68 (5): 1355–65. http://dx.doi.org/10.1016/j.ecolecon.2008.09.003.

Bernauer, T., and P. Kuhn. 2010. "Is There an Environmental Version of the Kantian Peace? Insights from Water Pollution in Europe." *European Journal of International Relations* 16 (1): 77–102. http://dx.doi.org/10.1177/1354066109344662.

Bernauer, T., and E. Meins. 2003. "Technological Revolution Meets Policy and the Market: Explaining Cross-National Differences in Agricultural Biotechnology Regulation." *European Journal of Political Research* 42 (5): 643–83. http://dx.doi.org/10.1111/1475-6765.00099.

Bernhagen, P. 2007. *The Political Power of Business: Structure and Information in Public Policy-Making*. London: Routledge.

Bernhagen, P. 2008. "Business and International Environmental Agreements: Domestic Sources of Participation and Compliance by Advanced Industrialized Democracies." *Global Environmental Politics* 8 (1): 78–110. http://dx.doi.org/10.1162/glep.2008.8.1.78.

Bernhagen, P., and M. Marsh. 2007. "The Partisan Effects of Low Turnout: Analyzing Vote Abstention as a Missing Data Problem." *Electoral Studies* 26 (3): 548–60. http://dx.doi.org/10.1016/j.electstud.2006.10.002.

Blair, D.J. 2003. "The CEC's Citizen Submission Process: Still a Model for Reconciling Trade and the Environment?" *Journal of Environment & Development* 12 (3): 295–324. http://dx.doi.org/10.1177/1070496503255577.

Blanc, F. 2013. *Inspections Reforms: Why, How and With What Results.* Paris: OECD.

Blossfeld, H., K. Golsch, and G. Rohwer. 2007. *Techniques of Event History Modeling Using Stata: New Approaches to Causal Analysis.* Mahwah, NJ: Erlbaum.

Blume, Y.B. 2000. "Key Issues for Ukrainian Acceptance of Genetically Modified Plants and a Comparison with Other Central and Eastern European Countries." In *Proceedings of the 6th International Symposium on the Biosafety of Genetically Modified Organisms,* ed. C. Fairbairn, G. Scoles and A. McHughen, 15–20. Saskatoon, SK: University Extension Press.

Borregaard, N., G. Volpi, H. Blanco, F. Wautiez, and A. Matte-Baker. 1999. *Environmental Impacts of Trade Liberalization and Policies for the Sustainable Management of Natural Resources: A Case Study on Chile's Mining Sector.* Geneva: UNEP.

Börzel, T., and A. Buzogány. 2010. "Environmental Organisations and the Europeanisation of Public Policy in Central and Eastern Europe: The Case of Biodiversity Governance." *Environmental Politics* 19 (5): 708–35. http://dx.doi.org/10.1080/09644016.2010.508302.

Botcheva, L. 1996. "Focus and Effectiveness of Environmental Activism in Eastern Europe: A Comparative Study of Environmental Movements in Bulgaria, Hungary, Slovakia, and Romania." *Journal of Environment & Development* 5 (3): 292–308. http://dx.doi.org/10.1177/107049659600500303.

Box-Steffensmeier, J., and B. Jones. 2004. *Event History Modeling.* Cambridge: Cambridge University Press. http://dx.doi.org/10.1017/CBO9780511790874.

Braun, D., and F. Gilardi. 2006. "Taking Galton's Problem Seriously: Towards a Theory of Policy Diffusion." *Journal of Theoretical Politics* 18 (3): 298–322. http://dx.doi.org/10.1177/0951629806064351.

Bravo, E. 2009. "La situación de los transgénicos en Venezuela." In *América Latina: La transgénesis de un continente. Visión Crítica de una Expansión Descontrolada,* ed. M.I. Manzur, G. Catacora, M.I. Cárcamo, E. Bravo, and M. Altieri, 68–71. Berkeley: SOCLA and Heinrich Böll Foundation.

Breunig, C., C. Koski, and P.B. Mortensen. 2010. "Stability and Punctuations in Public Spending: A Comparative Study of Budget Functions." *Journal of Public Administration: Research and Theory* 20 (3): 703–22. http://dx.doi.org/10.1093/jopart/mup028.

Brookes, G. 2008. "The Impact of Using Gm Insect Resistant Maize in Europe since 1998." *International Journal of Biotechnology* 10 (2–3): 148–66. http://dx.doi.org/10.1504/IJBT.2008.018351.

Brookes, G., and P. Barfoot. 2007. "GM Crops, the First Ten Years: Global Socio-economic and Environmental Impacts." *AgbioForum* 9 (3): 1–13.

Brown, H.S. 2007. "Transformation of the Environmental Regulatory System in Poland during the 1990s." *Knowledge, Technology & Policy* 19 (4): 26–43. http://dx.doi.org/10.1007/BF02914889.

Budapest Sun, The. 2005. "Science Split on GMO Issues." 28 January 2011. http://www.budapestsun.com/news/46347.

Budge, I., H. Klingemann, A. Volkens, J. Bara, and T. Tanenbaum, eds. 2001. *Mapping Policy Preferences: Estimates for Parties, Electors, and Governments, 1945–1998.* Oxford: Oxford University Press.

Bueno de Mesquita, B., A. Smith, R.M. Siverson, and J.D. Morrow. 2003. *The Logic of Political Survival.* Cambridge, MA: MIT Press.

Bugajski, J. 2002. *Political Parties of Eastern Europe: A Guide to Politics in the Post-Communist Era.* Armonk, NJ: M.E. Sharpe.

Buzogány, A. 2009a. "Hungary: Building Environmental Governance and the Limits of the Possible." In *Coping with Accession: New Modes of Governance in the New Member States,* ed. T. Börzel, 123–47. Basingstoke: Palgrave Macmillan.

Buzogány, A. 2009b. "Romania: Europeanization in the Shadow of Forms without Substance." In *Coping with Accession: New Modes of Governance in the New Member States,* ed. T. Börzel, 169–81. Basingstoke: Palgrave Macmillan.

Cameron, A.C., and P.K. Trivedi. 2010. *Microeconometrics Using Stata.* College Station, TX: Stata Press.

Campos, E.J. 2009. "La situación de los transgénicos en El Salvador." In *América Latina: La transgénesis de un continente. Visión Crítica de una Expansión Descontrolada,* ed. M.I. Manzur, G. Catacora, M.I. Cárcamo, E. Bravo, and M. Altieri, 88–90. Berkeley: SOCLA and Heinrich Böll Foundation.

Cantwell, J., J.H. Dunning, and S.A. Lundan. 2010. "An Evolutionary Approach to Understanding International Business Activity: The Co-Evolution of MNEs and the Institutional Environment." *Journal of International Business Studies* 41 (4): 567–86. http://dx.doi.org/10.1057/jibs.2009.95.

Cao, X., and A. Prakash. 2010. "Trade Competition and Domestic Pollution: A Panel Study, 1980–2003." *International Organization* 64 (3): 481–503. http://dx.doi.org/10.1017/S0020818310000123.

Capano, G. 2009. "Understanding Policy Change as an Epistemological and Theoretical Problem." *Journal of Comparative Policy Analysis* 11 (1): 7–31. http://dx.doi.org/10.1080/13876980802648284.

Capano, G., and M. Howlett. 2009. "Introduction: The Determinants of Policy Change: Advancing the Debate." *Journal of Comparative Policy Analysis* 11 (1): 1–5. http://dx.doi.org/10.1080/13876980802648227.

Carmin, J. 2010. "NGO Capacity and Environmental Governance in Central and Eastern Europe." *Acta Politica* 45 (1–2): 183–202. http://dx.doi.org/10.1057/ap.2009.21.

Carmin, J., and S.D. VanDeveer, eds. 2005. *EU Enlargement and the Environment: Institutional Change and Environmental Policy in Central and Eastern Europe.* London: Routledge.

Cashore, B., G. Auld, and D. Newsom. 2003. "Forest Certification (Eco-Labeling) Programs and Their Policy-Making Authority: Explaining Divergence among North American and European Case Studies." *Forest Policy and Economics* 5 (3): 225–47. http://dx.doi.org/10.1016/S1389-9341(02)00060-6.

Cashore, B., and M. Howlett. 2006. "Behavioural Thresholds and Institutional Rigidities as Explanations of Punctuated Equilibrium Processes in Pacific Northwest Forest Policy Dynamics." In *Punctuated Equilibrium and the Dynamics of U.S. Environmental Policy,* ed. R. Repetto, 137–61. New Haven: Yale University Press.

Cirtautas, A.M., and F. Schimmelfennig. 2010. "Europeanisation before and after Accession: Conditionality, Legacies and Compliance." *Europe-Asia Studies* 62 (3): 421–41. http://dx.doi.org/10.1080/09668131003647812.

Cleves, M., W.W. Gould, R.G. Gutierrez, and Y. Marchenko. 2008. *An Introduction to Survival Analysis Using Stata.* College Station, TX: Stata Press.

Close, D. 2010. *Latin American Politics: An Introduction.* Toronto: University of Toronto Press.

Cole, D. 1998. *Instituting Environmental Protection: From Red to Green in Poland.* Basingstoke: Macmillan.

Conaghan, C., and C. de La Torre. 2008. "The Permanent Campaign of Rafael Correa: Making Ecuador's Plebiscitary Presidency." *International Journal of Press/Politics* 13 (3): 267–84. http://dx.doi.org/10.1177/1940161208319464.

Copeland, B.R. 2008. "The Pollution Haven Hypothesis." In *Handbook on Trade and the Environment,* ed. K.P. Gallagher, 60–70. Cheltenham: Edward Elgar.

Copeland, B.R., and S. Gulati. 2006. "Trade and the Environment in Developing Countries." In *Economic Development and Environmental Sustainability: New Policy Options,* ed. R.E. Lopez and M. Toman, 178–216. Oxford: Oxford University Press.

Copeland, B.R., and S.M. Taylor. 2004. "Trade, Growth, and the Environment." *Journal of Economic Literature* 42 (1): 7–71. http://dx.doi.org/10.1257/002205104773558047.

Coppedge, M. 1997. "A Classification of Latin American Parties." Working paper, University of Notre Dame. http://nd.edu/~kellogg/publications/workingpapers/WPS/244.pdf.

Council of Ministers of the Republic of Poland. 2002. *National Environmental Policy for 2003–2006 and 2010 Outlook*. Warsaw: Council of Ministers.

Crawford, S.E., and E. Ostrom. 1995. "A Grammar of Institutions." *American Political Science Review* 89 (3): 582–600. http://dx.doi.org/10.2307/2082975.

Dahl, R.A. 1971. *Polyarchy: Participation and Opposition*. New Haven: Yale University Press.

Dai, X. 2006. "The Conditional Nature of Democratic Compliance." *Journal of Conflict Resolution* 50 (5): 690–713. http://dx.doi.org/10.1177/0022002706291048.

Dale, P.J., B. Clarke, and E.M.G. Fontes. Jun 2002. "Potential for the Environmental Impact of Transgenic Crops." *Nature Biotechnology* 20 (6): 567–74. http://dx.doi.org/10.1038/nbt0602-567. Medline:12042859.

Dalton, R., S. Recchia, and R. Rohrschneider. 2003. "The Environmental Movement and the Modes of Political Action." *Comparative Political Studies* 36 (7): 743–71. http://dx.doi.org/10.1177/0010414003255108.

Debus, M. 2008. "Office and Policy Payoffs in Coalition Governments." *Party Politics* 14 (5): 515–38. http://dx.doi.org/10.1177/1354068807088121.

Deere, C.L., and D.C. Esty, eds. 2002. *Greening the Americas: NAFTA's Lessons for Hemispheric Trade*. Cambridge, MA: MIT Press.

Demont, M., M. Cerovska, W. Daems, K. Dillen, J. Fogarasi, E. Mathijs, F. Muška, J. Soukup, and E. Tollens. 2008. "Ex Ante Impact Assessment under Imperfect Information: Biotechnology in New Member States of the EU." *Journal of Agricultural Economics* 59 (3): 463–86. http://dx.doi.org/10.1111/j.1477-9552.2008.00157.x.

Desai, U., ed. 1998. *Ecological Policy and Politics in Developing Countries: Economic Growth, Democracy, and Environment*. Albany: State University of New York Press.

DeSombre, E. 2000. *Domestic Sources of International Environmental Policy: Industry, Environmentalists, and U.S. Power*. Cambridge, MA: MIT Press.

De Vaus, D.A. 2001. *Research Design in Social Research*. London: Sage.

Diez, J. 2006. *Political Change and Environmental Policymaking in Mexico*. London: Routledge.

Digital Journal. 2012. "Poland Imposes Ban on Monsanto MON810 Genetically Modified Maize." 7 April 2012. http://digitaljournal.com/article/322551.

DiMaggio, P.J., and W.W. Powell. 1991. "The Iron Cage Revisited: Institutionalized Isomorphism and Collective Rationality in Organizational Fields." In *The New Institutionalism in Organizational Analysis*, ed. W.W. Powell and P.J. DiMaggio, 63–82. Chicago: Chicago University Press.

Diplomat, The. 2011. "Romania in Genetically Modified Dilemma." 1 March 2011. http://www.thediplomat.ro/articol.php?id=1819.

Downs, A. 1957. *An Economic Theory of Democracy.* New York: HarperCollins.

Drezner, D.W. 2007. *All Politics Is Global: Explaining International Regulatory Regimes.* Princeton: Princeton University Press.

Dubinyuk, Y. 2010. *Ukraine Agricultural Biotechnology Annual.* Washington, DC: USDA Foreign Agricultural Service.

Duquette, M. 1999. *Building New Democracies: Economic and Social Reform in Brazil, Chile, and Mexico.* Toronto: University of Toronto Press.

Earnhart, D. 1997. "Enforcement of Environmental Protection Laws under Communism and Democracy." *Journal of Law & Economics* 40 (2): 377–402. http://dx.doi.org/10.1086/467377.

Earnhart, D., and L. Lizal. 2008. "Pollution Reductions in the Czech Republic." *Post-Communist Economies* 20 (2): 231–52. http://dx.doi.org/10.1080/14631370802018999.

Ederington, J., and J. Minier. 2003. "Is Environmental Policy a Secondary Trade Barrier? An Empirical Analysis." *Canadian Journal of Economics / Revue Canadienne d'Économique* 36 (1): 137–54. http://dx.doi.org/10.1111/1540-5982.00007.

Ehrke, A. 2010. *An Ever Cleaner Union? The Impact of European Environmental Measures in Poland and Ukraine.* Wiesbaden: VS.

El Comercio. 2011. "Aprobaron moratoria de 10 años que impide el ingreso de transgénicos." 3 November 2011. http://elcomercio.pe/economia/1327984/noticia-aprobaron-moratoria-10-anos-que-impide-ingreso-transgenicos.

El Correo de la Diaspora Latinoaméricaine. 2004. "Chávez dice NO a los Transgénicos ... pero hace falta decretarlo." 24 April 2007. http://www.elcorreo.eu.org/?Chavez-dice-NO-a-los-Transgenicos&lang=fr.

El País. 2010. "Transgénicos y hormonas causan calvicie y homosexualidad, según Evo Morales." 21 April 2010. http://www.elpais.com/articulo/sociedad/Transgenicos/hormonas/causan/calvicie/homosexualidad/Evo/Morales/elpepusoc/20100421elpepusoc_7/Tes.

Environmental Technologies Action Plan. 2007. "Promotion of Sustainable Forestry in Germany and Romania." http://ec.europa.eu/environment/etap/inaction/pdfs/feb07_sustainable_forestry.pdf.

Epoch Times, The. 2008. "Food Prices Skyrocket amidst Growing Shortages." 11 April 2008. http://en.epochtimes.com/news/8-4-11/68956.html.

Esty, D.C. 1996. "Revitalizing Environmental Federalism." *Michigan Law Review* 95 (3): 570–653. http://dx.doi.org/10.2307/1290162.

Esty, D.C., and M.P. Porter. 2005. "National Environmental Performance: An Empirical Analysis of Policy Results and Determinants." *Environment and Development Economics* 10 (4): 391–434. http://dx.doi.org/10.1017/S1355770X05002275.

Europa Publications. 2005. *The Environment Encyclopedia and Directory 2005*. London: Routledge.

Fagan, A. 2004. *Environment and Democracy in the Czech Republic: The Environmental Movement in the Transition Process*. Cheltenham: Edward Elgar.

Fagan, A., and J.A. Carmin, eds. 2011. *Green Activism in Post-Socialist Europe and the Former Soviet Union*. London: Routledge.

Falkner, R., and A. Gupta. 2009. "The Limits of Regulatory Convergence: Globalization and GMO Politics in the South." *International Environmental Agreement: Politics, Law and Economics* 9 (2): 113–33. http://dx.doi.org/10.1007/s10784-009-9094-x.

Figurska, J. 2010. "Poland Considers Restrictive Biotech Law – Farmers Fighting Back." GAIN report no. PL 1004. Washington, DC: USDA Foreign Agricultural Service.

Fitting, E. 2006. "Importing Corn, Exporting Labor: The Neoliberal Corn Regime, GMOs and the Erosion of Mexican Biodiversity." *Agriculture and Human Values* 23 (1): 15–26. http://dx.doi.org/10.1007/s10460-004-5862-y.

Fitting, E. 2008. "Importing Corn, Exporting Labor: The Neoliberal Corn Regime, GMOs, and the Erosion of Mexican Biodiversity." In *Food for the Few: Neoliberal Globalism and Biotechnology in Latin America*, ed. G. Otero, 135–58. Austin: University of Texas Press.

Francis, P., J. Klarer, and B. Moldan. 1997. "Conclusions." In *The Environmental Challenge for Central European Economies in Transition*, ed. J. Klarer and B. Moldan, 271–80. New York: Wiley.

Frank, D., A. Hironaka, and E. Schofer. 2000. "Environmentalism as a Global Institution." *American Sociological Review* 65 (1): 122–7. http://dx.doi.org/10.2307/2657293.

Fredriksson, P.G., E. Neumayer, R. Damania, and S. Gates. 2005. "Environmentalism, Democracy, and Pollution Control." *Journal of Environmental Economics and Management* 49 (2): 343–65. http://dx.doi.org/10.1016/j.jeem.2004.04.004.

Freidenberg, F., and M. Alcántara, eds. 2001. *Partidos políticos de América Latina: Cono Sur*. Salamanca: Ediciones Universidad de Salamanca.

Galbreath, D.J., and D. Auers. 2009. "Green, Black and Brown: Uncovering Latvia's Environmental Politics." *Journal of Baltic Studies* 40 (3): 333–48. http://dx.doi.org/10.1080/01629770903086244.

Gallagher, K.P. 2002. "Industrial Pollution in Mexico: Did NAFTA Matter?" In *Greening the Americas: NAFTA's Lessons for Hemispheric Trade,* ed. C. Deere and D. Esty, 119–43. Cambridge, MA: MIT Press.

Gallagher, K.P. 2004. *Free Trade and the Environment: Mexico, NAFTA, and Beyond.* Stanford: Stanford University Press.

Gallagher, K.P. 2008. "Trading Away the Ladder? Trade Politics and Economic Development in the Americas." *New Political Economy* 13 (1): 37–59. http://dx.doi.org/10.1080/13563460701859686.

Gallagher, K.S. 2006. *China Shifts Gears: Automakers, Oil, Pollution, and Development.* Cambridge, MA: MIT Press.

Gallagher, K.S. 2008. "Foreign Direct Investment and Clean Technology Leapfrogging in China." In *Handbook on Trade and the Environment*, ed. K.P. Gallagher, 147–55. Cheltenham: Edward Elgar.

Gallardo, E.G., and F. Schmithüsen, eds. 2005. *La Contribución del Derecho Forestal-Ambiental al Desarrollo Sustentable en América Latina.* Vienna: IUFRO.

Ganghof, S. 2003. "Promises and Pitfalls of Veto Player Analysis." *Swiss Political Science Review* 9 (2): 1–25. http://dx.doi.org/10.1002/j.1662-6370.2003.tb00411.x.

Ganghof, S. 2011. "Veto Player." In *International Encyclopedia of Political Science*, ed. B. Badie, D. Berg-Schlosser, and L. Morlino, 2707–9. Los Angeles: Sage.

Garcia-Johnson, R. 2000. *Exporting Environmentalism: U.S. Multinational Chemical Corporations in Brazil and Mexico.* Cambridge, MA: MIT Press.

Garvie, D., and A. Keeler. 1994. "Incomplete Enforcement with Endogenous Regulatory Choice." *Journal of Public Economics* 55 (1): 141–62. http://dx.doi.org/10.1016/0047-2727(94)90085-X.

Geddes, B. 2003. *Paradigms and Sand Castles: Theory Building and Research Design in Comparative Politics.* Ann Arbor: University of Michigan Press.

Gelman, A., and J. Hill. 2007. *Data Analysis Using Regression and Multilevel/Hierarchical Models.* Cambridge: Cambridge University Press. http://dx.doi.org/10.1017/CBO9780511790942.

Gilardi, F. 2008. *Delegation in the Regulatory State: Independent Regulatory Agencies in Western Europe.* Cheltenham: Edward Elgar.

Gilardi, F. 2010. "Who Learns from What in Policy Diffusion Processes?" *American Journal of Political Science* 54 (3): 650–66. http://dx.doi.org/10.1111/j.1540-5907.2010.00452.x.

Gilley, B. 2008. "Legitimacy and Institutional Change – The Case of China." *Comparative Political Studies* 43 (3): 259–84.

Givel, M. 2006. "Punctuated Equilibrium in Limbo: The Tobacco Lobby and U.S. State Policy Making from 1990 to 2003." *Policy Studies Journal: The Journal of the Policy Studies Organization* 34 (3): 405–18. http://dx.doi.org/10.1111/j.1541-0072.2006.00179.x.

Gobbi, J. 2009. *Environmental Effects of Implementing Mercosur in Argentina: An Integrated Assessment.* Saarbrücken: Lambert Academic Publishing.

Goodman, J., and L. Pauly. 1993. "The Obsolescence of Capital Controls?: Economic Management in an Age of Global Markets." *World Politics* 46 (1): 50–82. http://dx.doi.org/10.2307/2950666.

Gray, W.B., and J.P. Shimshack. 2011. "The Effectiveness of Environmental Monitoring and Enforcement: A Review of the Empirical Evidence." *Review of Environmental Economics and Policy* 5 (1): 3–24. http://dx.doi.org/10.1093/reep/req017.

Greif, A., and D. Laitin. 2004. "A Theory of Endogenous Institutional Change." *American Political Science Review* 98 (4): 633–52. http://dx.doi.org/10.1017/S0003055404041395.

Grossman, G.M., and A.B. Krueger. 1995. "Economic Growth and the Environment." *Quarterly Journal of Economics* 110 (2): 353–77. http://dx.doi.org/10.2307/2118443.

Gudynas, E. 2009. "La ecología política del giro biocéntrico en la nueva Constitución de Ecuador." *Revista de Estudios Sociales* 32 (1): 34–47.

Gulbrandsen, L.H. 2010. *Transnational Environmental Governance: The Emergence and Effects of the Certification of Forests and Fisheries.* Cheltenham: Edward Elgar.

Gutiérrez, D. 2002. "La expropiación privada de la naturaleza." In *La vida en venta: Transgénicos, patentes y biodiversidad*, ed. C. Heineke, 235–49. San Salvador: Ediciones Heinrich Böll.

Haerpfer, C.W. 2009. "Post-Communist Europe and Post-Soviet Russia." In *Democratization*, ed. C.W. Haerpfer, P. Bernhagen, R.F. Inglehart, and C. Welzel, 309–20. Oxford: Oxford University Press.

Haerpfer, C.W., P. Bernhagen, R.F. Inglehart, and C. Welzel, eds. 2009. *Democratization.* Oxford: Oxford University Press.

Hajba, E. 1994. "The Rise and Fall of the Hungarian Greens." *Journal of Communist Studies and Transitional Politics* 10 (3): 180–91. http://dx.doi.org/10.1080/13523279408415267.

Hall, P.A. 1993. "Policy Paradigms, Social Learning, and the State: The Case of Economic Policymaking in Britain." *Comparative Politics* 25 (3): 275–96. http://dx.doi.org/10.2307/422246.

Hall, P.A., and R. Taylor. 1996. "Political Science and the Three New Institutionalisms." *Political Science* 44 (5): 936–57.

Hall, P.A., and K. Thelen. 2009. "Institutional Change in Varieties of Capitalism." *Socio-economic Review* 7 (1): 7–34. http://dx.doi.org/10.1093/ser/mwn020.

Halpin, D. 2011. "Explaining Policy Bandwagons: Organized Interest Mobilization and Cascades of Attention." *Governance: An International Journal of Policy, Administration and Institutions* 24 (2): 205–30. http://dx.doi.org/10.1111/j.1468-0491.2011.01522.x.

Hanisch, M., and A. Schlüter. 2000. "Institutional Analysis and Institutional Change – What to Learn from the Case of Bulgarian Land Reform?" In *Land Ownership, Land Markets and Their Influence on the Efficiency of Agricultural Production in Central and Eastern Europe*, ed. P. Tillack and E. Schulze, 152–70. Kiel: Vauk.

Harper, K. 2003. "Green Carnivores, Mad Cows and Gene Tech: The Politics of Food in Hungarian Environmentalism." University of Massachusetts – Amherst, Anthropology Department Faculty Publication Series. http://scholarworks.umass.edu/anthro_faculty_pubs/77.

Harty, S. 2005. "Theorizing Institutional Change." In *New Institutionalism: Theory and Analysis*, ed. A. Lecours, 51–79. Toronto: University of Toronto Press.

Henisz, W.J., and B.A. Zelner. 2005. "Legitimacy, Interest Group Pressures and Change in Emergent Institutions: The Case of Foreign Investors and Host Country Governments." *Academy of Management Review* 30 (2): 361–82. http://dx.doi.org/10.5465/AMR.2005.16387892.

Héritier, A. 2007. *Explaining Institutional Change in Europe.* Oxford: Oxford University Press. http://dx.doi.org/10.1093/acprof:oso/9780199298129.001.0001.

Herrera, M. 2008. "El Salvador Biotechnology Annual 2008." GAIN Report no. ES 8009. Washington, DC: USDA Foreign Agricultural Service.

Hewett, E.A. 2011. *Foreign Trade Prices in the Council for Mutual Economic Assistance.* Cambridge: Cambridge University Press.

Hibbs, D. 1977. "Political Parties and Macroeconomic Policies." *American Political Science Review* 71 (4): 1467–87. http://dx.doi.org/10.2307/1961490.

Hickey, G.M. 2008. "Evaluating Sustainable Forest Management." *Ecological Indicators* 8 (2): 109–14. http://dx.doi.org/10.1016/j.ecolind.2006.11.011.

Hillman, A.L. 1994. "The Transition from Socialism: An Overview from a Political Economy Perspective." *European Journal of Political Economy* 10 (1): 191–225. http://dx.doi.org/10.1016/0176-2680(94)90067-1.

Hillman, A.L., and H.W. Ursprung. 1988. "Domestic Politics, Foreign Interests, and International Trade Policy." *American Economic Review* 78 (4): 729–45.

Hoberg, G. 1991. "Sleeping with an Elephant: The American Influence on Canadian Environmental Regulation." *Journal of Public Policy* 11 (1): 107–31. http://dx.doi.org/10.1017/S0143814X00004955.

Hoberg, G. 2001. "Globalization and Policy Convergence: Symposium Overview." *Journal of Comparative Policy Analysis* 3 (2): 127–32. http://dx.doi.org/10.1080/13876980108412657.

Hoberg, G. 2003. "Science, Politics, and U.S. Forest Law: The Battle over the Forest Service Planning Rule." Discussion paper, Resources for the Future. Washington, DC. http://www.rff.org/rff/Documents/RFF-DP-03-19.pdf.

Hoberg, G., ed. 2002. *Capacity for Choice: Canada in a New North America.* Toronto: University of Toronto Press.

Hoberg, G., K. Banting, and R. Simeon. 2002. "The Scope for Domestic Choice: Policy Autonomy in a Globalized World." In *Capacity for Choice: Canada in a New North America*, ed. G. Hoberg, 252–99. Toronto: University of Toronto Press.

Hochstetler, K. 2003. "Fading Green? Environmental Politics in the Mercosur Free Trade Agreement." *Latin American Politics and Society* 45 (4): 1–32. http://dx.doi.org/10.2307/3177129.

Hogenboom, B. 1998. *Mexico and the NAFTA Environment Debate: The Transnational Politics of Economic Integration.* Utrecht: International Books.

Holzinger, K., and C. Knill. 2004. "Competition and Cooperation in Environmental Policy: Individual and Interaction Effects." *Journal of Public Policy* 24 (1): 25–47. http://dx.doi.org/10.1017/S0143814X04000029.

Holzinger, K., and C. Knill. 2005. "Causes and Conditions of Cross-National Policy Convergence." *Journal of European Public Policy* 12 (5): 775–96. http://dx.doi.org/10.1080/13501760500161357.

Holzinger, K., and C. Knill. 2008. "Theoretical Framework: Causal Factors and Convergence Expectations." In *Environmental Policy Convergence in Europe? The Impact of International Institutions and Trade*, ed. K. Holzinger, C. Knill, and B. Arts, 30–63. Cambridge: Cambridge University Press. http://dx.doi.org/10.1017/CBO9780511491962.004.

Holzinger, K., C. Knill, and B. Arts, eds. 2008. *Environmental Policy Convergence in Europe? The Impact of International Institutions and Trade.* Cambridge: Cambridge University Press. http://dx.doi.org/10.1017/CBO9780511491962.

Holzinger, K., C. Knill, and T. Sommerer. 2008. "Environmental Policy Convergence: The Impact of International Harmonization, Transnational Communication and Regulatory Competition." *International Organization* 62 (4): 553–87. http://dx.doi.org/10.1017/S002081830808020X.

Holzinger, K., C. Knill, and T. Sommerer. 2011. "Is There Convergence of National Environmental Policies? An Analysis of Policy Outputs in 24 OECD Countries." *Environmental Politics* 20 (1): 20–41. http://dx.doi.org/10.10 80/09644016.2011.538163.

Holzinger, K., and P. Knoepfel, eds. 2000. *Environmental Policy in a European Union of Variable Geometry? The Challenge of the Next Enlargement.* Basel: Helbing & Lichtenhahn.

Holzinger, K., and T. Sommerer. 2011. "Race to the Bottom or Race to Brussels? Environmental Competition in Europe." *Journal of Common Market Studies* 49 (2): 315–39. http://dx.doi.org/10.1111/j.1468-5965.2010.02135.x.

Howlett, M., and B. Cashore. 2009. "The Dependent Variable Problem in the Study of Policy Change: Understanding Policy Change as a Methodological Problem." *Journal of Comparative Policy Analysis* 11 (1): 33–46. http://dx.doi. org/10.1080/13876980802648144.

Howlett, M., and S. Joshi-Koop. 2011. "Transnational Learning, Policy Analytical Capacity, and Environmental Policy Convergence: Survey Results from Canada." *Global Environmental Change* 21 (1): 85–92. http:// dx.doi.org/10.1016/j.gloenvcha.2010.10.002.

Howlett, M., and M. Ramesh. 2002. "The Policy Effects of Internationalization: A Subsystem Adjustment Analysis of Policy Change." *Journal of Comparative Policy Analysis* 4 (1): 31–50. http://dx.doi. org/10.1080/13876980208412669.

Howlett, M., M. Ramesh, and A. Perl. 2009. *Studying Public Policy: Policy Cycles and Policy Subsystems.* Oxford: Oxford University Press.

Howlett, M., and J. Rayner. 2006. "Understanding the Historical Turn in the Policy Sciences: A Critique of Stochastic, Narrative, Path Dependency, and Process-Sequencing Models of Policy-Making over Time." *Policy Sciences* 39 (1): 1–18. http://dx.doi.org/10.1007/s11077-005-9004-1.

Hristova, V. 2011. "United in Diversity? Differentiation in Three EU Regulatory Policies." Paper presented at the ECPR Joint Sessions, St Gallen, Switzerland, April 2011.

Huba, M. 1997. "Slovak Republic." In *The Environmental Challenge for Central European Economies in Transition*, ed. J. Klarer and B. Moldan, 229–71. New York: Wiley.

Huber, E., J.D. Stephens, T. Mustillo, and J. Pribble. 2008. *Codebook: Social Policy in Latin America and the Caribbean Dataset, 1960–2006.* Chapel Hill: University of North Carolina Press.

Huntington, S.P. 1991. *The Third Wave: Democratization in the Late Twentieth Century.* Norman: University of Oklahoma Press.

Ibarra Turcios, A.M., C.E. Rauda, F.J. Rivera, and M.G. Murillo. 2004. *Por un El Salvador libre de Transgénicos: Como enfrentar y derrotar la amenaza de los OGMs*. San Salvador: Asociación Luterana de Servicios para el Desarrollo / Unidad Ecológica Salvadoreña.

Immergut, E.M. 1990. "Institutions, Veto Points, and Policy Results: A Comparative Analysis of Health Care." *Journal of Public Policy* 10 (4): 391–416. http://dx.doi.org/10.1017/S0143814X00006061.

Immergut, E.M., and K.S. Anderson. 2007. "Editors' Introduction: The Dynamics of Pension Politics." In *The Handbook of West European Pension Politics*, ed. E.M. Immergut, K.S. Anderson and I. Schulze, 1–45. Oxford: Oxford University Press.

Inglehart, R. 1997. *Modernization and Postmodernization: Cultural, Economic and Political Change in 43 Societies*. Princeton: Princeton University Press.

Inter Press Service. 2008. "Banging Empty Pots to Protest Food Prices." 13 March 2008. http://www.ipsnews.net/news.asp?idnews=41586.

Iturbe, R., C. Flores, A. Castro, and L.G. Torres. 2007. "Sub-soil Contamination Due to Oil Spills in Zones Surrounding Oil Pipeline-Pump Stations and Oil Pipeline Right-of-Ways in Southwest-Mexico." *Environmental Monitoring and Assessment* 133 (1–3): 387–98. http://dx.doi.org/10.1007/s10661-006-9593-y. Medline:17286169.

Jahn, D., and F. Müller-Rommel. 2010. "Political Institutions and Policy Performance: A Comparative Analysis of Central and Eastern Europe." *Journal of Public Policy* 30 (1): 23–44. http://dx.doi.org/10.1017/S0143814X09990250.

James, C. 2002. *Global Review of Commercialized Transgenic Crops. 2002 Feature: Bt Maize*. ISAAA Briefs no. 29-2002. Ithaca: ISAAA.

James, C. 2009. *Global Status of Commercialized Biotech/GM Crops: 2009*. ISAAA Briefs no. 41-2009. Ithaca: ISAAA.

Jancar-Webster, B. 1997. "Environmental Degradation and Environmental Politics in the Former Soviet Union." In *Latin American Environmental Policy in International Perspective*, ed. G.J. MacDonald, D.L. Nielson, and M.A. Stern, 211–36. Boulder: Westview Press.

Jänicke, M. 2006. "Ecological Modernisation: New Perspectives." In *Environmental Governance in Global Perspective: New Approaches to Ecological and Political Modernisation*, ed. M. Jänicke and K. Jacob, 9–29. Berlin: Freie Universität Berlin.

Jansen, K., and A. Roquas. 2008. "Biosafety Regulation and Global Governance: The Problem of Absentee Expertise in Latin America." In *Food for the Few: Neoliberal Globalism and Biotechnology in Latin America*, ed. G. Otero, 91–114. Austin: University of Texas Press.

Jepson, W.E., C. Brannstrom, and R. Stancato de Souza. 2008. "Brazilian Biotechnology Governance: Consensus and Conflict over Genetically Modified Crops." In *Food for the Few: Neoliberal Globalism and Biotechnology in Latin America*, ed. G. Otero, 217–42. Austin: University of Texas Press.

John, P. 2003. "Is There Life after Policy Streams, Advocacy Coalitions, and Punctuations: Using Evolutionary Theory to Explain Policy Change." *Policy Studies Journal: The Journal of the Policy Studies Organization* 31 (4): 481–98. http://dx.doi.org/10.1111/1541-0072.00039.

Jovanović, M.N. 2006. *The Economics of International Integration*. Cheltenham: Edward Elgar.

Jovanović, M.N., ed. 2011. *International Handbook on the Economics of Integration*. Volume 1: *General Issues and Regional Groups*. Cheltenham: Edward Elgar.

Julesz, M. 2010. "The Individual and the Environment: The New Hungarian Civil Code." *Open Law Journal* 3 (1): 1–5. http://dx.doi.org/10.2174/1874950X01003010001.

Karaczun, Z. 2005. "Preparing for EU Environmental Policy in Poland: The Case of the Nitrates Directive." *Land Use Policy* 22 (3): 245–53. http://dx.doi.org/10.1016/j.landusepol.2003.09.007.

Katzenstein, P.J. 1985. *Small States in World Markets: Industrial Policy in Europe*. Ithaca: Cornell University Press.

Kellman, J. 2002. "The Brazilian Legal Tradition and Environmental Protection: Friend or Foe." *Hastings International and Comparative Law Review* 25 (2): 145–67.

Keohane, R.O. 1984. *After Hegemony: Cooperation and Discord in the World Political Economy*. Princeton: Princeton University Press.

Keohane, R.O. 2002. *Power and Interdependence in a Partially Globalized World*. New York: Routledge. http://dx.doi.org/10.4324/9780203218174.

Kingdon, J.W. 2002. *Agendas, Alternatives, and Public Policies*. New York: Longman.

Kingston, C., and G. Caballero. 2009. "Comparing Theories of Institutional Change." *Journal of Institutional Economics* 5 (2): 151–80. http://dx.doi.org/10.1017/S1744137409001283.

Kittel, B. 1999. "Sense and Sensitivity in Pooled Analysis of Political Data." *European Journal of Political Research* 35 (2): 225–53. http://dx.doi.org/10.1111/1475-6765.00448.

Kittel, B., and H. Winner. 2005. "How Reliable Is Pooled Analysis in Political Economy? The Globalization–Welfare State Nexus Revisited." *European Journal of Political Research* 44 (2): 269–93. http://dx.doi.org/10.1111/j.1475-6765.2005.00228.x.

Klarer, J., and P. Francis. 1997. "Regional Overview." In *The Environmental Challenge for Central European Economies in Transition*, ed. J. Klarer and B. Moldan, 1–66. New York: Wiley.

Klingemann, H., A. Volkens, J. Bara, I. Budge, and M. McDonald, eds. 2006. *Mapping Policy Preferences II: Estimates for Parties, Electors and Governments in Central and Eastern Europe, European Union and OECD 1990–2003*. Oxford: Oxford University Press.

Knight, J. 1992. *Institutions and Social Conflict*. Cambridge: Cambridge University Press. http://dx.doi.org/10.1017/CBO9780511528170.

Knill, C. 2001. *The Europeanisation of National Administrations: Patterns of Institutional Change and Persistence*. Cambridge: Cambridge University Press. http://dx.doi.org/10.1017/CBO9780511491986.

Knill, C., M. Debus, and S. Heichel. 2010. "Do Parties Matter in Internationalized Policy Areas? The Impact of Political Parties on Environmental Policy Outputs in 18 OECD Countries 1970–2000." *European Journal of Political Research* 49 (3): 301–36. http://dx.doi.org/10.1111/j.1475-6765.2009.01903.x.

Knill, C., and A. Lenschow. 2000. "'New' Environmental Policy Instruments as a Panacea? Their Limitations in Theory and Practice." In *Environmental Policy in a European Union of Variable Geometry? The Challenge of the Next Enlargement*, ed. K. Holzinger and P. Knoepfel, 317–48. Basel: Helbing & Lichtenhahn.

Knill, C., and A. Lenschow. 2001. "Seek and Ye Shall Find! Linking Different Perspectives on Institutional Change." *Comparative Political Studies* 34 (2): 187–215. http://dx.doi.org/10.1177/0010414001034002003.

Knill, C., and D. Liefferink. 2007. *Environmental Politics in the European Union*. Manchester: Manchester University Press.

Knill, C., and J. Tosun. 2012. *Public Policy: A New Introduction*. Basingstoke: Palgrave Macmillan.

Knill, C., K. Schulze, and J. Tosun. 2012. "Regulatory Policy Outputs and Impacts: Exploring a Complex Relationship" *Regulation & Governance* 6 (4): 627–44. http://10.1111/j.1748-5991.2012.01150.x.

Knill, C., J. Tosun, and M.W. Bauer. 2009. "Neglected Faces of Europeanization: The Differential Impact of the EU on the Dismantling and Expansion of Domestic Policies." *Public Administration* 87 (3): 519–37. http://dx.doi.org/10.1111/j.1467-9299.2009.01768.x.

Knill, C., J. Tosun, and S. Heichel. 2008. "Balancing Competitiveness and Conditionality: Environmental Policy-making in Low-regulating Countries." *Journal of European Public Policy* 15 (7): 1019–40. http://dx.doi.org/10.1080/13501760802310512.

Konisky, D.M. 2007. "Regulatory Competition and Environmental Enforcement: Is There a Race to the Bottom?" *American Journal of Political Science* 51 (4): 853–72. http://dx.doi.org/10.1111/j.1540-5907.2007.00285.x.

Konisky, D., and N. Woods. 2010. "Exporting Air Pollution? Regulatory Enforcement and Environmental Free Riding in the United States." *Political Research Quarterly* 63 (4): 771–82. http://dx.doi.org/10.1177/1065912909334429.

Krasner, S.D. 1994. "International Political Economy: Abiding Discord." *Review of International Political Economy* 1 (1): 13–19. http://dx.doi.org/10.1080/09692299408434265.

Krüger, C., and A. Carius. 2001. *Environmental Policy and Law in Romania: Towards EU Accession*. Berlin: Ecoscript.

Krugman, P.R., and M. Obstfeld. 2010. *International Economics: Theory and Policy*. Amsterdam: Addison-Wesley Longman.

Kübler, D. 2001. "Understanding Policy Change with the Advocacy Coalition Framework: An Application to Swiss Drug Policy." *Journal of European Public Policy* 8 (4): 623–41. http://dx.doi.org/10.1080/13501760110064429.

Laaksonen-Craig, S. 2004. "Foreign Direct Investment in the Forest Sector: Implications for Sustainable Forest Management in Developed and Developing Countries." *Forest Policy and Economics* 6 (3–4): 359–70. http://dx.doi.org/10.1016/j.forpol.2004.03.011.

Latinamerican Press. 2011. "Transgenic Corn Moves Forward: Multinational Corporation Monsanto Begins Experimental Cultivation of Genetically Modified Corn. 2 March 2011. http://www.lapress.org/articles.asp?art=6300.

Lecours, A. 2005. "New Institutionalism: Issues and Questions." In *New Institutionalism: Theory and Analysis*, ed. A. Lecours, 3–25. Toronto: University of Toronto Press.

Lee, S., and S. McBride, eds. 2007. *Neo-Liberalism, State Power and Global Governance*. Berlin: Springer. http://dx.doi.org/10.1007/978-1-4020-6220-9.

León-Chaux, E.P. 2006. "Colombia." In Gobernanza del Agua en América del Sur: Dimensión Ambiental, ed. A. Iza and M.B. Rovere, 161–206. Gland, CH: IUCN.

Levinson, A., and M.S. Taylor. 2008. "Unmasking the Pollution Haven Effect." *International Economic Review* 49 (1): 223–54. http://dx.doi.org/10.1111/j.1468-2354.2008.00478.x.

Levitsky, S., and M.V. Murillo. 2005. *The Politics of Institutional Weakness: Argentine Democracy*. University Park: Pennsylvania State University Press.

Lewis, P.G. 2000. *Political Parties in Post-Communist Eastern Europe*. London: Routledge.

Lewis, P.G. 2001. "The 'Third Wave' of Democracy in Eastern Europe: Comparative Perspectives on Party Roles and Political Development." *Party Politics* 7 (5): 543–65. http://dx.doi.org/10.1177/1354068801007005002.

Lewis-Beck, M., and M. Stegmaier. 2008. "The Economic Vote in Transitional Democracies." *Journal of Elections, Public Opinions and Parties* 18 (3): 303–23. http://dx.doi.org/10.1080/17457280802227710.

Li, Q., and R. Reuveny. 2006. "Democracy and Environmental Degradation." *International Studies Quarterly* 50 (4): 935–56. http://dx.doi.org/10.1111/j.1468-2478.2006.00432.x.

Libecap, G.D. 1989. *Contracting for Property Rights*. Cambridge: Cambridge University Press.

Lieberman, E.S. 2005. "Nested Analysis as a Mixed-Method Strategy for Comparative Research." *American Political Science Review* 99 (3): 435–52. http://dx.doi.org/10.1017/S0003055405051762.

Lieberson, S. 1987. *Making It Count: The Improvement of Social Research and Theory*. Berkeley: University of California Press.

Lijphart, A., and C.H. Waisman. 1996. "Institutional Design and Democratization." In *Institutional Design in New Democracies*, ed. A. Lijphart and C.H. Waisman, 1–11. Boulder: Westview Press.

Lindblom, C. 1959. "The Science of Muddling Through." *Public Administration Review* 19 (2): 79–88. http://dx.doi.org/10.2307/973677.

Lindblom, C. 1977. *Politics and Markets*. New York: Basic Books.

Lipset, S.M., and S. Rokkan. 1967. *Party Systems and Voter Alignments*. New York: Free Press.

Long, S.J. 1997. *Regression Models for Categorical and Limited Dependent Variables*. Thousand Oaks: Sage.

Long, S.J., and J. Freese. 2006. *Regression Models for Categorical Outcomes Using Stata*. College Station, TX: Stata Press.

Macdonald, D. 2007. *Business and Environmental Politics in Canada*. Toronto: Broadview Press.

Mahoney, J., and K. Thelen. 2010. "A Theory of Gradual Institutional Change." In *Explaining Institutional Change Ambiguity, Agency, and Power*, ed. J. Mahoney and K. Thelen, 1–37. Cambridge: Cambridge University Press.

Magnani, E. 2001. "The Environmental Kuznets Curve: Development Path or Policy Result?" *Environmental Modelling & Software* 16 (2): 157–65. http://dx.doi.org/10.1016/S1364-8152(00)00079-7.

Mair, P., and C. Mudde. 1998. "The Party Family and Its Study." *Annual Review of Political Science* 1 (1): 211–29. http://dx.doi.org/10.1146/annurev.polisci.1.1.211.

Mauri, C. 2002. "Case Study on Environmental Law Enforcement and Compliance in Costa Rica: Water Pollution with Toxic Substances." In Sixth International Conference on Environmental Compliance and Enforcement, ed. J. Gerardu, K. Markowitz, P. Sturges, and D. Zaelke, 185–98. Washington, DC: INECE.

Mainwaring, S., and F. Hagopian. 2005. "Introduction: The Third Wave of Democratization in Latin America." In *The Third Wave of Democratization in Latin America: Advances and Setbacks*, ed. F. Hagopian and S. Mainwaring, 1–13. Cambridge: Cambridge University Press. http://dx.doi.org/10.1017/CBO9780511791116.001.

March, J.G., and J.P. Olsen. 2008. "Elaborating the 'New Institutionalism.'" In *The Oxford Handbook of Political Institutions*, ed. R.A.W. Rhodes, S.A. Binder, and B.A. Rockman, 3–21. Oxford: Oxford University Press. http://dx.doi.org/10.1093/oxfordhb/9780199548460.003.0001.

McAllister, L.K. 2008. *Making Law Matter: Environmental Protection and Legal Insitutions in Brazil*. Stanford: Stanford University Press.

McAllister, L.K., B. van Rooij, and R.A. Kagan. 2010. "Reorienting Regulation: Pollution Enforcement in Industrializing Countries." *Law & Policy* 32 (1): 1–13.

McCormick, J. 1993. "International Nongovernmental Organizations: Prospects for a Global Environmental Movement." In *Environmental Politics in the International Arena: Movements, Parties, Organizations, and Policy*, ed. S. Kamieniecki, 131–44. Albany: State University of New York Press.

Medina, E. 2001. "PROFEPA's Reorganization Strengthens Enforcement Powers." http://www.pulse-point.com/archive/jul2001/index.htm.

Meseguer Yebra, C. 2009. *Learning, Policy Making, and Market Reforms*. Cambridge: Cambridge University Press. http://dx.doi.org/10.1017/CBO9780511626685.

Migdal, J.S. 1988. *Strong Societies and Weak States: State–Society Relations and State Capabilities in the Third World*. Princeton: Princeton University Press.

Ministry of Waters and Environmental Protection 2003. "Report in the Field of Environmental Inspections according to Point VIII 1 of the Recommendation 2001/331/EC of 4 April 2001 Providing the Minimum Criteria for Environmental Inspection." http://ec.europa.eu/environment/impel/pdf/countries/romania.pdf.

Miroshnichenko, N.N. 2008. "Control and Assessment of the Hydrocarbon Contamination of Ukrainian Soils." *Eurasain Soil Science* 41 (5): 542–9. http://dx.doi.org/10.1134/S1064229308050098.

Montoro Zamora, Y. 2009. "La situación de los transgénicos en Perú." In *América Latina: La transgénesis de un continente. Visión Crítica de una Expansión Descontrolada*, ed. M.I. Manzur, G. Catacora, M.I. Cárcamo, E. Bravo, and M. Altieri, 44–6. Berkeley: SOCLA and Heinrich Böll Foundation.

Morrow, J.D., B. Bueno de Mesquita, R.M. Siverson, and A. Smith. 2008. "Retesting Selectorate Theory: Separating the Effects of W from Other Elements of Democracy." *American Political Science Review* 102 (3): 393–400. http://dx.doi.org/10.1017/S0003055408080295.

Mueller, B. 2010. "The Fiscal Imperative and the Role of Public Prosecutors in Brazilian Environmental Policy." *Law & Policy* 32 (1): 104–26.

Müller, K. 2003. *Privatising Old-Age Security: Latin America and Eastern Europe Compared*. Cheltenham: Edward Elgar.

Müller-Rommel, F., and T. Poguntke, eds. 2002. *Green Parties in National Governments*. London: Frank Cass.

Mumme, S.P. 1998. "Environmental Policy and Politics in Mexico." In *Ecological Policy and Politics in Developing Countries: Economic Growth, Democracy, and Environment*, ed. U. Desai, 183–204. Albany: State University of New York Press.

Mumme, S.R., and E. Korzetz. 1997. "Democratization, Politics, and Environmental Reform in Latin America." In *Latin American Environmental Policy in International Perspective*, ed. G.J. MacDonald, D.L. Nielson and M.A. Stern, 40–59. Boulder: Westview Press.

Nap, J.P., P.L.J. Metz, M. Escaler, and A.J. Conner. Jan 2003. "The Release of Genetically Modified Crops into the Environment, part I: Overview of Current Status and Regulations." *Plant Journal* 33 (1): 1–18. http://dx.doi.org/10.1046/j.0960-7412.2003.01602.x. Medline:12943538.

Nelson, R.R. 1995. "Recent Evolutionary Theorizing about Economic Change." *Journal of Economic Literature* 33 (1): 48–90.

Nelson, R.R., and S.G. Winter. 1982. *An Evolutionary Theory of Economic Change*. Cambridge, MA: Harvard University Press.

Nelson, R.R., and S.G. Winter. 2002. "Evolutionary Theorizing in Economics." *Journal of Economic Perspectives* 16 (2): 23–46. http://dx.doi.org/10.1257/0895330027247.

Neumayer, E. 2002. "Do Democracies Exhibit Stronger International Environmental Commitment? A Cross-country Analysis." *Journal of Peace Research* 39 (2): 139–64. http://dx.doi.org/10.1177/0022343302039002001.

Neumayer, E. 2003. "Are Left-Wing Party Strength and Corporatism Good for the Environment? Evidence from Panel Analysis of Air Pollution in OECD Countries." *Ecological Economics* 45 (2): 203–20. http://dx.doi.org/10.1016/S0921-8009(03)00012-0.

Neumayer, E. 2004. "The Environment, Left-Wing Political Orientation and Ecological Economics." *Ecological Economics* 51 (3–4): 167–75. http://dx.doi.org/10.1016/j.ecolecon.2004.06.006.

Newell, P. 2009. "Bio-Hegemony: The Political Economy of Agricultural Biotechnology in Argentina." *Journal of Latin American Studies* 41 (1): 27–57. http://dx.doi.org/10.1017/S0022216X08005105.

Nijnik, M., and A. Oskam. 2004. "Governance in Ukrainian Forestry: Trends, Impacts and Remedies." *International Journal of Agricultural Resources, Governance and Ecology* 3 (1–2): 116–33. http://dx.doi.org/10.1504/IJARGE.2004.004648.

Nikolova, S. 2010. "GMOs Ban in Bulgaria – Decision by Bulgarian Society." http://www.agrolink.org/agrolink/news.php?idarticles=157&idcategories=22.

Nohlen, D., ed. 2005. *Elections in the Americas: A Data Handbook.* Volume 2: *South America.* Oxford: Oxford University Press.

Nolte, G.E. 2011. *Peru Agricultural Biotechnology Annual.* Washington, DC: USDA Foreign Agricultural Service.

Nordberg, M. 2007. "Ukraine Reforms in Forestry 1990–2000." *Forest Policy and Economics* 9 (6): 713–29. http://dx.doi.org/10.1016/j.forpol.2006.07.002.

North, D.C. 1990. "A Transaction Cost Theory of Politics." *Journal of Theoretical Politics* 2 (4): 355–67. http://dx.doi.org/10.1177/0951692890002004001.

Novinite. 2010. "Public Opposition Slams Bulgaria's Door to GMOs." 26 May 2011. www.novinite.com/view_news.php?id=116542.

Novinite. 2011a. "Bulgaria Bans MON 810 GMO Maize." 1 February 2011. www.thebulgariannews.com/view_news.php?id=124797.

Novinite. 2011b. "Bulgaria Opposes GMO Invasion in EU." 2 February 2011. http://www.novinite.com/view_news.php?id=124815.

Oakley, S.M., A. Pocasangre, C. Flores, J. Monge, and M. Estrada. 2000. "Waste Stabilization Pond Use in Central America: The Experiences of El Salvador, Guatemala, Honduras and Nicaragua." *Water Science and Technology* 42 (10–11): 51–8.

Obinger, H. 2001. "Veto Players, Political Parties, and Welfare-State Retrenchment in Austria." *International Journal of Political Economy* 32 (2): 44–66.

OECD. 1999. *Environmental Performance Reviews, Czech Republic.* Paris: OECD.

OECD. 2005. *Environmental Performance Reviews, Chile.* Paris: OECD.

Oelsner, A., and M. Bain. 2009. "Latin America." In *Democratization,* ed. C.W. Haerpfer, P. Bernhagen, R.F. Inglehart and C. Welzel, 290–308. Oxford: Oxford University Press.

Otero, G., and G. Pechlaner. 2008. "Latin American Agriculture, Food, and Biotechnology: Temperate Dietary Pattern Adoption and Unsustainability."

In *Food for the Few: Neoliberal Globalism and Biotechnology in Latin America*, ed. G. Otero, 31–60. Austin: University of Texas Press.

Palacios, M., and C. Chávez. 2005. "Determinants of Compliance in the Emissions Compensation Program in Santiago, Chile." *Environment and Development Economics* 10 (4): 453–83. http://dx.doi.org/10.1017/S1355770X05002299.

Parker, D. 2008. "Chávez y la búsqueda de una seguridad y soberanía alimentarias." *Revista Venezolana de Economía y Ciencias Sociales* 14 (3): 121–43.

Parker, J.A., and V. Smelik. 2008. "Ukraine." *International Comparative Legal Guide: Environmental Law* 1 (1): 411–17.

Paun, G. 2011. *Report: Romania's Experience Shows GE Crops Do Not Meet European Quality Standards*. Bucharest: Agent Green.

Pavlínek, P., and J. Pickles. 2000. *Environmental Transitions: Transformation and Ecological Defence in Central and Eastern Europe*. London: Routledge.

Payne, R.A. 1995. "Freedom and the Environment." *Journal of Democracy* 6 (3): 41–55. http://dx.doi.org/10.1353/jod.1995.0053.

Pechlaner, G., and G. Otero. 2008. "The Third Food Regime: Neoliberal Globalism and Agricultural Biotechnology in North America." *Sociologia Ruralis* 48 (4): 351–71. http://dx.doi.org/10.1111/j.1467-9523.2008.00469.x.

Pelaez, V. 2009. "State of Exception in the Regulation of Genetically Modified Organisms in Brazil." *Science & Public Policy* 36 (1): 61–71. http://dx.doi.org/10.3152/030234209X403235.

Pelc, I. 2009. *The Role of GMOs in the New Member States – A Critical Appraisal*. Brussels: The Greens/European Free Alliance in the European Parliament.

Pennings, P., and J. Lane. 1998. "Introduction." In *Comparing Party System Change*, ed. P. Pennings and J. Lane, 1–20. London: Routledge.

Perkins, R., and E. Neumayer. 2009. "Transnational Linkages and the Spillover of Environment-Efficiency into Developing Countries." *Global Environmental Change* 19 (3): 375–83. http://dx.doi.org/10.1016/j.gloenvcha.2009.05.003.

Perkins, R., and E. Neumayer. 2012. "Does the 'California Effect' Operate across Borders? Trading- and Investing-Up in Automobile Emission Standards." *Journal of European Public Policy* 19 (2): 217–37. http://dx.doi.org/10.1080/13501763.2011.609725.

Petras, J., and H. Veltmeyer. 2010. "A Class Perspective on Social Ecology and the Indigenous Movement." *Critical Sociology* 36 (3): 437–52. http://dx.doi.org/10.1177/0896920510365208.

Pickvance, C. 1999. "Democratisation and the Decline of Social Movements: The Effects of Regime Change on Collective Action in Eastern Europe, Southern Europe and Latin America." *Sociology* 33 (2): 353–72.

Pickvance, C. 2003. *Local Environmental Regulation in Post-Socialism: A Hungarian Case Study*. Aldershot: Ashgate.

Pierson, P. 2001. "Coping with Permanent Austerity Welfare State Restructuring in Affluent Democracies." In *The New Politics of the Welfare State*, ed. P. Pierson, 410–56. Oxford: Oxford University Press. http://dx.doi.org/10.1093/0198297564.003.0014.

Plümper, T., V. Troeger, and P. Manow. 2005. "Panel Data Analysis in Comparative Politics: Linking Method to Theory." *European Journal of Political Research* 44 (2): 327–54. http://dx.doi.org/10.1111/j.1475-6765.2005.00230.x.

Poitras, M. 2008. "Social Movements and Techno-Democracy: Reclaiming the Genetic Commons." In *Food for the Few: Neoliberal Globalism and Biotechnology in Latin America*, ed. G. Otero, 267–88. Austin: University of Texas Press.

Pollack, D., J. Jacobs, O. Müller, and G. Pickel. 2003. *Political Culture in Post-Communist Europe: Attitudes in New Democracies*. Aldershot: Ashgate.

Pollack, M.A., and G.C. Shaffer. 2009. *When Cooperation Fails: The International Law and Politics of Genetically Modified Foods*. New York: Oxford University Press.

Pollack, M.A., and G.C. Shaffer. 2010. "Biotechnolog Policy: Between National Fears and Global Disciplines." In *Policy-Making in the European Union*, ed. H. Wallace, M.A. Pollack, and A.R. Young, 331–56. Oxford: Oxford University Press.

Porter, G. 1999. "Trade Competition and Pollution Standards: 'Race to the Bottom' or 'Stuck at the Bottom'?" *Journal of Environment & Development* 8 (2): 133–51. http://dx.doi.org/10.1177/107049659900800203.

Porter, M.E., K. Schwab, and A. Lopez-Claros. 2005. *The Global Competitiveness Report 2005–2006: Policies Underpinning Rising Prosperity*. Basingstoke: Palgrave Macmillan.

Prado, M., and M. Trebilcock. 2009. "Path Dependence, Development, and the Dynamics of Institutional Reform." *University of Toronto Law Journal* 59 (3): 341–80. http://dx.doi.org/10.3138/utlj.59.3.341.

Prakash, A. 2000. *Greening the Firm: The Politics of Corporate Environmentalism*. Cambridge: Cambridge University Press. http://dx.doi.org/10.1017/CBO9780511491863

Prakash, A., and M. Potoski. 2006. "Racing to the Bottom? Trade, Environmental Governance, and ISO 14001." *American Journal of Political Science* 50 (2): 350–61. http://dx.doi.org/10.1111/j.1540-5907.2006.00188.x.

Prakash, A., and M. Potoski. 2007. "Investing Up: FDI and the Cross Country Diffusion of ISO 14001 Management Systems." *International Studies Quarterly* 51 (3): 723–44. http://dx.doi.org/10.1111/j.1468-2478.2007.00471.x.

Princen, S. 2010. "Venue Shifts and Policy Change in EU Fisheries Policy."
    Marine Policy 34 (1): 36–41. http://dx.doi.org/10.1016/j.marpol.2009.04.006.
Przeworski, A. 1991. Democracy and the Market: Political and Economic Reforms
    in Eastern Europe and Latin America. New York: Cambridge University Press.
    http://dx.doi.org/10.1017/CBO9781139172493.
Przeworski, A., and H. Teune. 1970. The Logic of Comparative Social Inquiry.
    Malabar: Krieger.
Quist, D., and I.H. Chapela. 2001. "Transgenic Dna Introgressed into
    Traditional Maize Landraces in Oaxaca, Mexico." Nature 414 (6863): 541–3.
    http://dx.doi.org/10.1038/35107068. Medline:11734853.
Radaelli, C. 2009. "Measuring Policy Learning: Regulatory Impact
    Assessment in Europe." Journal of European Public Policy 16 (8): 1145–64.
    http://dx.doi.org/10.1080/13501760903332647.
Rauscher, M. 2005. "International Trade, Foreign Investment, and the
    Environment." In Handbook of Environmental Economics, vol. 3, ed.
    K.G. Mäler and J.R. Vincent, 1403–56. Amsterdam: Elsevier. http://dx.doi.
    org/10.1016/S1574-0099(05)03027-5.
Ready, R.C., J. Malzubris, and S. Senkane. 2002. "The Relationship between
    Environmental Values and Income in a Transition Economy: Surface Water
    Quality in Latvia." Environment and Development Economics 7 (1): 147–56.
    http://dx.doi.org/10.1017/S1355770X02000086.
Rénique, G. 2009. "Latin America: The New Neoliberalism and Popular
    Mobilization." Socialism and Democracy 23 (3): 1–26. http://dx.doi.
    org/10.1080/08854300903290801.
Reuters. 2010. "Bulgaria Parliament Bans GMO Crops to Soothe
    Fears." 18 March 2010. www.reuters.com/article/2010/03/18/
    us-bulgaria-gmo-idUSTRE62H3EJ20100318.
Reuters. 2011. "Monsanto Sees More Investment in Paraguay."
    4 April 2011. http://www.reuters.com/article/2011/04/04/
    us-latam-summit-paraguay-monsanto-idUSTRE7337FS20110404.
Rodrik, D. 1992. "The Rush to Free Trade in the Developing World: Why So
    Late? Why Now? Will it Last?" National Bureau of Economic Research Working
    Papers 3947: 1–20.
Rokkan, S. 1970. Citizens, Elections, Parties: Approaches to the Comparative Study
    of Political Development. Oslo: Universitetsforlaget.
Roller, E. 2005. The Performance of Democracies: Political Institutions and Public
    Policy. Oxford: Oxford University Press.
Rosas, G. 2005. "The Ideological Organization of Latin American Legislative
    Parties: An Empirical Analysis of Elite Policy Preferences." Comparative
    Political Studies 38 (7): 824–49. http://dx.doi.org/10.1177/0010414004274386.

Rose, R. 1991. "What Is Lesson-Drawing?" *Journal of Public Policy* 11 (1): 3–30. http://dx.doi.org/10.1017/S0143814X00004918.

Rudra, N. 2011. "Openness and the Politics of Potable Water." *Comparative Political Studies* 44 (6): 771–803. http://dx.doi.org/10.1177/0010414011401217.

Ruttan, V.W. 2006. "Social Science Knowledge and Induced Institutional Innovation: An Institutional Design Perspective." *Journal of Institutional Economics* 2 (3): 249–72. http://dx.doi.org/10.1017/S1744137406000403.

Ruttan, V.W., and Y. Hayami. 1984. "Towards a Theory of Induced Institutional Innovation." *Journal of Development Studies* 20 (4): 203–23. http://dx.doi.org/10.1080/00220388408421914.

Sabalza, M., B. Miralpeix, R.M. Twyman, T. Capell, and P. Christou. 2011. "EU Legitimizes GM Crop Exclusion Zones." *Nature Biotechnology* 29 (4): 315–17. http://dx.doi.org/10.1038/nbt.1840. Medline:21478843.

Sabatier, P.A. 1998. "The Advocacy Coalition Framework: Revisions and Relevance for Europe." *Journal of European Public Policy* 5 (1): 98–130. http://dx.doi.org/10.1080/13501768880000051.

Sabatier, P.A., and H.C. Jenkins-Smith. 1999. "The Advocacy Coalition Framework: An Assessment." In *Theories of the Policy Process*, ed. P.A. Sabatier, 117–66. Boulder: Westview Press.

Sabatier, P.A., and H.C. Jenkins-Smith, eds. 1993. *Policy Change and Learning: An Advocacy Coalition Approach*. Boulder: Westview Press.

Sabatier, P.A., and C.M. Weible. 2007. "The Advocacy Coalition Framework: Innovations and Clarifications." In *Theories of the Policy Process*, ed. P.A. Sabatier, 189–220. Boulder: Westview Press.

Salgado Ramírez, A. 2009. "La situación de los transgénicos en México." In *América Latina: La transgénesis de un continente. Visión Crítica de una Expansión Descontrolada*, ed. M.I. Manzur, G. Catacora, M.I. Cárcamo, E. Bravo, and M. Altieri, 96–101. Berkeley: SOCLA and Heinrich Böll Foundation.

Sandulescu, E., J.E. Wagner, S. Pailler, D.W. Floyd, and C.J. Davis. 2007. "Policy Analysis of a Government-Sanctioned Management Plan for a Community-Owned Forest in Romania." *Forest Policy and Economics* 10 (1–2): 14–24. http://dx.doi.org/10.1016/j.forpol.2007.01.002.

Sartori, G. 1997. *Comparative Constitutional Engineering*. New York: New York University Press.

Sbert, C. 2004. *Elementos para una gestión ambiental efective en El Salvador, Honduras, Nicaragua, Guatemala y Costa Rica: Informe Preliminar Para Discusión*. Montreal: Unisféra International Centre.

Schattschneider, E.E. 1960. *The Semisovereign People: A Realist's View of Democracy in America*. New York: Holt, Rinehart, and Winston.

Schiavoni, C., and W. Camacaro. 2009. "The Venezuelan Effort to Build a New Food and Agriculture System." *Monthly Review* 61 (3). http://monthlyreview.org/2009/07/01/the-venezuelan-effort-to-build-a-new-food-and-agriculture-system.

Schimmelfennig, F., and U. Sedelmeier. 2004. "Governance by Conditionality: EU Rule Transfer to the Candidate Countries of Central and Eastern Europe." *Journal of European Public Policy* 11 (4): 661–79. http://dx.doi.org/10.1080/1350176042000248089.

Schimmelfennig, F. and F. Trauner.2009. "Introduction: Post-Accession Compliance in the EU's New Member States." *European Integration online Papers*, special issue 2, vol. 13: 1–8.

Schmidt, M.G. 1996. "When Parties Matter: A Review of the Possibilities and Limits of Partisan Influence on Public Policy." *European Journal of Political Science* 30 (2): 155–83. http://dx.doi.org/10.1111/j.1475-6765.1996.tb00673.x.

Schmithüsen, F., P. Herbst, and D.C. Le Master, eds. 2000. *Forging a New Framework for Sustainable Forestry: Recent Developments in European Forest Law.* Vienna: IUFRO.

Scholz, J.T., J. Twombly, and B. Headrick. 1991. "Street-Level Political Controls over Federal Bureaucracy." *American Political Science Review* 85 (3): 829–50. http://dx.doi.org/10.2307/1963852.

Schulze, K. 2013. "Do Parties Matter for Environmental Cooperation? An Analysis of Environmental Treaty Participation by Advanced Industrialized Democracies." *Environmental Politics*, forthcoming.

Schwarz, G.E. 1978. "Estimating the Dimension of a Model." *Annals of Statistics* 6 (2): 461–4. http://dx.doi.org/10.1214/aos/1176344136.

Scoones, I. 2008. "Mobilizing against GM Crops in India, South Africa and Brazil." *Journal of Agrarian Change* 8 (2–3): 315–44. http://dx.doi.org/10.1111/j.1471-0366.2008.00172.x.

Scruggs, L. 2003. *Sustaining Abundance: Environmental Performance in Industrial Democracies.* Cambridge: Cambridge University Press.

Shadish, W., T. Cook, and D. Campbell. 2002. *Experimental & Quasi-Experimental Designs for Generalized Causal Inference.* Boston: Houghton Mifflin.

Shepsle, K.A. 2008. "Rational Choice Institutionalism." In *The Oxford Handbook of Political Institutions*, ed. B.A.W. Rhodes, S.A. Binder, and B.A. Rockman, 23–39. Oxford: Oxford University Press. http://dx.doi.org/10.1093/oxfordhb/9780199548460.003.0002

Sigman, H. 2005. "Transboundary Spillovers and Decentralization of Environmental Policies." *Journal of Environmental Economics and Management* 50 (1): 82–101. http://dx.doi.org/10.1016/j.jeem.2004.10.001.

Silva, E. 1996. "Democracy, Market Economics, and Environmental Policy in Chile." *Journal of Interamerican Studies and World Affairs* 38 (4): 1–33. http://dx.doi.org/10.2307/166257.

Silva, E. 1997. "The Politics of Sustainable Development: Native Forest Policy in Chile, Venezuela, Costa Rica and Mexico." *Journal of Latin American Studies* 29 (2): 457–93. http://dx.doi.org/10.1017/S0022216X97004756.

Simmons, B.A. 2010. "Treaty Compliance and Violation." *Annual Review of Political Science* 13 (1): 273–96. http://dx.doi.org/10.1146/annurev.polisci.12.040907.132713.

Simmons, B.A., and Z. Elkins. 2004. "The Globalization of Liberalization: Policy Diffusion in the International Political Economy." *American Political Science Review* 98 (1): 171–89. http://dx.doi.org/10.1017/S0003055404001078.

Sinn, H.-W. 1997. "The Selection Principle and Market Failure in Systems Competition." *Journal of Public Economics* 66 (2): 247–74. http://dx.doi.org/10.1016/S0047-2727(97)00043-1.

Sitch, S., P.M. Cox, W.J. Collins, and C. Huntingford. 2007. "Indirect Radiative Forcing of Climate Change Through Ozone Effects on the Land-Carbon Sink." *Nature* 448 (7155): 791–4. http://dx.doi.org/10.1038/nature06059. Medline:17653194.

Skogstad, G. 2006. "Regulating Food Safety Risks in the European Union: A Comparative Perspective." In *What's the Beef? The Contested Governance of European Food Safety*, ed. C. Ansell and D. Vogel, 213–36. Cambridge, MA: MIT Press.

Skogstad, G. 2011. "Contested Accountability Claims and GMO Regulation in the European Union." *Journal of Common Market Studies* 49 (4): 895–915. http://dx.doi.org/10.1111/j.1468-5965.2010.02166.x.

Sorsa, P. 1994. "Competitiveness and Environmental Standards: Some Exploratory Results." Washington, DC: World Bank Policy Research Working Paper Series 1249.

Sotirov, M., and M. Memmler. 2012. "The Advocacy Coalition Framework in Natural Resource Policy Studies: Recent Experiences and Further Prospects." *Forest Policy and Economic* 16 (1): 51–64. http://dx.doi.org/10.1016/j.forpol.2011.06.007.

Spatareanu, M. 2007. "Searching for the Pollution Havens: The Impact of Environmental Regulations on Foreign Direct Investment." *Journal of Environment & Development* 16 (2): 161–82. http://dx.doi.org/10.1177/1070496507302873.

Sprinz, D. 1999. "Empirical-Quantitative Approaches to the Study of International Environmental Policy." In *Policy Analysis Methods*, ed. S.S. Nagel, 41–64. Commack, NY: Nova Science.

Stata Corporation. 2005. *Stata Longitudinal/Panel-Data Reference Manual, Release 9*. College Station, TX: Stata Press.

Sterner, T. 2002. *Policy Instruments for Environmental and Natural Resource Management*. Baltimore: Johns Hopkins University Press.

Stevis, D., and S. Mumme. 2000. "Rules and Politics in International Integration: Environmental Regulation in NAFTA and the EU." *Environmental Politics* 9 (4): 20–42. http://dx.doi.org/10.1080/09644010008414549.

Stinchcombe, A.L. 1968. *Constructing Social Theories*. Chicago: University of Chicago Press.

Strock, J.M. 1990. "Environmental Crime Enforcement Priorities for the 1990s." *George Washington Law Review* 59 (4): 916–37.

Strøm, K., and W.C. Müller. 1999. "Political Parties and Hard Choices." In *Policy, Office, or Votes?* ed. W.C. Müller and K. Strøm, 1–35. Cambridge: Cambridge University Press.

Šulek, R. 2000. "Economic Principles of the Sloval Republic Forestry Policy and Legislation." In *Forging a New Framework for Sustainable Forestry: Recent Developments in European Forest Law,* ed. F. Schmithüsen, P. Herbst, and D.C. Le Master, 87–91. Vienna: IUFRO.

Tapiero, C.S. 2009. "Energy Consumption and Environmental Pollution: A Stochastic Model." *IMA Journal of Management Mathematics* 20 (3): 263–73. http://dx.doi.org/10.1093/imaman/dpn041.

Teeple, G., and S. McBride. 2011. "Introduction: Global Crisis and Political Economy." In *Relations of Global Power: Neoliberal Order and Disorder,* ed. G. Teeple and S. McBride, xi–xx. Toronto: University of Toronto Press.

Thelen, K. 2003. "How Institutions Evolve: Insights from Comparative Historical Analysis." In *Comparative Historical Analysis in the Social Sciences,* ed. J. Mahoney and D. Rueschemeyer, 208–40. Cambridge: Cambridge University Press.

Tiebout, C. 1956. "A Pure Theory of Local Expenditures." *Journal of Political Economy* 64 (5): 416–26. http://dx.doi.org/10.1086/257839.

Tietenberg, T.H. 2006. *Environmental and Natural Resource Economics*. Boston: Addison-Wesley.

Tobin, J. 1958. "Liquidity Preference as Behavior towards Risk." *Review of Economic Studies* 25 (2): 65–86. http://dx.doi.org/10.2307/2296205.

Tondl, G. 2008. "Trade and Integration in Latin America and with Its Main Trading Partners." In *Trade, Integration and Economic Development: The EU and Latin America,* ed. G. Tondl, 17–37. Berlin: Springer. http://dx.doi.org/10.1007/978-3-211-75150-3_2.

Tortajada, C. 1998. "Water Supply and Wastewater Management in Mexico: An Analysis of the Environmental Policies." *Water Resources Development* 14 (3): 327–37. http://dx.doi.org/10.1080/07900629849240.

Tosun, J. 2011. "When the Grace Period Is Over: Assessing the New Member States' Compliance with EU Requirements for Oil Stockholding." *Energy Policy* 39 (11): 7156–64. http://dx.doi.org/10.1016/j.enpol.2011.08.035.

Trapido, M. 1999. "Polycyclic Aromatic Hydrocarbons in Estonian Soil: Contamination and Profiles." *Environmental Pollution* 105 (1): 67–74. http://dx.doi.org/10.1016/S0269-7491(98)00207-3.

Traxler, G. 2006. "The GMO Experience in North and South America." *International Journal of Technology and Globalisation* 2 (1–2): 46–64.

True, J.L., B.D. Jones, and F.R. Baumgartner. 2007. "Punctuated Equilibrium Theory: Explaining Stability and Change in American Policymaking." In *Theories of the Policy Process*, ed. P.A. Sabatier, 155–88. Boulder: Westview Press.

Tsebelis, G. 1995. "Decision Making in Political Systems: Veto Players in Presidentialism, Parliamentarism, Multicameralism and Multipartism." *British Journal of Political Science* 25 (3): 289–325. http://dx.doi.org/10.1017/S0007123400007225.

Tsebelis, G. 2002. *Veto Players: How Political Institutions Work*. Princeton: Princeton University Press.

Tsebelis, G., and E. Alemán. 2005. "Presidential Conditional Agenda Setting in Latin America." *World Politics* 57 (3): 396–420. http://dx.doi.org/10.1353/wp.2006.0005.

Tsebelis, G., and T.P. Rizova. 2007. "Presidential Conditional Agenda Setting in the Former Communist Countries." *Comparative Political Studies* 40 (10): 1155–82. http://dx.doi.org/10.1177/0010414006288979.

UNECE. 2007. *Environmental Performance Reviews: Ukraine Second Review*. New York, Geneva: United Nations.

UNEP. 2008. *Justicia Ambiental – Órganos especializados*. www.pnuma.org/deramb/taller_peru_documentos.php?menusup=7&menuinf=5.

Urrutia Riesco, J.A., and M. Correa Achurra. 2010. "Chile." *International Comparative Legal Guide: Environmental Law* 1 (1): 69–76.

Van Alstine, J., and E. Neumayer. 2008. "The Environmental Kuznets Curve." In *Handbook on Trade and the Environment*, ed. K.P. Gallagher, 49–59. Cheltenham: Edward Elgar.

Versluis, E. 2007. "Even Rules, Uneven Practices: Opening the Black Box of EU Law in Action." *West European Politics* 30 (1): 50–67. http://dx.doi.org/10.1080/01402380601019647.

Vogel, D. 1995. *Trading Up: Consumer and Environmental Regulation in the Global Economy*. Cambridge, MA: Harvard University Press.

Vogel, D. 1997. "Trading Up and Governing Across: Transnational Governance and Environmental Protection." *Journal of European Public Policy* 4 (4): 556–71. http://dx.doi.org/10.1080/135017697344064.

Vogel, D., and R.A. Kagan, eds. 2004. *Dynamics of Regulatory Change: How Globalization Affects National Regulatory Policies*. Berkeley: University of California Press.

Vogel, D., and T. Kessler. 1998. "How Compliance Happens and Doesn't Happen Domestically." In *Engaging Countries: Strengthening Compliance with International Environmental Accords*, ed. E.B. Weiss and H. Jacobson, 19–37. Cambridge, MA: MIT Press.

von Sperling, M. 2007. "Standards for Wastewater Treatment in Brazil." In *Standards and Thresholds for Impact Assessment*, ed. M. Schmidt, J. Glasson, L. Emmelin, and H. Helbron, 125–32. Berlin: Springer.

Voszka, E. 1996. "Privatization in Central Europe: Can It Be Designed?" In *Institutional Design in New Democracies: Eastern Europe and Latin America*, ed. A. Lijphart and C. Waisman, 177–94. Boulder: Westview Press.

Walgrave, S., and F. Varone. 2008. "Punctuated Equilibrium, and Agenda-Setting: Bringing Parties Back In: Policy Change after the Dutroux Crisis in Belgium." *Governance: An International Journal of Policy, Administration and Institutions* 21 (3): 365–95. http://dx.doi.org/10.1111/j.1468-0491.2008.00404.x.

Wälti, S. 2004. "How Multilevel Structures Affect Environmental Policy in Industrial Countries." *European Journal of Political Research* 43 (4): 599–634. http://dx.doi.org/10.1111/j.1475-6765.2004.00167.x.

Weaver, R.K., and B.A. Rockman. 1993. "When and How Do Institutions Matter?" In *Do Institutions Matter? Government Capabilities in the United States and Abroad*, ed. R.K. Weaver and B.A. Rockman, 445–61. Washington, DC: The Brookings Institution.

Weible, C.M., P.A. Sabatier, and K. McQueen. 2009. "Themes and Variations: Taking Stock of the Advocacy Coalition Framework." *Policy Studies Journal: The Journal of the Policy Studies Organization* 37 (1): 121–40. http://dx.doi.org/10.1111/j.1541-0072.2008.00299.x.

Weidner, H., and M. Jänicke, eds. 2002. *Capacity Building in National Environmental Policy*. Berlin: Springer.

Weingast, B.R., and W.J. Marshall. 1988. "The Industrial Organization of Congress; or, Why Legislatures, Like Firms, Are Not Organized as Markets." *Journal of Political Economy* 96 (1): 132–63. http://dx.doi.org/10.1086/261528.

Weyland, K. 1999. "Neoliberal Populism in Latin America and ˒ Eastern Europe." *Comparative Politics* 31 (4): 379–401. http://dx.doi. org/10.2307/422236.

Whitehead, L. 2000. "Comparing East Asia and Latin America: Stirrings of Mutual Recognition." *Journal of Democracy* 11 (4): 65–79. http://dx.doi. org/10.1353/jod.2000.0089.

Wiarda, H.J., and H.F. Kline. 2007. *A Concise Introduction to Latin American Politics and Development*. Boulder: Westview Press.

Wijewardana, D. 2008. "Criteria and Indicators for Sustainable Forest Management: The Road Travelled and the Way Ahead." *Ecological Indicators* 8 (2): 115–22. http://dx.doi.org/10.1016/j.ecolind.2006.11.003.

Winham, G.R. 2009. "The GMO Panel: Applications of WTO Law to Trade in Agricultural Biotech Products." *Journal of European Integration* 31 (3): 409–29. http://dx.doi.org/10.1080/07036330902782261.

Witt, U. 2003. *The Evolving Economy: Essays on the Evolutionary Approach to Economics*. Cheltenham: Edward Elgar.

Wooldridge, J.M. 2006. *Introductory Econometrics: A Modern Approach*. Mason, OH: Thomson South-Western.

World Bank. 2008. *Rising Food Prices: The World Bank's Latin America and Caribbean Region Position Paper*. Washington, DC: World Bank.

Yankelevich, A. 2010. *Paraguay Biotechnology Annual Report*. Washington, DC: USDA Foreign Agricultural Service.

Yu, Z. 2005. "Environmental Protection: A Theory of Direct and Indirect Competition for Political Influence." *Review of Economic Studies* 72 (1): 269–86. http://dx.doi.org/10.1111/0034-6527.00332.

Zaelke, D., D. Kaniaru, and E. Kružíková. 2005. *Making Law Work: Environmental Compliance and Sustainable Development*. London: Cameron May International Law and Policy.

Zarsky, L. 1999. "International Investment Rules and the Environment: Stuck in the Mud?" *Foreign Policy in Focus* 4 (22): 1–3.

Zarsky, L. 2008. "Foreign Direct Investment and Sustainable Industrial Development." In *Handbook on Trade and the Environment*, ed. K.P. Gallagher, 83–96. Cheltenham: Edward Elgar.

Zohlnhöfer, R. 2009. "How Politics Matter When Policies Change: Understanding Policy Change as a Political Problem." *Journal of Comparative Policy Analysis* 11 (1): 97–115. http://dx.doi. org/10.1080/13876980802648300.

Index

Studies in Comparative Political Economy and Public Policy